PUNISHING ATROCITIES THROUGH A FAIR TRIAL

International Criminal Law from Nuremberg to the Age of Global Terrorism

Over the past decades, international criminal law has evolved to become the operative norm for addressing the worst atrocities. Tribunals have conducted hundreds of trials addressing mass violence in the former Yugoslavia, Rwanda, Sierra Leone, Cambodia, and other countries to bring to justice perpetrators of genocide, war crimes, and crimes against humanity. But international courts have struggled to hold perpetrators accountable for these offenses while still protecting the fair trial rights of defendants. *Punishing Atrocities through a Fair Trial* explores this tension, from criticism of the Nuremberg Trials as 'victor's justice' to the accusations of political motivations clouding prosecutions today by the International Criminal Court. It explains why international criminal law must adhere to transparent principles of legality and due process to ensure its future as a legitimate and viable legal regime.

Jonathan Hafetz is Professor of Law at Seton Hall University School of Law.

Punishing Atrocities through a Fair Trial

INTERNATIONAL CRIMINAL LAW FROM NUREMBERG
TO THE AGE OF GLOBAL TERRORISM

JONATHAN HAFETZ

Seton Hall University School of Law

CAMBRIDGE
UNIVERSITY PRESS

CAMBRIDGE
UNIVERSITY PRESS

University Printing House, Cambridge CB2 8BS, United Kingdom

One Liberty Plaza, 20th Floor, New York, NY 10006, USA

477 Williamstown Road, Port Melbourne, VIC 3207, Australia

314-321, 3rd Floor, Plot 3, Splendor Forum, Jasola District Centre, New Delhi - 110025, India

79 Anson Road, #06-04/06, Singapore 079906

Cambridge University Press is part of the University of Cambridge.

It furthers the University's mission by disseminating knowledge in the pursuit of education, learning and research at the highest international levels of excellence.

www.cambridge.org
Information on this title: www.cambridge.org/9781107476592
DOI: 10.1017/9781316147627

First published 2018
First paperback edition 2018

A catalogue record for this publication is available from the British Library

Library of Congress Cataloging in Publication data
NAMES: Hafetz, Jonathan, author.
TITLE: Punishing atrocities through a fair trial : international criminal law from Nuremberg to the age of global terrorism / Jonathan Hafetz.
DESCRIPTION: Cambridge [UK] ; New York : Cambridge University Press, 2017. | Includes bibliographical references and index.
IDENTIFIERS: LCCN 2017033477 | ISBN 9781107094550 (alk. paper)
SUBJECTS: LCSH: International criminal law. | International Criminal Court. | International criminal courts. | Criminal liability. | Fair trial. | War crime trials – Germany – Nuremberg – History – 20th century. | Atrocities. | Terrorism.
CLASSIFICATION: LCC KZ7050 .H34 2017 | DDC 345–dc23
LC record available at https://lccn.loc.gov/2017033477

ISBN 978-1-107-09455-0 Hardback
ISBN 978-1-107-47659-2 Paperback

Contents

Acknowledgments

Many people helped make this book possible. I am indebted to the following individuals who shared their expertise and provided guidance at various stages of the project: Kristen Boon, Meg deGuzman, Megan Fairlie, Alexander K.A. Greenawalt, Fred Hafetz, Kevin Jon Heller, Aziz Huq, Michael Karnavas, Margaret Lewis, Jaya Ramji-Nogales, Alice Ristroph, Peter Robinson, Gregory Townsend, Jennifer Trahan, Jenia Iontcheva Turner, Beth Van Schaack, and Richard Wilson.

I am also grateful to the following people who generously shared their time when I conducted research at The Hague and at Nuremberg: Helen Brady, Daryl Mundis, Klaus Rackwitz, Alan Tieger, Gregory Townsend, and Alex Whiting. Several chapters in the book benefitted from presentations at the American Society of International Law Annual Meeting and Annual Research Forum, the SMU Dedman School of Law, Seton Hall Law School, and Temple University Beasley School of Law. The Program in Law and Public Affairs at Princeton University provided me with critical support in developing this book during my year there as a fellow. I would like to thank my editor, John Berger for his guidance and support, and Rebecca Jackaman and others at Cambridge University Press who assisted with the preparation and publication of the book.

Additionally, I would like to thank Hendrik van Hemmen, Daniel Hewitt, Mark Linscott, and Ryan Malloy for their invaluable research assistance, and Risa Pollack for her editorial assistance. I am grateful to Barbara Mol and Dianne Oster for their help in tracking down countless sources. I wish to express my gratitude to Seton Hall Law School for enabling me to undertake this project. Above all, I am grateful for the love and support of my parents, Fred and Myra, and my family, Martha, Ben, and Sam.

Introduction

International criminal law (ICL) has achieved a degree of permanence and prominence that seemed unforeseeable just decades ago. International criminal tribunals have conducted numerous trials and created an important body of jurisprudence on a range of substantive and procedural issues. Hybrid tribunals, which combine international and domestic features, have contributed significantly to this growth. National jurisdictions have also prosecuted individuals responsible for past atrocities and strengthened international norms.

But despite what Kathryn Sikkink has described as a "justice cascade,"[1] questions about ICL's effectiveness and legitimacy persist. The International Criminal Court (ICC) has neither ushered in an age of global justice nor ended impunity for atrocities. The ICC's jurisdiction remains limited in important respects, and the Court faces criticism over how its cases are selected and its trials are conducted. Meanwhile, domestic prosecutions under the Rome Statute's complementarity framework, which gives states the first responsibility and right to investigate and prosecute international crimes, are still impeded by local resistance.

One of the most important challenges ICL faces is how to resolve the recurring tension between holding perpetrators accountable for grave crimes, on the one hand, and conducting criminal trials that maintain principles of fairness, on the other. That tension is the subject of this book.

The impulse to punish mass atrocities and prevent impunity continues to drive ICL's growth. It underlies the rationale for overriding state sovereignty and subjecting individuals to the jurisdiction of international criminal tribunals as well as for increasing the capacity of national courts to prosecute international crimes. Yet, international tribunals also remain committed to principles of due process and legality in adjudicating charges against those individuals accused of the gravest offenses. Multiple factors help explain this commitment, including the influence of international human rights law, the desire to entrench rule-of-law norms in countries devastated by war and civil strife, and, above all, the goal of subjecting the most egregious forms of human violence to the controlling power of law rather than to other forms of retribution.

The quest to hold perpetrators accountable within the framework of an international criminal proceeding that conforms to prevailing fair trial standards and principles of legality dates to Nuremberg. Widely regarded as the birth of modern international criminal law, Nuremberg famously established that individuals may be prosecuted under international law for crimes committed against others, including against their own citizens. Nuremberg, however, also exposed the friction that can result when pursuing that goal. At Nuremberg, that friction took various forms, including conflicts between legal theories of individual and collective responsibility, controversy over criminal law's retroactive application in the service of broader notions of justice, and the prosecution of senior leaders of the defeated powers by the winning side whose own international law violations went unaddressed. Some of these issues have since been resolved: prosecutors no longer need, for example, to show a nexus to armed conflict to prosecute crimes against humanity to avoid concerns about the legality of the charges, as they had to do at Nuremberg. But tensions between the goals of accountability and fairness still lie at the heart of many important issues in ICL today.

This tension is not unique to ICL. ICL, however, operates on a separate plane from national criminal law. It has overlapping, but ultimately distinct, goals and audiences than national criminal law, and faces unique challenges. International criminal tribunals, for example, lack their own enforcement mechanisms and depend heavily on the cooperation of states where the crimes occurred. They also must grapple with issues that domestic courts ordinarily do not confront, such as the need to protect victims and witnesses in distant conflict zones. Moreover, because ICL addresses the gravest crimes, the pressure to hold individuals responsible is greater than in most domestic prosecutions, which encompass a far wider range of offenses.

The book explains how the tension between accountability and fairness continues to drive many debates in ICL. While the book focuses significantly on procedural safeguards, it also examines other issues that can affect ICL's fairness from the perspective of the accused, such as the use of expansive modes of criminal responsibility and the selection of situations and cases for investigation and prosecution. In the face of continued concerns about ICL's future, the book offers guarded optimism. It describes the significant progress international and hybrid courts have made in protecting the rights of defendants while conducting trials for some of the world's worst atrocities. The book, however, also highlights the continuing obstacles these courts face in achieving this goal.

Chapter 1 describes how the trials conducted at Nuremberg after World War II created the overarching template for modern ICL. Nuremberg's most important achievement was to establish a paradigm that provides legal accountability for atrocities by holding individuals responsible through a criminal trial. Nuremberg also established that the legitimacy of any such trial depends ultimately on its adherence to prevailing fair trial standards and that the enormity of the crimes increases, rather than diminishes, the importance of those standards. Nuremberg's legal procedures may appear rudimentary by today's metrics, but its articulation of this overarching principle remains critical to its legacy. Additionally, Nuremberg offers a notable contrast to the war crimes trial of Japanese political and military leaders conducted in Tokyo, which was marred by procedural flaws. Nuremberg, however, also illustrates many of the challenges international criminal tribunals face. Those challenges include: navigating between the competing forces of justice and legality; punishing collective criminality without abandoning principles of individual culpability; creating a historical record of mass violence without sacrificing the due process rights of individual defendants; and overcoming the enduring problem of victor's justice.

Chapter 2 examines the revival of ICL in the mid-1990s. It focuses mainly on the creation of the two *ad hoc* international tribunals, the International Criminal Tribunal for the former Yugoslavia (ICTY) and the International Criminal Tribunal for Rwanda (ICTR), while also briefly noting related developments at hybrid tribunals. It describes how these two *ad hoc* tribunals, and the ICTY in particular, expanded the fair trial protections provided to defendants by building on international human rights law and other post-Nuremberg developments. But it also notes how these tribunals illustrated the continuing tension between ICL's goal of providing accountability for mass atrocities while ensuring the fair treatment of defendants. The chapter first discusses the development of modes of liability designed to hold individuals criminally responsible even where, for example, they did not physically perpetrate the crime or some of the crimes fell outside a common criminal plan but were nevertheless reasonably foreseeable. It then describes other developments affecting the fair trial rights of accused persons, such as the growing reliance by judges on written evidence in place of live testimony, limits on the disclosure of evidence to the defense, restrictions on the pretrial release of defendants despite the presumption of innocence, and a lack of equality of arms between the defense and prosecution (defined generally as an equal ability for each side to present its respective case). Although these developments resulted largely from the limited enforcement powers of the ICTY and ICTR and their dependence on state cooperation, they also stemmed from the tribunals' embrace of goals beyond punishing guilty individuals, including promoting peace and stability in affected countries and securing justice for victims.

Chapter 3 focuses on the ICC, the first permanent international criminal tribunal, established by the Rome Statute of 1998. In contrast to the ICTY and ICTR, which were established by the UN Security Council, the ICC was created by an international treaty. The ICC provides a window into how tensions between accountability and fairness play out before a permanent international criminal court and the challenges of maintaining fair trial standards in this context. The chapter begins by examining modes of liability employed by the ICC and their relationship to fundamental criminal law principles. It then describes how the

ICC has expanded the procedural safeguards available to defendants. Yet, as the chapter explains, various factors can hinder implementation of these protections. The chapter discusses, for example, the conflict between the Court's rules obligating the prosecution to disclose material to defendants and those rules designed to protect the confidentiality of certain information supplied by states or organizations; the Court's reliance on written testimony rather than on oral testimony subject to cross-examination; and the Court's use of case management tools, which can limit a defendant's ability to challenge the evidence against him and to present evidence in his defense. The chapter also explores how the ICC's multiple goals – such as its recognition of the participatory rights of victims – can conflict with the due process rights of accused individuals. It then examines another dimension of fairness: the selection of situations and cases for investigation and prosecution. It suggests how selection decisions that favor powerful countries and interests or that disproportionately target weaker countries, particular regions, or non-state forces generally can undermine the equal application of law.

Chapter 4 examines how fair trial standards can develop within what remains a largely decentralized system of international criminal justice. The chapter describes the different roles that criminal procedure plays within this system. While the multiplicity of tribunals at the national and international level increases the risk of deviation from due process requirements, it also provides opportunities for elaborating upon and entrenching those requirements across different countries and legal systems. The chapter suggests how the ICC could more effectively use the Rome Statute's complementarity framework to advance fair trial safeguards at the national level. It also examines how those safeguards factored into decisions by the ICTY and ICTR (and their successor residual mechanism) on whether to refer cases to national jurisdictions and how those referrals contributed to the inclusion of more due process protections at the national level. The chapter then turns to hybrid tribunals. It explains how hybrid tribunals have developed procedural safeguards and their comparative advantages in embedding those safeguards within domestic legal systems. But it also notes the potential risks posed by hybrid tribunals, which include both shielding powerful officials from criminal responsibility and relaxing fair trial standards in a quest for vengeance.

Chapter 5 explores the question of fairness from the perspective of decisions by international criminal tribunals about which cases to investigate and prosecute. Selection decisions have long been among the thorniest issues in ICL, historically giving rise to claims of victor's justice and reinforcing realist critiques of ICL as a tool wielded by the strongest nations and their allies against weaker countries. Such critiques have become more pronounced as a result of the ICC's disproportionate focus on Africa and the evidence of major power influence over the Court's ability to investigate and punish atrocities. This chapter explains why failing to address concerns about the selection of situations and cases undermines the fairness and legitimacy of international criminal tribunals even where they afford individual defendants robust due process protections. The chapter examines various proposals to address selection decisions in ICL, focusing particularly on the ICC. It then proposes an alternative approach: placing more emphasis on expressing the principle that no individual is above the law when selecting situations and cases for investigation and prosecution.

Chapter 6 examines the recurring debate over whether terrorism should be treated as an international crime. The proliferation of global terrorism has generated increased pressure to bring terrorism within the orbit of international criminal justice. Elevating terrorism to the status of an international crime would, for example, serve a valuable expressive function, communicating the gravity of this extraordinarily destructive and destabilizing form of violence and the opprobrium it warrants. But prosecuting terrorism as an international crime poses significant challenges. The definition of terrorism still remains insufficiently precise and prone to overbroad interpretations. Further, terrorism prosecutions often involve the type of evidentiary issues that could jeopardize due process safeguards in international criminal prosecutions, given those prosecutions' dependence on state cooperation. Additionally, international terrorism prosecutions would likely result in the continued selection of situations and cases that embed major power influence and shield government forces even when they commit the same crimes as non-state actors. The chapter concludes that these concerns outweigh the potential benefits of subjecting terrorism to international criminal prosecution in light of ICL's overarching goals of accountability and fairness.

NOTE

1. Kathryn Sikkink, *The Justice Cascade: How Human Rights Prosecutions Are Changing World Politics* (New York: W.W. Norton, 2011).

1

Creating the Template: Nuremberg and the Post-World War II International Prosecutions

Today, the trial of major Nazi war criminals at Nuremberg is regarded as the foundation of modern international criminal law (ICL) and the birth of a movement that has expanded the principles and institutions of international justice. Yet, it bears remembering that the trial, which began on November 20, 1945, and concluded on October 1, 1946, almost never occurred.

The leaders of the major Allied powers did not initially support war crimes trials for senior Nazi officials. At the Tehran Conference in 1943, Soviet leader Josef Stalin advocated shooting between 50,000 and 100,000 Germans. British Prime Minister Winston Churchill opposed the Soviet plan for mass executions, but agreed that Nazi leaders should be shot, arguing that circumstances called for a political rather than judicial approach and that a trial would give the Nazis a public platform to propagate their hateful ideology.[1]

In the United States, Treasury Secretary Henry Morgenthau Jr. was the most prominent and vocal advocate for a punitive peace. Morgenthau not only backed summary executions of German leaders, but also sought Germany's overall economic destruction to ensure it would never again threaten world peace. Both President Franklin D. Roosevelt and General Dwight D. Eisenhower, at different junctures, gravitated towards Morgenthau's view, as did a clear majority of Americans, according to polls taken at the time.[2]

US Secretary of War Henry L. Stimson initially provided a dissenting voice in demanding criminal trials for individual Nazi leaders. Stimson feared that summary executions would tarnish the legitimacy of the war effort and fuel resentment within Germany, thus breeding a desire for future war rather than preventing it.[3] Trials, on the other hand, would bring long-term benefits by eradicating the Nazi system and preventing its recurrence, as long as they were conducted in "a dignified manner consistent with the advance of civilization."[4] "[P]unishment," Stimson said, "is for the purpose of prevention and not for vengeance."[5] Stimson maintained that a comprehensive war crimes trial would best further the goals of future peace and security.[6]

States had punished war crimes for centuries. But in the past, the victorious state had typically punished individuals from the vanquished state for war crimes committed against its own soldiers. Proposals for Nuremberg instead sought an international trial for crimes against the international legal order.

The trials envisaged after World War I offered scant encouragement to Stimson and others who sought to prosecute Nazi atrocities. At the conclusion of World War I, the Treaty of Versailles provided for the creation of an *ad hoc* international trial of the German Kaiser for initiating the war, which it described as "a supreme offense against international morality and the sanctity of treaties," and for the prosecution of German military personnel for war crimes against the Allied military.[7] But no tribunal was ever convened to try Kaiser Wilhelm II, who died in exile in the Netherlands where he had been granted political asylum. The Commission on the Responsibilities of the Authors of the War and on Enforcement of Penalties, established by the Allied Powers at the Paris Peace Conference in 1919, initially identified a list of German military personnel who might be prosecuted as criminals. Combined pressure by Germany, which declined to extradite any German citizens to Allied governments, and diminished interest among the Allies themselves caused that list to be whittled down. Eventually, the Allied powers agreed that only forty-five individuals should be prosecuted for war crimes committed during World War I, and that Germany should conduct those prosecutions. Only twelve individuals were brought to trial before the German Supreme Court at Leipzig in 1921, and the six defendants who were convicted received only minor sentences.[8]

Stimson's proposal for addressing Nazi atrocities after World War II received a boost when Morgenthau's plan of pastoralizing Germany was leaked to the press and eventually gained the upper hand.[9] Roosevelt, who had always been concerned that devastating Germany might create resistance, started to gravitate towards a framework for trials outlined by Murray Bernays, a colonel in the War Department, that followed Stimson's approach. In May 1945, President Harry Truman appointed Supreme Court Justice Robert H. Jackson as chief counsel for addressing Nazi crimes and authorized him to enter into negotiations for an international trial of the major Nazi war criminals with representatives of the United Kingdom, Soviet Union, and France. Those negotiations resulted in the London Charter of August 8, 1945, providing the basis for international criminal trials of Nazi officials and establishing rules for those trials.

The Nuremberg Trials attempted to achieve several broader goals beyond deciding a particular defendant's guilt or innocence and imposing punishment. The trials, which included the trial of both major Nazi military and civilian leaders before the International Military Tribunal (IMT) at Nuremberg and the twelve further trials of high-ranking German officials conducted by the US military under Control Council Law No. 10 (Subsequent Proceedings), sought to create the basis for postwar international peace and security by punishing the crime of aggression. As Jackson explained in his opening statement before the IMT, "This trial is part of the great effort to make the peace more secure."[10] The focus on crimes against the peace (or the crime of aggression) in the London Charter and at trial illustrates the aspiration for Nuremberg to become "the Trial to End All Wars."[11] The IMT deemed war "essentially an evil thing" and aggression the "supreme international crime."[12]

Nuremberg's architects chose criminal trials to achieve this goal not only because of their deterrent effect. They also believed that a judicial process would allow Germans to accept the criminality of their leaders, create a record of Nazi atrocities that would forever discredit the Nazi regime, and facilitate Germany's postwar transition.[13] Trials would demonstrate both the world's abhorrence for the Third Reich and the moral superiority of the Allied powers. The Nuremberg Trials thus pioneered what scholars have described as a model of closure: using criminal proceedings to provide a definitive account of and accounting for mass atrocity that evokes, in participants and observers, a sense of social solidarity premised on the "common values" of what Emile Durkheim called the "collective conscience."[14]

Criminal trials, in this regard, appeared superior to other forms of accountability. Yet, while Morgenthau opposed trials, at least for the Nazi leadership, he was closer to the spirit of ICL today in one respect. Morgenthau's focus on Nazi atrocities against Jews and other groups, rather than on sovereigntist concerns about Germany's launching of aggressive war, anticipated ICL's subsequent focus on crimes against humanity and genocide. On the other hand, Morgenthau wanted an extralegal form of justice, swift and merciless, which is antithetical to the basic premise of a judicialized process underpinning modern ICL.[15]

Nuremberg's singular achievement was to seek justice through a paradigm that defines crimes under international law and holds individuals responsible through the mechanism of a criminal proceeding. That paradigm represents the triumph of what Judith Shklar has termed legalism: "the ethical attitude that holds moral conduct to be a matter of rule following, and moral relationships to consist of duties and rights determined by rules."[16]

The Nuremberg Trials, however, were not merely deciding individual cases nor using those cases Solely to build a historical record of Nazi barbarity. In seeking to punish those responsible for Nazi atrocities and to prevent their recurrence, the United States and other Allied Powers were deliberately setting an example. They intended to show that principles of criminal justice could – and should – be applied to the gravest of crimes. Nuremberg thus resisted the proposition that some crimes were so extraordinary that, as Hannah Arendt later put it, they "explode[d] the limits of the law" and defied the structure of a judicial proceeding.[17] But adopting the form of a judicial proceeding meant that Nuremberg's success would be measured not only by whether, but also by *how* justice was imposed. Stimson and others did not believe that Nazi leaders deserved rights. They thus did not share the view associated with contemporary human rights discourse, which asserts the universal rights of all defendants regardless of the enormity of the alleged crimes or the form of proceeding in which they are tried. But Stimson and others did believe that the success of all criminal trials depends ultimately on the perception that the defendants are treated fairly and afforded due process. Jackson famously conveyed this sentiment in his opening statement, emphasizing, "We must never forget that the record on which we judge these defendants today is the record on which history will judge us tomorrow."[18]

Despite its aspiration to adhere to principles of legality and due process, the IMT faced significant obstacles that it did not – and could not – always overcome. Central charges of the indictment were vulnerable on the ground that they constituted impermissible *ex post facto* punishment – a violation of the principle of legality known as *nullum crimen sine lege* (no crime without law). That principle requires that the law be defined clearly in advance of a crime's commission. The related principle *nulla poena sine lege* (no penalty without law) similarly requires that the punishment be defined in advance. The indictment at Nuremberg consisted of four counts: conspiracy (Count 1); crimes against peace (Count 2); war crimes (Count 3); and crimes against humanity (Count 4).[19] The main charge (Count 2) alleged that the Nazi defendants had committed a crime against the peace by participating in "the planning, preparation, initiation, and waging of wars of aggression."[20] Prosecutors relied for this charge on the Kellogg-Briand Peace Pact of 1928, a treaty signed by Germany and sixty-three other countries that renounced aggressive war. The treaty, however, did not define aggressive war. Nor did the treaty provide for criminal sanctions or assign criminal responsibility to any national leader who violated it.

In their challenge to the indictment, the Nazi defendants argued that because crimes against peace had never been codified, their trial was "repugnant to a principle of jurisprudence sacred to the civilized world."[21] In rejecting the defendants' argument, the IMT determined that the *nullum crimen sin lege* principle "is not a limitation of sovereignty, but is in general a principle of justice."[22] Thus, rather than strict legality, the tribunal adopted a more flexible standard that considered whether the Nazis knew the conduct was wrong when they carried out a policy of invasion and aggression. As US Nuremberg prosecutor Telford Taylor framed the question: "It has never been a defense that a robber is surprised by the resistance of his victim and has to commit murder in order to get money."[23] The IMT also determined that the defendants could be held criminally responsible even though the Kellogg-Briand Pact spoke only to state responsibility, since "[c]rimes against international law are committed by men, not by abstract entities, and only by punishing individuals who commit such crimes can the provisions of international law be enforced."[24]

The fourth count was similarly vulnerable to attack. The indictment charged defendants with crimes against humanity, defined in the charter as "murder, extermination, enslavement, deportation, and other inhumane acts against any civilian population," whether or not in violation of the domestic law of the country where perpetrated.[25] From today's perspective, this charge best captures the egregious criminality of the Nazi regime – the mass murder of millions of Jews and other innocent civilians that constitutes the Holocaust. But at the time, the legal prohibition was less clear. Crimes against humanity, which had been suggested to Jackson by a prominent scholar, Hersch Lauterpacht, invoked familiar norms about the treatment of civilians, set forth in international treaties such as the Hague Conventions of 1899 and 1907. The term had also been used in the context of atrocities committed against Armenians in World War I. But no one had been held criminally responsible for this offense, and the offense was not specifically codified in any treaty.[26] The United States and Japan, moreover, had objected vociferously after World War I to the proposition that crimes against humanity existed under international law.[27] While the law of war provided some support for prosecuting crimes committed in occupied territory, international law generally did not regulate how a country treated individuals within its own borders. Prosecutors attempted to address the vulnerability of charging crimes against humanity by requiring a nexus to crimes against the peace or war crimes, thus requiring a connection to the war itself. Prewar atrocities thus had to be linked to preparations to wage aggressive war. The IMT's judgment reflected the uncertain status of crimes against humanity: it tended to find that defendants accused of war crimes and crimes against humanity were guilty of both, thus avoiding the need to distinguish the two offenses. In the two cases where the IMT found the defendants guilty solely of crimes against humanity (those of Nazi publisher and propagandist Julius Streicher and Nazi youth leader and local administrator Baldur Benedikt von Schirach), the tribunal did not elaborate on the nexus between crimes against humanity and war crimes (Streicher) or between crimes against humanity and aggression (von Schirach).[28]

The IMT did not address whether conviction for crimes against humanity constituted *ex post facto* punishment in its decision. Austrian jurist and legal philosopher Hans Kelsen provided one of the strongest defenses of the charge, appealing to notions of fundamental fairness and higher principles of justice. Even if positive law did not expressly outlaw their conduct, Kelsen argued, the defendants "were certainly aware of [its] immoral character," thus satisfying the principle of justice that requires fairness to the accused.[29] And when two postulates of justice are in conflict with each other – here, the principle of *nullum crimen* and the defendants' moral responsibility for aggressive war and atrocities – the higher principle prevails.[30] The alternative – not holding Nazi officials individually responsible for what were universally regarded as grave offenses – was considered unacceptable, as Taylor has explained.[31] But the Subsequent Proceedings convened by the US military in the American Zone from 1946 to 1949, after the main trials before the IMT had concluded, continued to endorse the principle of strict legality, with the exception of the trial of Nazi judges and prosecutors, known as the *Justice Case*.[32] There, the prosecution prevailed by establishing that the defendants knew or should have known that they could be brought to justice for acts so offensive to "the moral sense of mankind."[33]

The establishment of crimes against humanity as a basis for individual criminal responsibility under international law for atrocities committed within a country, including against that country's own citizens, is today considered among Nuremberg's most important legacies.[34] In that regard, Jackson's defense of the proceedings for providing the "sources of a newer and strengthened international law," notwithstanding the lack of precedent, has proven prescient.[35] Yet, Nuremberg also underscored the enduring tension in ICL between rigorous adherence to the principle of legality and the countervailing impulse to hold accountable those who transgress basic moral norms in committing atrocities.

Another potential legal infirmity at Nuremberg lay in the London Charter's provision for conspiracy liability. For Jackson, conspiracy supplied a means of reaching the main architects of aggressive war.[36] For Bernays, it offered a way to assign liability for prewar atrocities by the Nazis against their own nationals, particularly German Jews, by treating those atrocities as overt acts in a conspiracy to commit war crimes. Bernays' original proposal sought to avoid *ex post facto* problems since under traditional war crimes jurisprudence a person could not be guilty of war crimes committed before the outbreak of war.[37]

Article 6 of the London Charter expressly provided for the substantive offense of crimes against the peace as well as for "participation in a common plan or conspiracy for the accomplishment of any [crime against peace]."[38] Article 6, however, was ambiguous as to whether it intended to extend conspiracy liability to the other two substantive offenses under the London Charter: war crimes and crimes against humanity.[39] Most accounts agree that the London Charter's conspiracy provision was intended to apply only to crimes against the peace, which explains the emphasis at trial on that offense.[40]

Conspiracy provided an attractive vehicle for establishing liability in a case of mass criminality, such as the Nazi regime, and served Nuremberg's goal of bringing perpetrators to justice. But it proved highly controversial. Conspiracy triggered two interrelated concerns. First, the crime of conspiracy was an integral part of Anglo-American common law systems, but less familiar to Nuremberg's civil law participants (Germany, France, and Russia), although conspiracy was more widespread in civil law systems, including in Germany, than is generally acknowledged.[41] Second, the typical conspiracy in common law systems involved a relatively small number of individuals seeking limited goals. Extending that mode of liability to a nation's decision to wage war could jeopardize the principle of personal responsibility and potentially drag innocent people into the prosecution's net. As Bradley Smith has noted, the French and Russians initially "seemed unable to grasp all the implications of the concept," but once they did, "[t]he French viewed it entirely as a barbarous legal mechanism unworthy of modern law, while the Soviets seemed to have shaken their head in wonderment – a reaction, some cynics may believe, prompted by envy."[42]

The IMT, therefore, interpreted conspiracy liability narrowly. It rejected conspiracy as a basis of liability for war crimes and crimes against humanity, applying the conspiracy charge only to crimes against peace and limiting conspiracy's scope to acts closely involving planning of the war.[43] Twenty-two defendants were charged with conspiracy at Nuremberg, but only eight were convicted of this charge, and a conviction for conspiracy did not factor heavily in their sentences.[44] Judges further restricted conspiracy liability during the Subsequent Proceedings.[45]

Similar concerns surrounded the second path for achieving broader liability: Bernays' plan to try German organizations as well as individual defendants at Nuremberg. Convicting an organization before the IMT, Bernays believed, would facilitate the conviction of its individual members in subsequent proceedings for the lesser crime of membership, especially if defendants bore the burden of showing that they did not join the organization voluntarily.[46] Allied planners, especially Jackson, viewed organizational liability as essential to pursuing the numerous individuals whose participation the Allies could not prove, but whose membership in a criminal organization, such as the SS or Gestapo, they could easily demonstrate.[47]

The IMT judges, however, exhibited concerns about the case against criminal organizations and narrowed organizational liability in several ways. They insisted that prosecutors show both that the organization had an existence as a group entity, such that its members would have understood that they were participating in a collective purpose, and that the organization's criminal objectives were pervasive and shared among its members.[48] Under this more restrictive test, the IMT acquitted four of the seven organizations that had been charged (convicting only the Leadership Corps, Gestapo, and SS). The judges further concluded that the prosecution would bear the burden of proving that any person prosecuted for membership in a criminal organization joined that organization voluntarily and knew that the organization engaged in crimes within the jurisdiction of the London Charter.[49] In the Subsequent Proceedings held before US military tribunals, the prosecution had to establish each person's knowing and voluntary participation in a group with criminal aims, thus negating the procedural advantage Bernays had hoped would result from the conviction of criminal organizations.[50] The administrative denazification program established by the Allies eventually replaced Bernays' plan for thousands of summary trials, and subsequent trials for membership in criminal organizations did not occur on a wide scale.[51]

The Nuremberg Trials reflected the natural impulse to obtain justice for mass atrocities perpetrated by the Nazi regime by imposing criminal responsibility on guilty individuals. But the IMT and tribunals in the Subsequent Proceedings nonetheless recognized that justice had to be implemented in a manner that adhered to principles of legality and fairness to individual defendants. While the Nuremberg Trials highlighted the utility of doctrines that captured the collective nature of Nazi criminality, they also recognized the need for placing limits on conspiracy and organizational liability. Those limits, the IMT explained, were rooted in "well settled legal principles, one of the most important of which is that criminal guilt is personal, and that mass punishments should be avoided."[52]

* * *

Studies of Nuremberg generally pay less attention to its procedures than to its substantive innovations in international law. But Nuremberg's legacy is significant in the procedural domain as well. The defendants, as Jackson wrote in his report on the London Charter, must have the "fundamentals of procedural 'due process of law.'"[53]

Nuremberg's contribution in this area, however, is less to specific procedural requirements, which seem skeletal by today's international fair trial standards, than to broader principles of fairness.[54] The accused were accorded a presumption of innocence and the prosecution was required to prove beyond a reasonable doubt the guilt of each defendant. The London Charter and Rules of Procedure provided the defendants with a basic list of protections. Before trial, they were entitled to an explanation of their right to trial, receipt of the indictment, and a list of defense counsel. At trial, they had the right to an explanation of the charges, to a translation of the proceedings (if needed), to the assistance of counsel, to present evidence, and to cross-examine witnesses called by the prosecution.[55] The IMT also had the power to summon witnesses to testify.[56]

Defendants, however, had no right against self-incrimination, no right of appeal, and no protection against double jeopardy,[57] and *in absentia* trials were permitted if the defendant had not been found or if the tribunal deemed it necessary in the interests of justice to conduct the trial in the defendant's absence.[58] The London Charter was designed to give the tribunal flexibility in the admission of evidence. The IMT could admit any evidence "deemed to have probative value" and was not "bound by technical rules of evidence."[59] The use of written affidavits was intended to help expedite the IMT proceedings, and was seen by Jackson as critical to progress in the cases.[60] At trial, a large number of affidavits were admitted into evidence.[61] Such reliance on untested affidavit evidence in place of oral testimony subject to cross-examination under the London Charter[62] represents a procedural limitation of Nuremberg, even if the trial was generally fair overall.[63] While the London Charter specified that the IMT had the authority to summon witnesses, order the production of documents and other evidence, and appoint court officers to collect such evidence, those powers were not typically exercised in favor of the defense.[64] Further, the prosecution had greater resources than defense counsel.[65] Even the presumption of innocence was not codified, but was provided *de facto*, primarily at Jackson's insistence.[66]

Defendants' lack of any right of appeal is a significant deficiency of Nuremberg, particularly given the importance of the proceedings and the complexity of the issues. The IMT's authority both to try a defendant *in absentia* and to impose the death penalty exacerbated this shortcoming.[67] In the Subsequent Proceedings, defendants were given a limited right of appeal to the US Military Governor, from whom they could seek clemency and pardons.[68]

Several factors help put these procedural limitations in perspective. The IMT sought to combine the distinct Anglo-American common law and Continental civil law systems of the participating states.[69] This blending was reflected, for example, in Nuremberg's extensive reliance on documentary evidence.[70] Also, the defense lacked adequate conditions and resources to undertake independent investigations, a key feature of adversarial systems.[71] Beyond the challenges presented by the attempted marriage between civil and common law systems, the sheer gravity of the Nazi crimes exerted a downward pressure on procedural rights. Most importantly, Nuremberg predated the postwar development of due process standards in international human rights and international humanitarian law.[72] In this regard, Nuremberg did not seek to deviate from recognized rules so much as attempt to create baseline fair trial procedures in a *sui generis* context.

Nuremberg's main contribution was in establishing the principle that due process must be maintained in bringing perpetrators of the severest crimes to justice. Nuremberg thus not only created a lasting precedent for addressing mass atrocity through an international criminal trial, but also reinforced the notion that the trial's ultimate success hinged on its fairness and integrity. The finest jurists were sent to Nuremberg, indicating the significance that the Allied Powers attached not only to the proceedings, but also to the perception that those proceedings be viewed as lawful and legitimate. As with its approach to the *nullum crimen* principle, the Nuremberg Trials aspired to a basic sense of fairness. Jackson set the tone early on in a speech to the American Society of International Law in Washington, DC: "You must put no man on trial under the forms of judicial proceedings if you are not willing to see him freed if not proven guilty. . . the world yields no respect to courts that are merely organized to convict."[73]

The judges, who came only from the Allied side, were not necessarily free from bias or immune to the overwhelming public demand that Nazi leaders be held accountable.[74] Further, the proceedings were characterized by frequent *ex parte* communications between Jackson and Francis Biddle, the primary US judge at Nuremberg (and Jackson's friend and former colleague). Jackson, for example, directly voiced his disapproval to Biddle on multiple occasions, including about the tribunal's decision overruling Jackson's objections to Hermann Göring's answers on cross-examination and its admitting (what Jackson deemed) irrelevant documents introduced by the defense,[75] while also sharing his opinion with Biddle of the defense's case.[76] Such communications tainted the proceedings and constituted clear violations of professional ethics standards in place at the time.[77]

Yet, the IMT nonetheless demonstrated impartiality in important ways. Due to an internal mix-up, the original indictment substituted German industrialist Gustav Krupp for his son Alfried. The Krupp family had long been Germany's leading arms manufacturer and had managed more than 138 concentration camps. However,

Gustav, who had previously suffered a stroke, had become senile and was deemed medically unfit for trial. Gustav's condition made Alfried, an ardent Hitler supporter who had taken control of the family firm in 1943, the more logical choice for prosecution. When Jackson's prosecution team proposed delaying the trial to allow Alfried to replace Gustav in the indictment, the judges denied the motion; the charges against the father were severed and adjourned without future date. Gustav was never tried, and while Alfried was charged and convicted in the Subsequent Proceedings in the American occupied zone, he was released after three years in prison, pardoned, and restored to his property by the United States. Alfried thus likely received far more lenient treatment than he would have received if originally tried by the IMT since by the time of his trial America's focus had shifted from punishing Nazi war crimes to solidifying Germany's support in the emerging Cold War.[78]

Judges at Nuremberg also demonstrated impartiality in their treatment of German Admiral Karl Doenitz, who was charged with waging unrestricted submarine warfare in violation of the laws of war, including by failing to rescue survivors of attacks. The London Charter was confined strictly to the crimes of the defendants and thus precluded the judges from considering a *tu quoque* defense – that the conduct was excused or mitigated because the other side had engaged in similar conduct.[79] Doenitz's attorney, Otto Kranzbuehler, nevertheless sought and obtained an affidavit from Admiral Chester Nimitz, the US Navy's commander in the Pacific, stating that the United States had likewise waged unrestricted submarine warfare there. Kranzbuehler explained to the judges that he was not offering *tu quoque* evidence, but rather was demonstrating that Doenitz (like Nimitz) had acted in conformance with international law. The IMT convicted Doenitz of other charges, but not the offense of waging unrestricted submarine warfare, and gave him a lesser sentence than it otherwise would have imposed.[80]

Perhaps the most compelling evidence of Nuremberg's aspiration to ensure the fair treatment of the defendants is the outcome itself. Despite the trial's proximity in time to Nazi aggression and atrocities, of the twenty-two high-ranking defendants ultimately tried by the IMT at Nuremberg, nineteen were convicted, while three were acquitted. (The twenty-third defendant, Martin Bormann, was tried and convicted *in absentia*.) Of those nineteen defendants, the IMT acquitted several of some charges, and sentenced only twelve to death.[81] While some defendants may have received sentences that seemed too lenient and others too harsh, the tribunal generally sought to calibrate the sentences to the crimes.[82] The IMT sought not only to demonstrate respect for legality and due process, but also to ensure that international criminal justice not devolve into a show trial, in which, as Vaclav Havel put it, judges are "manipulated by power" and "incapable of defying [it]."[83]

One of the most prominent criticisms of Nuremberg was its exclusive focus on Nazi crimes, which prompted accusations of "victor's justice." US Supreme Court Justice (and Jackson's colleague) Harlan Fiske Stone called the IMT a "high-grade lynching party."[84] Jackson recognized the need for international criminal justice to be even-handed: "If certain acts and violations of treaties are crimes, they are crimes whether the United States does them or Germany does them," he said. "We are not prepared to lay down a rule of criminal conduct against others which we would not be willing to have invoked against us."[85] The Allied Powers recognized that they were creating an international legal regime that could, in the future, be applied to their own actions as well.[86] But at Nuremberg this principle was honored more in the breach than the observance. The IMT limited prosecutions to the defeated European Axis powers and did not consider war crimes committed by the Allied Powers.[87] The Allied Powers, moreover, did not prosecute Germans for the aerial bombings of Coventry, Belgrade, Warsaw, and Rotterdam because they knew it would trigger legal scrutiny of their bombings of Dresden, Darmstadt, and Hamburg.[88] While prosecutorial selection decisions did not delegitimize Nuremberg,[89] they remain Nuremberg's most complicated legacy and point to a dimension of fairness that international criminal tribunals continue to grapple with today.[90]

* * *

Nuremberg should also be viewed in connection with the proceedings conducted by the International Military Tribunal for the Far East (also known as the Tokyo Tribunal). Established to prosecute Japanese war crimes, the Tokyo Tribunal has a checkered history. If Nuremberg highlights ICL's potential to impose criminal responsibility for the commission of atrocities while upholding principles of legality and due process, Tokyo underscores the risk that these principles will be sacrificed to hold alleged perpetrators accountable. The Tokyo Tribunal, moreover, has cast a long shadow over international justice mechanisms in nonwestern societies by reinforcing the perception that those mechanisms are biased in their design and implementation.[91]

Although less studied than the Nuremberg Trials, the Tokyo Tribunal's flaws have been well documented.[92] All twenty-five defendants before the Tokyo Tribunal were convicted, excluding the two who died during the trial and the one who was discharged because of a mental disorder. Nine of the eleven judges signed the majority opinion; five wrote separate opinions; and two authored dissenting opinions.[93]

Unlike the IMT, which was created through negotiation among the Big Four powers, the Tokyo Tribunal was established by the Special Proclamation of General Douglas MacArthur, acting as Supreme Commander for the Allied Powers.[94] The Tokyo Tribunal's charter did not bind it to any technical rules of evidence. The tribunal not only relied heavily on second or third-hand hearsay, including newspaper reports, but also expressed less caution than the IMT in exercising this latitude.[95] Resources were heavily skewed in favor of the prosecution. Japanese defendants, although permitted to have American lawyers in addition to Japanese attorneys, remained at a disadvantage because they faced an unfamiliar legal system and a criminal proceeding conducted in a language with which they were not completely proficient.[96] Similar criticisms have been directed at the separate trial of General Tomoyuki Yamashita, whose conviction by a US military commission in the Philippines was upheld on appeal by the US Supreme Court.[97] In a scathing dissent from the Supreme Court's opinion, Justice Frank Murphy asserted that Yamashita had been "rushed to trial under an improper charge, given insufficient time to prepare an adequate defense, deprived of the benefits of some of the most elementary rules of evidence, and summarily sentenced to be hanged."[98]

As at Nuremberg, defendants at Tokyo claimed that the trial violated the principle of *nullum crimen sine lege*. The Tokyo Tribunal rejected this challenge, citing the Nuremberg judgment as precedent. In his separate opinion, Justice Röling of the Netherlands explained that *nullum crimen sine lege* "is not a principle of justice but a rule of policy, valid only if expressly adopted, so as to protect citizens against arbitrariness of courts ... as well as against arbitrariness of legislators.... [It] may, if circumstances necessitate it, be disregarded even by powers victorious in a war fought for freedom."[99] Röling's opinion captures the notion that strict legal principles could – and sometimes must – be sacrificed for higher aims of justice, particularly that of holding perpetrators of mass crimes responsible to prevent their recurrence.[100]

Justice Radhabinod Pal of India attacked both this premise and the overall conduct of the Tokyo Tribunal in a lengthy and caustic dissent. In addition to objecting to the *ex post facto* imposition of punishment, Pal maintained that the conspiracy charge had not been proven and that the rules of evidence were biased in favor of the prosecution.[101] He labeled the trial a "sham employment of legal process for the satisfaction of a thirst for revenge" and maintained that it did "not correspond to any idea of justice."[102]

Pal's dissent crystalized concerns about victor's justice that are still widely shared in Japan today.[103] This concern centers not only on the conduct of the Tokyo trials, but also on the selection of defendants, which was influenced more by strategic calculations and trade-offs than by the neutral application of legal principles.[104] Justice Pal characterized the creation of the Tokyo Tribunal as essentially a political affair, "cloaked by a juridical appearance," and an exercise in "[f]ormalized vengeance."[105] Notably, Chief Prosecutor Joseph Keenan did not indict Japanese Emperor Hirohito, even though Japan could not have gone to war without his approval, because MacArthur and his advisers believed that keeping Hirohito in power would facilitate a successful postwar transition and help prevent the spread of communism in Japan.[106] The Tokyo Tribunal also failed to examine the conduct of a special Japanese unit that engaged in research into and experiments with biological weapons in China because the United States was eager both to hide the information from the Soviet Union and to profit from the information obtained from the experiments.[107]

There is a risk in overstating the differences between the Nuremberg and Tokyo trials especially since a number of criticisms of the latter (including the imposition of *ex post facto* punishment, the use of hearsay evidence in place of live testimony, the lack of a right of appeal, and the exclusion of crimes committed by the Allied Powers) applied to Nuremberg as well. Several factors contribute to the different perceptions of the two tribunals, such as the higher caliber and prominence of the US legal team at Nuremberg (including the top judge and chief prosecutor) and the IMT's acquittal of three defendants, itself a powerful rejoinder to accusations that Nuremberg was merely a show trial.[108] Despite its flaws, the Nuremberg Trials came closer than the Tokyo Tribunal to achieving an essential goal of any credible and legitimate criminal proceeding, whether aimed at prosecuting garden-variety domestic offenses like theft or murder or the gravest international crimes: to hold a defendant accountable while ensuring his fair treatment.

Nuremberg's effort to protect itself against legal challenge – for example, by requiring a link between crimes against humanity and the crime of aggressive war, and by limiting conspiracy liability to the latter charge – has exposed it to criticism for minimizing the mass extermination of European Jews, the most significant Nazi crime of all.[109] This critique highlights a broader challenge in ICL: the constraints that a criminal trial's procedural requirements impose on its capacity to render a complete or accurate history of mass atrocity. For some, such as Hannah Arendt, the pursuit of other ends beyond determining the guilt or innocence of an individual defendant compromises the integrity of any criminal trial. Arendt, for example, famously critiqued Israel's trial in 1961 of senior-level Nazi bureaucrat Adolf Eichmann for placing history, rather than the actions of the accused, at the center of the trial.[110] Yet, as Lawrence Douglas has explained, even if Nuremberg's approach to crimes against humanity and conspiracy restricted its ability to "do justice" to the Holocaust, the trials still performed an important didactic function. The vast archive of documentary material assembled for the proceedings supplied the basis for subsequent accounts by leading historians of the Holocaust.[111] The Nuremberg Trials, as Richard Wilson has shown, also provided a model for pursuing historical goals within the parameters of an international criminal proceeding that is adversarial in nature.[112] Nuremberg's success in contributing to the historical record, however, depended partly on its reputation for overall procedural fairness when documenting Nazi criminality and the evils of the Third Reich.

* * *

Nuremberg's legal significance is widely recognized. Before Nuremberg, states were generally considered the only proper subjects of international law and a state's treatment of its own citizens within its territory was regarded as an internal affair.[113] Nuremberg altered that Westphalian paradigm by making a state's treatment of its citizens a subject of international law and articulating norms of international criminal responsibility.[114] Nuremberg established that individuals could be held criminally responsible under international law for leading their country into a war of aggression and for atrocities committed within their own state's territory, even when the acts involved only the state's own citizens and were permitted under the state's laws.[115]

The Subsequent Proceedings at Nuremberg conducted by US military tribunals pursuant to Control Council Law No. 10 built on the precedents established by the IMT.[116] The Subsequent Proceedings provided the first case in which the defendants were specifically convicted of genocide (albeit as a crime against humanity), helped develop and refine the doctrine of command responsibility, and rejected the defense of superior orders where an order was manifestly illegal.[117] The Subsequent Proceedings also contributed to the eventual elimination of a required nexus between crimes against humanity and armed conflict. Control Council Law No. 10 did not restrict a tribunal's jurisdiction over crimes against humanity to offenses committed in connection with crimes against the peace or war crimes,[118] and the tribunals in the *Justice* and *Einsatzgruppen* cases suggested that no such nexus was required.[119]

After Nuremberg, the substance and procedure of international criminal law proceeded on divergent paths. Substantive international criminal law continued to develop based on the foundation laid at Nuremberg. In 1946, the UN General Assembly endorsed "the principles of international law recognized by the Charter of the Nuremberg Tribunal and the judgment of the Tribunal."[120] The following year, the General Assembly tasked the newly created International Law Commission (ILC) with preparing a draft code of offenses against the peace and security of mankind,[121] which the Commission completed in 1950 and revised in 1954.[122] Genocide, which was not specifically prosecuted as an offense at Nuremberg, but which was referenced by name in closing arguments of the British and French prosecutors, was prohibited under the Genocide Convention of 1948.[123] The four Geneva Conventions of 1949, which provided a comprehensive codification of international humanitarian law, adopted the Nuremberg principles by strengthening the basis for domestic prosecution of war crimes and providing for international cooperation in the prosecution and punishment of those crimes.[124] The scope of international criminal responsibility established at Nuremberg expanded over time in several ways, such as through the elimination of a required nexus to armed conflict for crimes against humanity.[125]

In 1954, however, the UN General Assembly postponed approval of the ILC's revised draft code of offenses because of disagreements over the politically charged issue of defining aggression.[126] With Cold War tensions mounting, progress largely halted on establishing a system of international criminal justice. Without a workable framework or judicial mechanism, the development of rules and procedures that accompany criminal law's application likewise stagnated.

Other developments, however, helped sow the seeds for the revival of international criminal justice. Most significantly, the post-World War II expansion of international human rights law reinforced the universal nature of states' obligations regarding the treatment of individuals, including those within their own borders.

The development of an international human rights system, with bodies authorized to investigate violations and tribunals empowered to issue judgments, helped establish a right to truth and compensation and foster a victim-centered approach to account-ability. Regional human rights tribunals, particularly in Europe and Latin America, began adjudicating state responsibility for the commission of torture, extrajudicial killing, forced disappearance, and other abuses. Human rights law also helped galvanize domestic prosecutions against senior officials responsible for grave crimes. Beginning in the late 1970s, for example, prosecutors brought cases against former officials, including senior officials, in several countries in Latin America for wide-spread human rights violations committed during previous authoritarian regimes. These developments strengthened accountability norms, empowered civil actors, and generated momentum for the creation of new international criminal tribunals.

While international human rights law bolstered the pursuit of accountability for atrocities through prosecutions, it also strengthened the protections owed to those accused of crimes. For example, the International Covenant on Civil and Political Rights (ICCPR), a foundational international human rights treaty, outlines a series of fair trial rights for defendants, including the right to a presumption of innocence, the right not to be compelled to testify against oneself, the right to equality of arms, and the right to impartial judges.[127] The ICCPR further identifies various pretrial rights, including freedom from arbitrary arrest and a prompt hearing before a judicial officer.[128] These and other guarantees are also contained in UN documents and in regional human rights treaties, including the American Convention on Human Rights, European Convention on Human Rights, and African Charter on Human and Peoples' Rights.[129] Decisions by the UN Human Rights Committee (the treaty body that monitors the ICCPR's implementation), regional human rights tribu-nals, and domestic courts have elaborated on the rights of individuals investigated, detained, and prosecuted by states. The fair trial protections under international human rights law that began to take shape after World War II seek mainly to protect individuals against the coercive authority of the state and to prevent government officials from arbitrarily wielding that authority against disfavored or dissident groups. But these human rights guarantees are universal in scope and thus apply to all defendants, regardless of the alleged crime or the type of proceeding. In this regard, human rights law reinforces one of Nuremberg's central legacies: that legal proceedings established to hold accountable individuals, including state offi-cials, accused of the most heinous crimes must still respect prevailing fair trial norms.

The postwar development of fair trial guarantees under international humanitarian law has also helped cement this legacy. The right to a fair trial is contained in all four Geneva Conventions and in Additional Protocols I and II.[130] The Third and Fourth Geneva Conventions and Additional Protocol I treat depriving a defendant of a fair trial as a war crime.[131] Common Article 3 to the 1949 Geneva Conventions prohibits the imposition of sentences except by regularly constituted courts affording all the judicial guarantees recognized as indispensable by civilized peoples.[132] As the

International Committee of the Red Cross notes, the right to a fair trial has become a rule of customary international law in both international and noninternational armed conflict.[133]

In theory, ICL's overarching goals of accountability and fairness not only can be reconciled, but also are mutually reinforcing. A fair trial is more likely to be perceived as legitimate. Yet, in practice, these goals are often in tension. In the context of international criminal justice, the victim-oriented focus of human rights law, the practical challenges of obtaining evidence in countries devastated by war and political violence, and the sheer gravity of the crimes themselves create pressure to hold alleged perpetrators responsible even at the expense of strict adherence to due process guarantees and principles of legality.

During the hiatus in international criminal justice that followed Nuremberg, substantive norms governing accountability and procedures protecting the rights of defendants continued to develop. But this underlying tension remained. It resurfaced with the revival in the mid-1990s of international criminal tribunals to address atrocities committed in the former Yugoslavia and Rwanda and, thereafter, with the establishment of a permanent international criminal court. The next two chapters trace the evolution of the template established at Nuremberg through these subsequent critical stages in ICL's development.

NOTES

1. Gary J. Bass, *Stay the Hand of Vengeance: The Politics of War Crimes Tribunals* (New Jersey: Princeton University Press, 2000), 182.
2. Ibid., 160.
3. Madoka Futamura, *War Crimes Tribunals and Transitional Justice: The Tokyo Trial and the Nuremberg Legacy* (London: Routledge Press, 2008), 43.
4. David Bosco, *Rough Justice: The International Criminal Court in a World of Power Politics* (New York: Oxford University Press, 2014), 25.
5. Bass, *Stay the Hand*, 157.
6. Bradley F. Smith, *Reaching Judgment at Nuremberg* (New York: Basic Books, Inc., 1977), 25.
7. Treaty of Peace with Germany, arts. 227–29, June 28, 1919, Consol. T. S. 188, 285.
8. M. Cherif Bassiouni, "Combatting Impunity for International Crimes," *University of Colorado Law Review* 71 (2008), 409, 411–13.
9. Bass, *Stay the Hand*, 148.
10. Robert H. Jackson, "Opening Address for the United States," in Michael R. Marrus ed., *The Nuremberg War Crimes Trial 1945–46: A Documentary History* (New York: St. Martin's Press, 1997), 79.
11. David Luban, *Legal Modernism* (Ann Arbor: University of Michigan Press, 1994), 336.
12. *Trial of the Major War Criminals before the International Military Tribunal, Nuremberg, November 14, 1945–October 1, 1946* (1947), vol. 1, 186 (*Trial of the Major War Criminals before the IMT*).
13. Futamura, *War Crimes Tribunals*, 42–43.
14. Jose E. Alvarez, "Rush to Closure: Lessons of the Tadic Judgment," *Michigan Law Review* 96 (1998), 2031, 2032–33. See also Mark J. Osiel, *Mass Atrocity, Collective Memory, and the*

Law (New Jersey: Transaction Publishers, 1997), 22, 24; Salvatore Zappalà, *Human Rights in International Criminal Proceedings* (Oxford: Oxford University Press, 2001), 22–24.

15. Bass, *Stay the Hand of Vengeance*, 152.

16. Judith Shklar, *Legalism: Law, Morals, and Political Trials* (Cambridge: Harvard University Press, 1986), 1.

17. *Hannah Arendt and Karl Jaspers, Correspondence, 1929–1969*, ed. Lotte Kohler and Hans Saner, trans. Robert Kimber and Rita Kimber (New York: Harcourt Brace Jovanovich, Inc., 1992), 54.

18. Jackson, "Opening Address for the United States," 81.

19. Indictment, *Trial of the Major War Criminals before the IMT* (vol. 1), 29–68.

20. Ibid., 42.

21. Ibid., 169.

22. Ibid., 219.

23. Telford Taylor, "Statement of the Prosecution" (August 30, 1946), *Trial of the Major War Criminals before the IMT* (vol. 22), 280.

24. *Trial of the Major War Criminals before the IMT* (vol. 1), 223.

25. Agreement for the Prosecution and Punishment of the Major War Criminals of the European Axis, with annexed Charter of the International Military Tribunal, August 8, 1945, 59 Stat. 1544, 82 UNTS 279 (London Charter).

26. Jonathan A. Bush, "Nuremberg: The Modern Law of War and Its Limits," *Columbia Law Review* 93 (1993), 2022, 2031–32.

27. David Matas, "Prosecuting Crimes against Humanity: The Lessons of World War I," *Fordham International Law Journal* 13 (1989), 3, 87–90.

28. Antonio Cassese, *International Criminal Law*, 3rd ed. (Oxford, England: Oxford University Press, 2013), 88.

29. Hans Kelsen, "Will the Judgment in the Nuremberg Trial Constitute a Precedent in International Law?" *International Law Quarterly* 1 (1947), 153, 165.

30. Ibid.

31. Telford Taylor, *The Anatomy of the Nuremberg Trials: A Personal Memoir* (New York: Alfred A. Knopf, 1992), 629.

32. Kevin Jon Heller, *The Nuremberg Military Tribunals and the Origins of International Criminal Law* (New York: Oxford University Press, 2011), 126.

33. *United States v. Alstoetter (Justice Case), Trials of War Criminals Before the Military Tribunals under Control Council Law No. 10*, vol. 3 (1948), 977; William Schabas, *Unimaginable Atrocities: Justice, Politics, and Rights at the War Crimes Tribunals* (Oxford: Oxford University Press, 2012), 43–44.

34. Theodore Meron, "The Humanization of Humanitarian Law," *American Journal International Law* 94 (2000), 239, 263.

35. Robert H. Jackson, "Opening Statement before the International Military Tribunal," November 21, 1945, *The Robert H. Jackson Center*, www.roberthjackson.org/speech-and -writing/opening-statement-before-the-international-military-tribunal/.

36. Bush, "Nuremberg: The Modern Law of War," 2043.

37. Ibid., 2044.

38. London Charter, art. 6.

39. Raha Wala, Note, "From Guantanamo to Nuremberg and Back: An Analysis of Conspiracy to Commit War Crimes under International Humanitarian Law," *Georgetown Journal of International Law* 41 (2010), 683, 694.

40. Ibid.; Taylor, *The Anatomy of the Nuremberg Trials*, 75–76.

41. Heller, *The Nuremberg Military Tribunals*, 132.

42. Smith, *Reaching Judgment at Nuremberg*, 51.
43. *Trial of the Major War Criminals before the IMT* (vol. 1), 224–25; Steven R. Ratner and Jason S. Abrams, *Accountability for Human Rights Violations in International Law* (Oxford: Oxford University Press, 1997), 118–19; Jonathan A. Bush, "Lex Americana: Constitutional Due Process and the Nuremberg Defendants," *Saint Louis University Law Journal* 45 (2001), 515, 534.
44. Stanislaw Pomorski, "Conspiracy and Criminal Organization," in George Ginsburgs and V. N. Kudriavtsev eds., *The Nuremberg Trial and International Law* (Netherlands: Kluwer Academic Publishers, 1990), 229.
45. Bush, "Nuremberg: Modern Law of War," 2077; *Trials of War Criminals before the Nuremberg Military Tribunals under Control Council Law No. 10*, vol. 15 (1949), 1077.
46. Jonathan A. Bush, "The Prehistory of Corporations and Conspiracy in International Criminal Law: What Nuremberg Really Said," *Columbia Law Review* 109 (2009), 1094, 1141; Pomorski, "Conspiracy and Criminal Organization," 213–20.
47. Pomorski, "Conspiracy and Criminal Organization," 213–20.
48. Allison Marston Danner and Jenny S. Martinez, "Guilty Associations, Joint Criminal Enterprise, Command Responsibility, and the Development of International Criminal Law," *California Law Review* 93 (2005), 75, 113–14.
49. Ibid.
50. Ibid., 114.
51. Ibid.
52. *Trial of the Major War Criminals before the IMT* (vol. 1), 256.
53. Report of Robert H. Jackson, *United States Representative to the International Conference on Military Trials* (London, 1945), xi.
54. M. Cherif Bassiouni, *Introduction to International Criminal Law* (Leiden: Martinus Nijhoff, 2012), 552–53.
55. London Charter, art. 16; Nuremberg Trial Proceedings, Rules of Procedure (vol. 1), http://avalon.law.yale.edu/imt/imtrules.asp; Gregory S. Gordon, "Toward an International Criminal Procedure: Due Process Aspiration and Limitations," *Columbia Journal of Transnational Law* 45 (2007), 635, 642.
56. London Charter, art. 17(a).
57. Gordon, "Toward an International Criminal Procedure," 645.
58. London Charter, art. 12.
59. Report of Robert H. Jackson, xi.
60. Taylor, *The Anatomy of the Nuremberg Trials*, 242.
61. Richard May and Marieke Wierda, "Trends in International Criminal Evidence: Nuremberg, Tokyo, The Hague, and Arusha," *Columbia Journal of Transnational Law* 37 (1999), 725, 749; Megan A. Fairlie, "The Abiding Problem of Witness Statements in International Criminal Trials," *New York University Journal of International Law and Politics* 50 (forthcoming), Florida International University Legal Studies Research Paper No. 17-08 (April 2017), 2–3, https://papers.ssrn.com/sol3/papers.cfm?abstract_id=2956413.
62. London Charter, art. 16(e).
63. Gordon, "Toward an International Criminal Procedure," 644; Fairlie, "The Abiding Problem of Witness Statements," 3–4.
64. Zappála, *Human Rights in International Criminal Proceedings*, 19–20.
65. Robert Cryer, *An Introduction to International Criminal Law and Procedure* (Cambridge: Cambridge University Press, 2007), 95.
66. Norbert Ehrenfreund, *The Nuremberg Legacy: How the Nazi War Crimes Trials Changed the Course of History* (New York: Palgrave Macmillan, 2007), 32.

67. Tessa McKeown, "The Nuremberg Trial: Procedural Due Process at the International Military Tribunal," *Victoria University of Wellington Law Review* 45 (2014), 109, 131.
68. Ibid.
69. Jens David Ohlin, "A Meta-Theory of International Criminal Procedure: Vindicating the Rule of Law," *UCLA Journal of International Law and Foreign Affairs* 14 (2009), 77, 79–80.
70. Gordon, "Toward an International Criminal Procedure," 642–44.
71. Ibid., 644.
72. Laura A. Dickinson, "Using Legal Process to Fight Terrorism: Detentions, Military Commissions, International Tribunals, and the Rule of Law," *Southern California Law Review* 75 (2002), 1407, 1431.
73. Henry T. King, Jr., "The Legacy of Nuremberg," *Case Western Journal of International Law* 34 (2002), 335, 336.
74. Smith, *Reaching Judgment at Nuremberg*, 76.
75. Ehrenfreund, *The Nuremberg Legacy*, 75–77.
76. Taylor, *The Anatomy of the Nuremberg Trials*, 134; Ehrenfreund, *The Nuremberg Legacy*, 81–82.
77. Ehrenfreund, *The Nuremberg Legacy*, 76–78.
78. Ibid., 179–85; Taylor, *The Anatomy of the Nuremberg Trials*, 89–94, 151–64.
79. London Charter, art. 18.
80. Ehrenfreund, *The Nuremberg Legacy*, 60–63.
81. Marrus, *The Nuremberg War Crimes Trial*; Brian F. MacPherson, "Building an International Criminal Court for the 21st Century," *Connecticut Journal of International Law* 13 (1998), 9–10.
82. Bush, "Nuremberg: Modern Law of War," 2037 (comparing the relatively lenient sentencing of Albert Speer and the relatively harsh sentencing of Julius Streicher).
83. Bass, *Stay the Hand*, 28.
84. Alpheus Thomas Mason, "Extra-Judicial Work for Judges: The Views of Chief Justice Stone," *Harvard Law Review* 67 (1953), 193, 212.
85. Report of Robert H. Jackson, 330.
86. Schabas, *Unimaginable Atrocities*, 74–75.
87. London Charter, art. 1; Gerry J. Simpson, "Didactic and Dissident Histories in War Crimes Trials," *Albany Law Review* 60 (1997), 801, 804–06.
88. Mark Lewis, *The Birth of the New Justice: The Internationalization of Crime and Punishment, 1919–1950* (Oxford: Oxford University Press, 2014), 274.
89. Benjamin Ferencz, *An International Criminal Court: A Step toward World Peace* (New York: Oceana Publishing, 1980), 88–89.
90. Lyal S. Sunga, *Individual Responsibility in International Law for Serious Human Rights Violations* (Leiden: Brill/Nijhoff, 1992).
91. Simon Chesterman, "International Criminal Law with Asian Characteristics?," *Columbia Journal of Asian Law* 27 (2014), 129, 143.
92. Futamura, *War Crimes Tribunals*, 8; Richard H. Minear, *Victor's Justice: The Tokyo War Crimes Trial* (Princeton: Princeton University Press, 1971), 74–75.
93. Futamura, *War Crimes Tribunals*, 54. The two dissenting opinions were filed by Justice Radhabinod Pal of India and Justice Henri Bernard of France.
94. Arnold Brackman, *The Other Nuremberg: The Untold Story of the Tokyo War Crimes Trials* (New York: Morrow, 1987), 59.
95. May and Wierda, "Trends in International Criminal Evidence," 745–46.
96. Futamura, *War Crimes Tribunals*, 60.

97. *In re Yamashita*, 327 U.S. 1 (1946).

98. Ibid., 27.

99. *United States v. Araki et al.*, "Separate Opinion of Justice Röling," in *The Tokyo Major War Crimes Trial: The Records of the International Military Tribunal for the Far East* (vol. 109) R. John Pritchard ed., (Lewiston: The Edword Mellen Press, 1981), 44–45.

100. Beth Van Schaack, "*Crimen Sine Lege*: Judicial Lawmaking at the Intersection of Law and Morals," *Georgetown Law Journal* 97 (2008), 119, 132.

101. Dissenting Opinion of Justice Radhabinod Pal, in *The Tokyo Major War Crimes Trial* (vol. 105).

102. Ibid., 37.

103. Futamura, *War Crimes Tribunals*, 148.

104. Chris Mahony, "The Justice Pivot: U.S. International Criminal Law Influence from Outside the Rome Statute," *Georgetown Journal of International Law* 46 (2015), 1071, 1076–77.

105. Dissenting Opinion of Justice Radhabinod Pal in *Tokyo Major War Crimes Trial* (vol. 105), 37.

106. Elizabeth Borgwardt, "A New Deal for the Nuremberg Trial: The Limits of Law in Generating Human Rights Norms," *Law and History Review* 26 (2008), 679, 699–700.

107. Antonio Cassese ed., *The Tokyo Trial and Beyond: Reflections of a Peacemonger* (London: Polity Press, 1993), 47–50.

108. Borgwardt, "A New Deal for the Nuremberg Trial," 701–02.

109. Michael Marrus, *The Holocaust in History* (Hanover: University Press of New England, 1987).

110. Hannah Arendt, *Eichmann in Jerusalem: A Report on the Banality of Evil*, Revised ed. (New York: Penguin Press, 1994), 285–86. Arendt specifically criticized the prosecution for presenting witness after witness who did not address Eichmann's personal guilt. Ibid., 9.18. Eichmann, as another scholar observed, became peripheral to his own trial, which mainly addressed Nazi crimes against the Jews. Osiel, *Mass Atrocity*, 60.

111. Lawrence Douglas, *The Memory of Judgment: Making Law and History in the Trials of the Holocaust* (New Haven: Yale University Press, 2001), 2–3.

112. Richard Ashby Wilson, *Writing History in International Criminal Trials* (Cambridge: Cambridge University Press, 2011), 225.

113. Michael Scharf, "Seizing the 'Grotian Moment': Accelerated Formation of Customary International Law in Times of Fundamental Change," *Cornell International Law Journal* 43 (2010), 454.

114. Anne-Marie Slaughter and William Burke-White, "An International Constitutional Moment," *Harvard International Law Journal* 43 (2002), 1, 8; Paul R. Dubinsky, "Human Rights Law Meets Private Law Harmonization: The Coming Conflict," *Yale Journal of International Law* 20 (2005), 212.

115. Schabas, *Unimaginable Atrocities*, 51–55; Meron, "The Humanization of Humanitarian Law," 263.

116. Control Council Law No. 10 authorized subsequent proceedings against German military and civilian personnel by the Allied powers in their respective occupying zones. Commanders in the French zone also established a tribunal to conduct prosecutions pursuant to Control Council Law No. 10; the British did not conduct trials pursuant to this law, but instead conducted a series of military prosecutions confined to charges based on the laws of war; the Soviet Union did not pursue any prosecutions pursuant to Control Council Law No 10. Allison Marston Danner, "The Nuremberg Industrialist Prosecutions and Aggressive War," *Virginia Journal of International Law* 46 (2006), 651, 659.

117. Heller, *The Nuremberg Military Tribunals*, 388, 392–93, 395.
118. Control Council Law No. 10, Punishment of Persons Guilty of War Crimes, Crimes against Peace and against Humanity (December 20, 1945), http://avalon.law.yale.edu /imt/imt10.asp.
119. W. J. Fenrick, "International Humanitarian Law and Criminal Trials," *Transnational Law and Contemporary Problems* 7 (1997), 23, 41–42, and n. 61.
120. U.N. G.A. Res. 95(I), U.N. Doc. A/64/Add.1 (December 11, 1946).
121. U.N. G.A. Res. 177(II), U.N. Doc. A/RES/174(II) (November 21, 1947).
122. Principles of International Law Recognized by the Charter of the Nuremburg Tribunal and in the Judgment of the Tribunal, adopted by the UN International Law Commission, August 2, 1950, reprinted in *Yearbook of the International Law Commission* 2 (1950).
123. Geneva Convention for the Prevention and Punishment of the Crime of Genocide, December 9, 1948, 78 U.N. T.S. 277; William A. Schabas, "Origins of the Genocide Convention: From Nuremberg to Paris," *Case Western Journal of International Law* 40 (2007–08), 36–37.
124. The 1949 Geneva Conventions, for example, strengthened the basis for individual criminal responsibility for the mistreatment of prisoners of war and civilians during armed conflict. Geneva Convention Relative to the Treatment of Prisoners of War, August 12, 1949, art. 129, 6 U.S.T. 3316, 75 U.N. T.S. 135; Geneva Convention Relative to the Protection of Civilian Persons in Time of War, August 12, 1949, art. 146, 6 U.S.T. 3516, 75 U.N. T.S. 287.
125. Meron, "The Humanization of Humanitarian Law," 263.
126. G.A. Res. 898 (IX), U.N. GAOR, 9th Sess., Supp. No. 21, at 50, U.N. Doc. A/2890 (1954).
127. International Covenant on Civil and Political Rights, art. 14, December 16, 1966, 6 I.L.M. 368 (entered into force March 23, 1976).
128. Ibid., art. 9.
129. Andrew B. Friedman, "Transitional Justice and Local Ownership: A Framework for the Protection of Human Rights," *Akron Law Review* 46 (2013), 727, 742–43; Sara Stapleton, Note, "Ensuring a Fair Trial in the International Criminal Court: Statutory Interpretation and the Impermissibility of Derogation," *New York University Journal of International Law and Politics* 3 (1999), 535, 545, and n. 3.
130. Jean-Marie Henckaerts and Louise Doswald-Beck, *Customary International Humanitarian Law, Volume 1: Rules* (Cambridge: Cambridge University Press, 2005), 352–53.
131. Ibid., 353.
132. 1949 Geneva Conventions, Common Article 3.
133. Henckaerts and Doswald-Beck, *Customary International Humanitarian Law*, 352.

2

International Criminal Law's Revival and the Challenges of Implementation

The mass violence that erupted in the territory of the former Yugoslavia in the early 1990s helped spark the second era of modern international criminal law. In response to widespread killings and atrocities, the United States and Europe pressed for the creation of an international criminal tribunal to punish those most responsible. A similar impulse propelled the creation the following year of an international criminal tribunal for Rwanda, where nearly one million people were murdered in a genocide perpetrated by Hutu extremists during a 100-day period in 1994. After the international community failed to intervene or prevent the violence, it sought to impose legal accountability for it.

The waning of the Cold War had made possible the international cooperation necessary to establish an international criminal tribunal. In May 1993, the United Nations (UN) Security Council passed Resolution 827, creating the International Criminal Tribunal for the former Yugoslavia (ICTY), the first international criminal tribunal since the Nuremberg and Tokyo tribunals were created after World War II. The resolution announced that the tribunal would seek to bring to justice those individuals responsible for the commission of mass killings, ethnic cleanings, and other serious violations of international law in the former Yugoslavia.[1] In November 1994, the Security Council passed Resolution 955 creating the International Criminal Tribunal for Rwanda (ICTR) to prosecute and punish those responsible for the genocide and other atrocities committed in Rwanda.[2] In both instances, the Security Council invoked its powers under Chapter VII of the UN Charter to address what it identified as a threat to international peace and security.[3]

Like the IMT at Nuremberg, the ICTY and ICTR – also known as the *ad hoc* tribunals – sought to punish grave criminality, while also protecting the rights of the accused. But unlike Nuremberg, the ICTY and ICTR were truly international; rather than being composed of judges from the winning side of the conflict, they were supranational entities established by the international community. The ICTY and ICTR, moreover, could exercise jurisdiction over all individuals within the territory covered by their governing statutes during the relevant time period, another measure with the potential to avoid the pitfalls of victor's justice. Most importantly, the design and structure of the *ad hoc* tribunals reflected significant post-Nuremberg developments in the field of international law. By the mid-1990s, international human rights law had expanded the protections afforded individuals accused of crimes, regardless of the nature of the proceedings or gravity of the offense. The UN Secretary-General thus explained that it was "axiomatic that the [ICTY] must fully respect the internationally recognized standards regarding the rights of the accused at all stages of its proceedings."[4] The statutes of the ICTY and ICTR both incorporated numerous legal protections for the accused recognized under human rights treaties, including the presumption of innocence, the right to trial without undue delay, and the right to examine and confront the prosecution's witnesses.[5] Each tribunal's respective Rules of Procedure and Evidence supplemented these protections.[6] Additionally, the *ad hoc* tribunals extended legal protections to defendants at other phases of international criminal proceedings, including the pretrial, sentencing, and appeals phases.[7] For example, at both Nuremberg and Tokyo, defendants did not have a right to appeal their conviction. The ICTY, ICTR, and other second-generation international criminal tribunals expressly recognized this right, reflecting both the influence of human rights norms and an appreciation of the value of appellate review to ICL's development.[8]

Through these enhanced legal protections, the ICTY and ICTR reinforced the notion that international criminal tribunals should provide accountability within a framework of procedural fairness. Additionally, the *ad hoc* tribunals highlighted the potential for ICL to promote respect for human rights protections through the prosecution of grave crimes. Bringing fair trial norms to war-torn societies by articulating and enforcing fair trial standards has been described as an additional benefit of international criminal tribunals.[9] These tribunals could both elevate and model human rights norms by respecting them even in prosecutions of the most extraordinary crimes.

Since its establishment, the ICTY has indicted more than 160 individuals for serious violations of international humanitarian law committed in the territory of the former Yugoslavia, and concluded proceedings in all except a handful of those cases.[10] The Completion Strategy adopted by the UN Security Council in 2003 required the ICTY to focus on the most senior leaders and transfer intermediate and lower level officials to domestic jurisdictions.[11] The ICTY is expected to conclude its final trial and appeals by 2017.[12] The ICTR concluded proceedings for more than eighty accused individuals; a small number of its remaining cases have been referred to national courts[13] or to the International Residual Mechanism for Criminal Tribunals (MICT), which the UN Security Council established in 2010 to continue the essential functions of the ICTY and ICTR after the tribunals' closure.[14]

The ICTY and ICTR have made significant contributions to the development of international criminal law and procedure. They have provided the modern template for an organizational structure of an international criminal tribunal, elaborated substantive doctrines of international criminal responsibility, set precedents in international humanitarian law, and developed practices and procedures to address the multitude of issues that can arise during an international criminal prosecution. But despite their many successes, the ICTY and ICTR also highlight the tensions between ICL's goals of holding perpetrators accountable and protecting the fair trial rights of the accused. This chapter focuses on these two *ad hoc* tribunals. It also briefly describes corresponding developments at hybrid tribunals – courts that combine international and domestic features and which are discussed at greater length in Chapter 4.

***

Early scholarship on the ICTY often focused on the challenge of blending two disparate legal systems: the adversarial systems of common law countries such as the United States and United Kingdom; and the inquisitorial, civil law systems of continental Europe and other civil law countries. As a general matter, in adversarial legal systems, judges serve as neutral referees, while the parties – the prosecution and defense – bear primary responsibility for marshaling and presenting evidence. In inquisitorial systems of civil law countries, judges traditionally play an active role in the proceedings, including by examining the charges and requesting necessary modifications, requesting and reviewing documentary evidence, and examining witnesses.[15] The ICTY initially more closely resembled adversarial models, in part because of significant US influence on the drafting of the ICTY statute and Rules of Procedure and Evidence.[16] Over time, however, the ICTY incorporated more features of civil law systems to address concerns about the lengthy and cumbersome nature of international criminal trials. The ICTY, for example, adopted a rule for and practice of appointing a pretrial judge, increasingly utilized documentary and other non-oral evidence, and relied on greater judicial management.[17] The ICTY thus increased its use of inquisitorial procedures to increase efficiency.[18] Some observers have argued that melding the two systems jeopardizes important safeguards present in each system.[19] Adversarial systems, for example, rely heavily on zealous advocacy by defense counsel to test the prosecution's evidence because judges act more like neutral umpires rather than active investigators of the facts on behalf of both sides, as in civil law systems. An amalgamated system that limits the latitude of defense counsel to challenge the evidence without retaining the prominent judicial role in scrutinizing that evidence – an important safeguard of inquisitorial systems – can produce imbalances between the opposing sides that may undermine a trial's fairness.[20]

One area in which international criminal tribunals have had to mediate between divergent common law and civil law traditions is the prosecution's right to appeal an acquittal. Common law countries, such as the United States, typically prohibit the government from appealing judgments of acquittal, whereas civil law systems generally allow for appeals of legal errors and questions of fact, as they view the appeal as part of the same proceeding.[21] The ICTY and ICTR adopted the civil law model by giving the prosecution a broad right of appeal. This feature has exposed those tribunals to criticism for unnecessarily tipping the scale in favor of the prosecution, particularly with respect to appeals of factual questions.[22] Human rights instruments, however, contemplate this result, prohibiting the trial of an individual twice for the same offense,[23] but leaving the determination of what constitutes a final conviction or acquittal – thereby triggering this prohibition – to the law and procedure of each country's respective legal system.

Scholars today focus less on the collision of disparate legal systems than on how international criminal tribunals navigate the challenges they face in achieving their multiple, disparate, and sometimes conflicting goals.[24] Like all prosecutions, international criminal trials depend on a judicial forum designed to determine if a particular defendant is guilty and, if so, to impose punishment in accordance with specified rules and procedures. Yet, the ICTY and successor tribunals have also pursued other goals. Those goals include ending impunity for international crimes and preventing their reoccurrence; restoring international peace and security (the principal justification for the UN Security Council's establishment of the ICTY and ICTR); creating a historical record of mass atrocity; spreading respect for human rights and fair trial principles to national justice systems; and honoring the rights and interests of crime victims, including by enabling their meaningful participation in legal proceedings.[25]

Maintaining ICL's commitment to the rights of the accused can advance each of these various goals. Convictions achieved through fair procedures, for example, strengthen their legitimacy. Protecting the rights of the accused can help restore peace and security by demonstrating respect for the rule of law even where it might lead to an undesirable outcome in a particular case. And modeling fair trial procedures in international prosecutions can strengthen respect for those procedures at the national level.

But pursuit of these broader goals can also conflict with an international criminal tribunal's commitment to upholding fair trial standards in individual cases. Prioritizing the creation of a historical record can infuse trials with a didactic purpose, such as establishing the root cause of a conflict or genocide, potentially delaying proceedings and weakening the presumption of innocence. Giving a voice to victims can prejudice defendants, as can measures designed to protect witnesses by limiting a defendant's right to understand the case against him and to confront and cross-examine his accusers. And because the stakes are so high, prosecutions of grave crimes tend to accentuate the tension inherent in all criminal proceedings between the impulse to punish the perpetrator and the obligation to protect the rights of the accused.

Pursuit of ICL's broader aims can create a proclivity towards victim-focused teleological reasoning that maximizes victim protection through expansive doctrines of liability and construes ambiguous legal questions against the defendant.[26] The desire to adhere to classic liberal principles designed to safeguard the rights of defendants while also pursuing a victim-oriented focus urged by human rights groups and other broader goals has led to what one scholar termed ICL's "identity crisis."[27] Some have responded by insisting that international tribunals scale back their ambitions and focus more on criminal law's traditional purpose: determining if individual defendants are guilty or not.[28] Others, however, have instead called for even greater flexibility by jettisoning the goal of applying fair trial standards developed in domestic contexts to international criminal prosecutions.[29]

The ICTY statute provides various textual hooks that judges have used to balance the rights of the accused with the goal of achieving accountability through criminal prosecutions. Article 21 of the ICTY statute, for example, is the primary provision addressing the right of the accused to a fair trial and is derived from Article 14 of the International Covenant on Civil and Political Rights (ICCPR), a core human rights treaty.[30] Although Article 21 mainly enumerates the rights of the accused, its first subsection provides that "all persons shall be equal" before the tribunal.[31] ICTY judges have relied on this provision to grant rights to the prosecution, explaining that the principle of equality prohibits favoring one party at the expense of another.[32] In one case, the ICTY Appeals Chamber ordered a partial retrial because the Trial Chamber had refused the prosecutor additional time to secure the testimony of witnesses.[33] In other cases, the ICTY has similarly viewed requests by the prosecutor to present certain evidence through the lens of the prosecution's right to a fair trial, rather than asking whether the prosecution was unduly hampered in presenting its case, thus effectively pitting the prosecutor's right to a fair trial against that of the defendant.[34] The corresponding fair trial clauses of the ICTR and the Special Court for Sierra Leone (SCSL), the hybrid tribunal created to prosecute international war crimes committed during that country's civil war, also contain provisions regarding the equality of the parties. (The former references the rights of all persons, the latter the rights of all accused.)[35] The SCSL has extended the right to trial without undue delay beyond the prosecution to victims and their family members.[36]

A more powerful counterweight to the rights of the accused is the challenge of trying mass crimes, particularly those perpetrated by senior government and military officials, in an international court with limited enforcement power. While tribunals established to prosecute international crimes purport to transcend state sovereignty, they depend heavily on the cooperation of individual states for critical functions, from arresting suspects to gathering evidence. The First President of the ICTY, Antonio Cassese, compared the tribunal to "an armless and legless giant which needs artificial limbs to act and move." Those limbs, Cassese said, are state authorities, and if those authorities "fail to carry out their responsibilities, the giant is paralyzed, no matter how determined its efforts."[37] This dependence on states can make it difficult for international tribunals to fulfill their aspiration of protecting the rights of the accused while bringing perpetrators of grave crimes to justice.[38] At the ICTY and ICTR, this dependence, along with other obstacles, created pressure to expand modes of criminal responsibility and to restrict the procedural rights of defendants in several ways.

***

Some of the sharpest critiques of the *ad hoc* tribunals relate to the scope of international criminal responsibility. An extensive body of literature examines the development of modes of liability – mainly, joint criminal enterprise and command responsibility – that impose responsibility on individuals other than those who physically committed the offense.[39] These modes of liability can be critical legal tools for prosecuting mass crimes, where those most culpable in terms of seniority or decision-making authority are often remote from the locus of the physical commission of the crime itself. Yet, they also risk sweeping in lower-level officials or improperly assigning responsibility to higher-level officials when those officials lack the necessary *mens rea* (criminal intent). Additionally, retroactively applying arguably novel doctrines of criminal responsibility to past conduct clashes with the principle of legality.

The ICTY's use of joint criminal enterprise (JCE) has prompted significant criticism. In several respects, concerns over the ICTY's application of JCE echoes those expressed at Nuremberg over the use of conspiracy and organizational liability to address collective criminality. JCE provides for criminal responsibility where an individual acts together with others pursuant to a common plan, design, or purpose in committing an international crime. JCE is thus not a crime itself, but rather a mode of liability. It can be applied to crimes that have multiple participants, who each played a different role in planning, organizing, or executing the criminal conduct. In the case of torture, for example, one person might order the crime, another might physically execute it, and still another might observe it to determine if the victim reveals useful information. All these individuals could potentially be held criminally responsible under JCE based on their respective participation in the common plan of torture.[40] JCE also can enable prosecutors to reach, among others, the criminal masterminds in a context where a mastermind's direct link – and evidence of that link – is often lacking. In the case of offenses committed in concentration camps or prisons, for example, the person ultimately responsible for the criminal conduct typically remains separated from its physical commission by several levels of bureaucracy.

The ICTY first recognized JCE in the seminal *Tadić* case, the first full trial before the tribunal. The ICTY convicted Duško Tadić, a low-level Serbian perpetrator, of several counts of war crimes and crimes against humanity, but acquitted him of murder as a crime against humanity for the killing of five Muslim men in a Bosnian village, the most serious charge against him. The Trial Chamber found that although Tadić was a member of the armed group that had entered the village and beat its inhabitants, there was insufficient evidence that Tadić himself had participated in the murder of five men during the time that the group was in the village.[41] The Appeals Chamber reversed the acquittal, finding that under JCE Tadić could be held criminally responsible for the murders because he had shared and participated in a common plan with the individuals who carried them out, even if he himself did not commit them.[42]

The Appeals Chamber in *Tadić* identified three forms of JCE liability: (i) where the defendant belongs to a group with a common plan but is not the physical perpetrator of the crime intended by the group (JCE I); (ii) where the defendant has knowledge of and actively participates in an organized system of violence and repression, such as a concentration camp (JCE II); and (iii) where the defendant who participates in a common plan is held criminally responsible for acts committed by other group members that are a "natural and foreseeable consequence" of the original plan (JCE III).[43] Although proponents of JCE have sought to distance it from conspiracy because the latter is histori-cally viewed as a common law doctrine without sufficient support in interna-tional law, JCE functions in many respects like conspiracy by placing the focus on a shared understanding or arrangement between two or more people amount-ing to an agreement that they will commit a crime.[44]

The ICTY statute provided five modes of liability but did not expressly recognize JCE as a basis for criminal responsibility. The Appeals Chamber nonetheless concluded that JCE liability was supported by the statute's object and purpose, which extended the tribunal's authority over those "responsible for serious violations of international humanitarian law" committed within the territory of the former Yugoslavia so that the perpetrators could be "brought to justice."[45] In support of this conclusion, it cited cases from military courts established after World War II.[46] Those cases involved concentration camps and the unlawful killings of Allied prisoners of war (POWs) by German soldiers (or German soldiers and German townspeople). The concentration camp cases provide solid support for JCE II, but the POW cases provide support only for more limited versions of JCE I and JCE III.[47] Because the POW cases involved murders by small groups of individuals within a specific time and place, they are weak precedents for more expansive forms of JCE liability based on a common plan that extends several years and across multiple regions, and particularly for the broadest form of the doctrine – JCE III or extended joint criminal enterprise – used to hold defendants responsible for crimes committed outside the common plan based on their foreseeability.[48] That JCE III permits liability for the acts of coconspirators, as long as the results are reasonably foreseeable, suggests its close link to the doctrine of conspiracy and especially to the *Pinkerton* doctrine developed by US courts, which provides for the attribution of criminal responsibility based on the acts of coconspirators.[49] Notably, however, several US courts have recognized the fairness concerns posed by *Pinkerton* liability where the link between an individual's wrongdoing and criminal liability is highly attenuated, and have accordingly narrowed the doctrine's reach in such circumstances.[50]

At the time the ICTY prosecutor indicted Tadić in 1995, the tribunal suffered from "a lack of individuals to try and a surfeit of judges with no cases to adjudicate."[51] JCE offered new opportunities to hold individuals responsible – including high-level officials who were the tribunal's main focus – for atrocities committed in the former Yugoslavia. Yet, the ICTY's innovative approach was in tension not only with the principle of *nullum crimen sin lege* given the limited support for JCE provided by the World War II era precedents, but also with the tribunal's mandate to employ only that part of international criminal law that had become "beyond doubt" part of customary international law,[52] or law that results from "a general and consistent practice of states followed by them from a sense of legal obligation."[53]

JCE also can jeopardize the principle of personal culpability. After *Tadić*, the ICTY applied JCE to atrocities committed throughout an entire region and to a nationwide government-organized system.[54] As one Trial Chamber explained, "[a] joint criminal enterprise can exist whenever two or more people participate in a common criminal endeavor. This criminal endeavor can range anywhere along a continuum from two persons conspiring to rob a bank to the systematic slaughter of millions during a vast criminal regime comprising thousands of participants."[55] Judges at the ICTY confirmed indictments that alleged, for example, that the defendant participated in the JCE of forcibly removing a majority of the non-Serbian population from approximately one-third of the territory of Croatia and from large parts of Bosnia and Herzegovina.[56] Because the ICTY considered "all of the participants in the . . . enterprise to be equally guilty of the crime regardless of the part played by each in its commission," it made low-level individuals perpetrators of all the crimes committed within the enterprise.[57] Attributing responsibility to an individual without regard to his role and function in the commission of a crime conflicts with the principle that individuals should be punished based on their personal culpability.[58] Also, while the ICTY pointed to the need to show each defendant's contribution to the common plan as a limitation on JCE, it did not impose a high threshold, rejecting that the contribution necessarily be substantial and failing to specify what would make a contribution significant.[59] Additionally, ICTY decisions weakened the requirement that the defendant share the common intent of the enterprise – a central justification for JCE – by finding that a person could intend a consequence, even if it was not the person's immediate aim, as long as he could foresee a substantial possibility that his course of action would produce that outcome.[60]

Under JCE III, moreover, individuals may be held responsible for any foreseeable crime committed by members of the group even if it falls outside the common plan. Several ICTY chambers interpreted foreseeable to mean "objectively foreseeable," thus making defendants liable for consequences that they did not themselves anticipate as long as a reasonable person in the defendant's position would have foreseen the risk that crimes beyond the criminal purpose of the JCE were likely. This interpretation effectively lowers the mental state from purposeful culpability to recklessness, if not negligence,[61] and represents a powerful tool for prosecutors given how easy it is to characterize a particular consequence as foreseeable.[62] The ICTY also defined foreseeability broadly to include crimes that might possibly have occurred when determining the *mens rea* requirement for JCE III.[63] The ICTY's expansive view of JCE effectively situates the potential limits on criminal responsibility not primarily in the law itself, but rather in the exercise of a prosecutor's discretion not to bring cases against less culpable individuals or in a judge's decision to make more fine-grained distinctions about a particular defendant's relative culpability at verdict and sentencing.

After *Tadić*, the ICTY relied on JCE in many prosecutions, which, as a practical matter, made it more difficult to revisit prior conclusions since it would have jeopardized the legitimacy of much of the tribunal's work.[64] The ICTR also adopted JCE liability. Although the ICTR did not use JCE widely,[65] it relied on another potentially expansive mode of liability – conspiracy to commit genocide – in a majority of its indictments.[66] The SCSL also adopted JCE.[67] The Extraordinary Chambers in the Courts of Cambodia (ECCC), the hybrid tribunal established to prosecute atrocities committed by the Khmer Rouge, adopted JCE I and II, but notably rejected the ICTY's analysis and conclusion in *Tadić* on JCE III.[68] Based on a comprehensive analysis, the Pre-Trial Chamber of the ECCC ruled that JCE III did not previously exist as a mode of criminal responsibility under customary international law.[69] The Trial Chamber adopted this ruling, casting additional doubt on *Tadić's* analysis of JCE III and *Tadić's* conclusion that the use of JCE III conformed to the principle of legality since, the ECCC determined, JCE III was not an established basis for individual criminal responsibility when the acts in question were committed.[70] Commentators and practitioners, as well as an ICTY judge,[71] have expressed similar views, questioning JCE III's status under customary international law and noting the tension it creates with fairness-based principles of notice, individual criminal responsibility, and foreseeability.[72]

The ICTY has properly observed that its precedents "expanded the boundaries of international humanitarian and international criminal law."[73] Its adoption of JCE helped address collective criminality in instances where the perpetrator shared with others a common plan to commit international crimes, such as the persecution of a particular group within a town or city, but did not physically carry out the torture, beatings, or other unlawful conduct.[74] The ICTY's use of JCE thus facilitated the conviction of individuals who participated in serious violations of human rights.[75] JCE, for example, recently constituted the mode of liability under which an ICTY trial chamber convicted former Bosnian Serbian leader Radovan Karadžić of genocide and crimes against humanity for his role in the genocide in Srebrenica, the persecution and Bosnians and Croats in Bosnia and Herzegovina, and the spread of terror among the population of Sarajevo.[76]

JCE's defenders maintain that, in general, the doctrine is consistent with the principle of individual criminal responsibility because the defendant must be aware of the common purpose of the criminal action and share the requisite criminal intent.[77] The ICTY Appeals Chamber has also taken steps to cabin the scope of JCE liability, for example, by interpreting JCE to require a strict definition of common purpose.[78] But JCE nonetheless underscores how ICL's far-reaching goals – including holding perpetrators of mass crimes responsible under international law, ending impunity, establishing peace and security in affected countries and regions, and bringing justice to victims – can conflict with its commitment to the fair treatment of the accused, particularly as the doctrine is stretched to reach more marginal figures or acts more remote from an agreed upon criminal plan.

Some similar concerns surround the doctrine of command responsibility, although that doctrine has been used more sparingly and provoked less controversy than JCE.[79] The ICTY prosecuted the first international cases using command responsibility since *Yamashita* and other post-World War II trials. Following World War II, the Tokyo Tribunal employed the doctrine to hold Japanese commanders responsible for war crimes committed by subordinates without evidence of a commander's direct involvement.[80] Most notably, a US military tribunal in the Philippines convicted Japanese General Tomoyuki Yamashita and sentenced him to death, despite his denying any knowledge of or involvement in the massacres of civilians committed in the Philippines by Japanese troops under his authority.[81] The US Supreme Court's ruling affirming Yamashita's conviction helped establish the precedent that superiors may be held responsible for crimes committed by their subordinates.[82] But the doctrine of command responsibility, and Yamashita's case in particular, proved controversial for jeopardizing the principle of individual culpability by allowing superiors to be prosecuted without demonstrating their personal knowledge of or causal contribution to the crimes committed.[83] Yamashita argued that the US military counteroffensive had effectively cut off his chain-of-command, rendering him incapable of knowing about, preventing, or punishing the crimes.[84] In his dissent from the Supreme Court's decision upholding Yamashita's conviction, Justice Murphy maintained that "[t]o use the very inefficiency and disorganization created by the victorious forces as the primary basis for condemning officers of the defeated armies bears no resemblance to justice or to military reality."[85]

The ICTY helped develop the doctrine of command responsibility, providing a model that successor tribunals have largely adopted. The ICTY statute identifies two main ways for holding responsible a superior officer. The tribunal may hold a superior officer responsible where he orders, pressures, or encourages his subordinates to commit war crimes.[86] It may also hold a superior officer responsible where he knew or had reason to know the subordinate was about to commit crimes or had done so, and the superior failed either to take necessary and reasonable steps to prevent those crimes or to punish the perpetrators after their commission.[87] Most command responsibility cases proceed under a failure to prevent or punish theory since evidence of active involvement by a commander in the commission of war crimes is rare.[88] A UN Secretary-General report describes command responsibility as a type of "imputed responsibility or criminal negligence."[89] Command responsibility requires that the prosecution establish three main elements: the existence of a superior-subordinate relationship; that the superior knew, or had reason to know, a crime was about to be, was being, or had been committed; and that the superior failed to take adequate measures to prevent or respond to the crime.[90]

Command responsibility serves important purposes. It provides a means of penetrating the upper echelons of the military or civilian establishment whose members often bear the primary responsibility for atrocities committed by individuals on the ground. Command responsibility thus furthers ICL's aim to bring the main culprits to justice. It also serves a deterrent function.[91] Commanders are well situated to ensure that those under them obey international criminal and humanitarian law. The specter of liability for war crimes, even when not directly ordered or encouraged by superior officers, may incentivize those officers to take steps to prevent and punish their commission.

Yet, the same rationale behind command responsibility highlights its potential risks to ICL's commitment to the fair treatment of the accused. Holding superior officers responsible for their failure to prevent or punish atrocities jeopardizes the principle of personal responsibility where evidence of knowledge of the atrocities or control over the individuals who committed them is weak or nonexistent. It also runs counter to commonly held moral perceptions that distinguish between someone who fails to prevent or punish a crime and the person who commits it.[92] Because a superior officer is convicted of committing the crime itself, command responsibility can stigmatize individuals as war criminals in circumstances where their main failure may have been in not punishing a crime committed by others after the fact. Such inaction may warrant internal disciplinary action and even criminal prosecution under a country's domestic law. But, as Darryl Robinson observes, punishing an individual for the underlying international crime itself under a theory of command responsibility without any causal contribution to or impact on the crime's commission conflicts with basic criminal law principles of personal responsibility and fair labelling (the notion that the label of the offense should fairly capture and express the wrongdoing of the offender).[93] It risks conflating the procedural duty international humanitarian law imposes on a commander to investigate and punish the past crimes of his subordinates with a principle of criminal responsibility that makes the commander personally guilty for those crimes even if he has no causal connection to them.[94]

Judges have been more successful in limiting the expansion of command responsibility than JCE. Both the ICTY and ICTR resisted either a strict liability or negligence standard for convictions under command responsibility. In its first judgment, the ICTR rejected the application of a broad version of command responsibility to the civilian mayor of a town in Rwanda where the local militia had carried out abuses against displaced ethnic Tutsi seeking refuge in the town. In addressing *mens rea*, the Trial Chamber stated that command responsibility should be based on malicious intent or, at minimum, negligence "so serious as to be tantamount to acquiescence or even malicious intent."[95] Shortly thereafter, the ICTY addressed the command responsibility standard in an important case involving the Čelebići prison camp, where Bosnian Muslim and Bosnian Croat forces subjected Bosnian Serb detainees to torture, beatings, sexual assault, and other abuses. In applying the doctrine of command responsibility, the ICTY Trial Chamber ruled in *Prosecutor v. Delalić* (the *Čelebići* case) that a superior cannot "remain willfully blind to the acts of his subordinates."[96] The Appeals Chamber, however, refused to treat command responsibility as a form of strict liability, adopting a "had reason to know" standard and maintaining that a court may convict a superior only where "information was available to him which would have put him on notice of offenses committed by subordinates."[97] Applying this standard, the Appeals Chamber affirmed the acquittal of one of the defendants, a Bosnian Muslim deputy commander assigned to the camp, of command responsibility for crimes committed by lower ranked guards.[98] The Appeals Chamber's ruling in *Čelebići* settled lingering uncertainty at the ICTY over the reach of command responsibility. The ICTY Trial Chamber had previously interpreted the doctrine expansively in *Prosecutor v. Blaškić*, where widespread crimes had occurred in territory under a Croatian commander's control, but where there was no direct evidence of the commander's knowledge of most of the crimes. The Trial Chamber in *Blaškić* had suggested that criminal responsibility could be established based on an absence of knowledge that resulted from a commander's negligence in the discharge of his duties.[99] The Appeals Chamber later not only overturned *Blaškić's* conviction on most counts and reduced his sentence from forty-five to nine years, but also rejected that command responsibility could be imposed under a simple negligence theory.[100] The ICTY imposed a further limitation on command responsibility by requiring that a superior have effective control over his or her subordinate at the time of the offense, thus preventing the imposition of criminal liability where a superior lacked effective authority or assumed his position as commander after the crimes had occurred.[101]

Aiding and abetting liability in the context of foreign assistance to organizations is another area that can pit efforts to establish accountability for international crimes against fairness to the accused. In 2013, the ICTY Appeals Chamber acquitted former Yugoslav army chief Momčilo Perišić of aiding and abetting international crimes committed in Bosnia and Herzegovina during the early years of the conflict in the former Yugoslavia.[102] The ICTY Trial Chamber had previously found that Perišić, the top military officer in the Yugoslav Army in Belgrade, Serbia, had provided weapons and ammunition, technical expertise and training, and other critical support to Bosnian Serb separatist forces engaged in widespread and systematic atrocities, and that Perišić was aware of the atrocities being committed by Bosnian Serb forces.[103] Those atrocities included the shelling of Sarajevo from August 1993 to November 1995 and the massacre at Srebrenica in July 1995.[104] The Appeals Chamber ruled, however, that the Bosnian Serb Army was also a legitimate armed force engaged in lawful combat activities, and that Perišić, who was remote from the crimes of the principals, could not be convicted for the military assistance that the Yugoslav Army provided absent evidence that he specifically directed that assistance towards the Bosnian Serb Army's criminal activities and not merely towards its general war effort.[105]

However, less than one year later, in *Prosecutor v. Šainović*, the ICTY Appeals Chamber rejected the specific direction requirement articulated in *Perišić* in upholding the conviction of another Serbian general, Vladimir Lazarević, for aiding and abetting crimes committed during the forcible displacement of part of the Kosovo Albanian population by Serb forces.[106] In *Šainović*, the Appeals Chamber instructed that the focus should be on whether the accused had substantially and knowingly contributed to the commission of the relevant crimes.[107] The SCSL Appeals Chamber also subsequently rejected the specific direction standard as an element of aiding and abetting in upholding the conviction of Charles Taylor, the former president of Liberia, for providing military, financial, and other support to rebel forces in Sierra Leone who killed and tortured civilians, abducted children, and engaged in other crimes there.[108] The SCSL Appeals Chamber concluded, moreover, that aiding and abetting liability could be established based not only on intentional or knowing assistance of a crime, but also on recklessness.[109] The International Criminal Court (ICC), which is the focus of Chapter 3, has yet to confront this issue. But its statute adopts a different approach, requiring that the aider and abettor purposely facilitate the commission of crimes by the principal.[110] While the ICC provision places greater emphasis on intent, and thus could help prevent aiding and abetting liability from eroding the principle of personal responsibility, it would not necessarily reach commanders who continue to supply assistance to an organization even after they become aware of the nefarious uses to which that assistance is being put.[111]

The Appeals Chamber's decision in *Perišić* has prompted significant criticism for setting forth an overly stringent standard for aiding and abetting liability under ICL.[112] Because organizations engaged in illegal activity typically also engage in some legitimate acts, proving that a foreign state's assistance was specifically directed towards an organization's criminal actions – effectively drawing a straight line from the defendant's conduct to the offending behavior – can be difficult without the rare presence of smoking gun evidence.[113] *Perišić*, critics argue, thus risks foreclosing accountability for government officials, particularly military or political leaders, who remotely support foreign groups that manifestly engage in human rights violations as long as those groups also engage in legitimate activities and the support is not specifically targeted towards a group's criminal ends.[114]

But the Appeals Chamber's approach in *Perišić* has also been defended by those concerned with the potential breadth of aiding and abetting in the context of organizational liability. Kevin Jon Heller argues, for example, that because the *mens rea* of aiding and abetting liability requires only knowledge of an organization's criminal activities, requiring specific direction for the *actus reus* (physical elements of a crime) of aiding and abetting, as the ICTY Appeals Chamber did in *Perišić*, can help prevent overbroad applications.[115] Otherwise, he argues, individuals who inter-act with organizations engaged in lawful and unlawful acts cannot provide any assistance that might end up facilitating those unlawful acts, as long as they are aware of them. For example, US or UK officials who provide assistance to rebel groups in Syria could be held responsible for aiding and abetting even without any intention to further a group's criminal activities and even if they take measures to prevent those illegal activities.[116] Indeed, during trial proceedings in *Perišić*, Judge Bakone Justice Moloto, who ultimately dissented from the Trial Chamber's judg-ment of conviction, pressed the prosecution on whether its theory of aiding and abetting liability would effectively inculpate all NATO commanders in Afghanistan based on their knowledge of war crimes committed by some participants against detainees.[117] In that respect, aiding and abetting has the potential to exceed JCE III liability, which at least requires that the accused be part of an agreement with a criminal objective.

Aiding and abetting liability must be sufficiently flexible to cover situations such as those in the former Yugoslavia where generals, like Perišić, had every reason to know that the vast assistance they were supplying to Bosnian Serb forces would be used in the commission of war crimes and crimes against humanity, and where such crimes were being committed as part of a deliberate and systematic policy of ethnic cleansing.[118] An overly restrictive approach to aiding and abetting can also under-mine broader goals of accountability. In Serbia, for example, the government has sought to treat the Appeals Chambers' acquittal of Perišić as a collective exoneration of Serbia for its involvement in mass atrocities in Bosnia and Croatia.[119] Yet, allowing for aiding and abetting liability under a more malleable standard of knowledge coupled with assistance could lead to prosecutions of government officials that fail to provide the type of notice and predictability necessary to safeguard the liberty of the accused in a way consistent with the principle of legality.[120] It could also excessively deter constructive foreign aid programs that pursue foreign policy goals due to a fear that the aid will unavoidably fall into the wrong hands.[121] To address such chal-lenges, some scholars have proposed adoption of a reasonable due diligence require-ment before providing arms or other assistance to an organization.[122] Another proposal places less emphasis on distinctions among formal legal standards for aiding and abetting, viewing them as inevitably indeterminate, and instead focuses on ensuring that adjudicators assign criminal responsibility in a manner that is sufficiently predictable and maintains a normatively meaningful distinction between guilt and innocence.[123] Such an approach would attribute responsibility where a balance of factors overwhelmingly supports a finding of criminal guilt as a way of steering between the following extremes: the prosecutorial overreach that can result from a standard based merely on knowledge and substantial assistance; and the accountability gap that can result from requiring that the accused either share the criminal purposes of the principal perpetrators and extend significant support with the specific aim of furthering their crimes or provide aid that is specifically directed towards the criminal activity, as in *Perišić*.[124]

Liability under JCE, aiding and abetting, and command responsibility often boils down to a question of proof. Pressure to expand these doctrines frequently results from the commission of mass atrocities and the absence of direct or strong circumstantial evidence linking the physical commission of those atrocities to the person who bears significant, if not ultimate, responsibility for them. Increasing the legal requirements for criminal responsibility under one doctrine can divert prosecutions to an alternative mode of liability. The additional requirements of command responsibility, for example, helped cause international prosecutors to rely more heavily on JCE. Narrowing doctrines of criminal responsibility can also increase pressure on judges to dilute procedural safeguards and adopt more flexible standards of evidence to prove an individual defendant's guilt.

***

The ICTY and ICTR inherited from Nuremberg a commitment to procedural fairness and a recognition that the soundness and legitimacy of any criminal judgment, no matter how grave the offense, rests ultimately on the fairness of the process itself. Yet, the two *ad hoc* tribunals did not inherit a procedural system so much as a commitment to a broader principle of fairness and a skeletal set of standards for prosecuting crimes in international courts. Under the heading Rights of the Accused, Article 21 of the ICTY statute delineates core safeguards such as the presumption of innocence, the right to be informed of the charges, the right to have adequate time to prepare a defense and communicate with counsel of one's choosing, the right to trial without undue delay, the right to examine adverse witnesses, and the right not to be compelled to testify against oneself or confess guilt.[125] The ICTR statute contains a virtually identical provision.[126] Pursuant to the authority delegated under the tribunals' respective statutes,[127] ICTY and ICTR judges subsequently drafted Rules of Procedure and Evidence (RPE) establishing the procedural framework for pretrial, trial, appellate, and sentencing phases of proceedings.[128] The rules filled various gaps in the tribunals' respective statutes, such as by describing when the parties could seek appeals of a trial chamber's interlocutory (nonfinal) orders.[129] The judges have frequently amended their tribunals' respective RPE over time, helping to develop a set of *sui generis* procedures that combine aspects of different legal traditions.[130] The ICTY, in particular, has moved from an adversarial model rooted in common law legal systems to a model that includes significant features of civil law systems, such as greater judicial involvement and management at all stages of a case[131] and increased use of non-oral testimony.[132] Some view these judicial adaptations not merely as necessary, but also as a positive development because they represent a flexible response to emerging challenges on the ground.[133] Critics, however, maintain that some changes, particularly those designed to increase efficiency, disproportionately burden the defense, limit the defendant's ability to contest the prosecution's case, and diminish equality of arms between the parties.[134]

The *ad hoc* tribunals, and the ICTY in particular, developed a significant body of procedural law that has served as an example for international and hybrid courts that followed. Yet, the work of the ICTY and ICTR underscores that procedural systems are to some degree a product of their specific context. In ICL, various factors help shape procedure, including the gravity of the crimes, the challenges of gathering evidence in countries devastated by war, mass violence, and social upheaval, and the limits on a court's power of enforcement and reliance on states for cooperation. These features tend to exert pressure to diminish procedural protections and create friction with ICL's competing commitment to ensuring that defendants receive a fair trial.

Cracks in the ICTY's commitment to the procedural rights of the accused surfaced in *Tadić*, the tribunal's first trial, where the prosecution sought anonymity for several witnesses. In a divided decision, a majority of the Trial Chamber granted the prosecution's request.[135] It acknowledged that the ICTY statute gave the defendant the right to examine the prosecution's witnesses and to receive a fair and public hearing, but it also said that those protections had to be balanced against the statute's provision for the protection of witnesses.[136] The Trial Chamber distinguished the widespread prohibition on anonymous witnesses in domestic criminal proceedings based on the exceptional nature of the crimes and ongoing conflict in the former Yugoslavia, which it said could warrant departures from generally accepted criminal law principles.[137] The dissent noted that the use of anonymous witnesses could lead to unreliable testimony and prejudice the fair trial rights of the accused.[138] Although only one witness testified in a manner completely anonymous and shielded from the view of the defendant, the Trial Chamber's decision on protective measures received significant criticism.[139] The ICTY has not granted complete witness anonymity since *Tadić*, but the decision nonetheless exposed tensions between the tribunal's goal of punishing perpetrators of grave crimes and protecting witnesses, on the one hand, and safeguarding the fair trial rights of defendants, on the other.[140]

In general, the ICTY has demonstrated a preference for flexibility, giving judges discretion to consider and weigh evidence within the context of a particular case. The tribunal's rules permit judges to admit evidence that is relevant and probative, while allowing them to exclude evidence if it is substantially outweighed by the need to ensure a fair trial.[141] In its first trial, the ICTY upheld the admissibility of hearsay evidence as long as the evidence was reliable and had sufficient probative value.[142] One common explanation for the ICTY's approach is that the prohibition against hearsay evidence traditionally developed in common law systems in response to the mistrust of jurors, whom judges considered unable to assess properly such evidence. International tribunals such as the ICTY, however, employ professional judges capable of discounting irrelevant evidence and giving hearsay evidence its proper weight.[143] Another explanation is that the ICTY does not depend on cross-examination to the same extent as common law adversarial systems, where the party-led nature of evidence gathering generates a need for cross-examination to enable the factfinder to assess the credibility of declarants. The ICTY's more flexible approach to the admission of hearsay evidence additionally reflects the influence of civil law systems, whose commitment to discovering the truth generally militates against the exclusion of credible evidence, and the gravity of international crimes themselves, which makes exclusion of evidence less palatable.

The ICTY accordingly imposed a high bar on the exclusion of evidence, explaining that "it would be utterly inappropriate to exclude relevant evidence due to procedural considerations, as long as the fairness of the trial is guaranteed."[144] The tribunal underscored that the exclusion of relevant and probative evidence would conflict with its other goals of holding perpetrators of serious international law violations accountable, affording justice to victims, deterring future violations, and contributing to the restoration of peace in the territory of the former Yugoslavia.[145] ICTY judges also imposed minimal requirements on the authentication of documents, allowing them to consider large volumes of evidence that might otherwise prove too difficult or time-consuming to authenticate through traditional procedures.[146]

The ICTY's rules initially expressed a strong preference for in-person testimony, notwithstanding the tribunal's otherwise flexible approach to the admissibility of relevant hearsay evidence.[147] Depositions, for example, could be introduced only in exceptional circumstances and only where the opposing party could cross-examine the deponent.[148] A series of amendments intended to expedite proceedings in large trials like that of former Yugoslav president Slobodan Milošević and to address the challenges of producing witnesses from zones of armed conflict and social collapse gradually eroded that preference.[149]

Tribunal judges initially amended their rules to allow the parties to seek to introduce affidavits to corroborate live witness testimony, without requiring that the affiant be subject to cross-examination.[150] They subsequently amended the rules to give them the flexibility to accept evidence of a witness orally or, where the "interests of justice allow," in written form.[151] Judges also replaced the earlier amendment on corroboration of live witness testimony by affidavit with a provision, Rule 92 *bis*, allowing for the admission of evidence in written form where the evidence concerns issues other than the defendant's acts and conduct, such as evidence providing background about the conflict or establishing commission of a crime itself (as opposed to the defendant's role in it).[152] The admission of such crime-base evidence is common in international tribunals where political or military leaders facing indictment did not physically perpetrate the offense, but instead committed the crime as part of a joint criminal enterprise or through their exercise of superior responsibility over others, such as subordinate soldiers or paramilitaries.[153] As a result, crime-base evidence may bear on contextual elements of a crime, such as the widespread or systematic nature of the attacks for a crime against humanity, or on the accused's state of mind as it relates to establishing his guilt under different modes of liability.[154]

Rule 92 *bis* became one of the ICTY's most frequently used rule amendments, including in prominent cases such as the *Karadžić* trial.[155] It dispenses, however, with any requirement of cross-examination of witnesses who provide statements; instead, the opportunity to cross-examine such witnesses is left to judicial discretion.[156] While judges in some instances authorized cross-examination because of the importance of the evidence to the prosecution's case, they were inconsistent in their approach to Rule 92 *bis* and sometimes lacked sufficient information to determine whether the particular background evidence was, in fact, connected to the acts of the accused.[157] At the same time, the provision's efficiency gains remain contested.[158]

Another rule amendment, Rule 92 *ter*, which was prompted by challenges encountered during the trial of Slobodan Milošević, permits witnesses who testify to the acts of the defendant to submit written testimony as long as they come to court and are subject to cross-examination by the defense.[159] A separate rule amendment, Rule 92 *quater*, allows judges to admit written statements or transcripts from witnesses who have died, who are no longer able to testify orally due to their physical or mental condition, or who can no longer be found even after exhausting reasonable efforts.[160] A further rule amendment, Rule 92 *quinquies*, permits the admission of written evidence from witnesses who elect not to testify because of fear of intimidation, provided that the interests of justice will be served by such admission,[161] although the ICTY does not appear ever to have relied upon this provision.[162] The ICTY's reliance on written testimony increased as a result of the tribunal's Completion Strategy, which imposed deadlines for the conclusion of its work,[163] and the fact that a growing number of witnesses had testified before the tribunal more than once.[164] The ICTR and hybrid tribunals, such as the SCSL, exhibited similar flexibility on the admission of written evidence,[165] although they appear to have relied on such evidence less than the ICTY.[166]

Some view a flexible approach to the admission of evidence by international criminal tribunals as a pragmatic response to an array of challenges, including: evidence lost due to deceased witnesses; witness intimidation in territory over which international prosecutors lack the type of enforcement authority possessed by domestic prosecutors armed with the full power and support of their sovereign state; and the difficulties of gathering evidence in countries afflicted by protracted armed conflict and political and social disintegration.[167] The ICTY, for example, adopted its provision on the admission of evidence by persons who did not testify due to improper interference in response to concerns encountered in specific cases, namely that of Serbian politician Vojislav Šešelj, who reportedly succeeded in delaying proceedings through witness intimidation.[168]

This increased reliance on written evidence has nonetheless prompted concerns about limiting a defendant's ability to probe the prosecution's evidence through cross-examination and thereby weakening the defendant's fair trial rights.[169] Critics note, for example, that permitting the use of directly incriminating hearsay evidence, such as under Rule 92 *quater*'s provision for unavailable witnesses, can increase the risk of error, particularly where the trial chamber lacks the necessary information to assess its reliability.[170] Defense lawyers have been particularly outspoken. The Association of Defense Counsel for the ICTY, for example, has criticized the tribunal's wide latitude to admit written statements and to limit or deny cross-examination.[171] Additionally, critics note that the ICTY Prosecutor, who does not have an obligation to establish the truth or to investigate incriminating and exonerating information equally, has engaged in excessive adversarialism, thus undercutting a common justification for departing from a requirement of oral testimony.

The ICTY and ICTR's increased reliance on taking judicial notice of adjudicated facts has also generated controversy, pitting concerns about fairness to the accused against the need to minimize unnecessary delays in prosecuting international crimes, the main purpose behind the practice.[172] The *ad hoc* tribunals' respective RPE permit judicial notice to be taken of facts adjudicated in other proceedings before the tribunal.[173] As the ICTY explained, by taking judicial notice of an adjudicated fact from another case, the court "proceeds from the assumption that the fact is accurate" and "does not need to be re-established at trial."[174] Hybrid tribunals contain similar provisions.[175] Several trial chambers viewed this authority expansively. In *Karadžić*, the ICTY Trial Chamber took judicial notice of more than 2,000 adjudicated facts, including that Serb forces removed non-Serbs from certain areas, engaged in abuses of detainees, and attacked Muslim areas.[176] The ICTR took judicial notice of the genocide in Rwanda.[177] While taking judicial notice of a particular fact does not prevent the defense from challenging its accuracy, it does shift the burden onto the defense to rebut that fact rather than requiring the prosecution to prove it.[178] The challenge for international tribunals is to utilize provisions governing adjudicated facts to expedite proceedings without jeopardizing the integrity of the judicial fact-finding process.

Another area of contention concerns the scope and timing of the prosecution's disclosure of evidence to the accused. The ICTY's statute and rules mandate the disclosure of specific categories of information, such as materials that supported the indictment, prior statements of the accused, and prior statements of witnesses the prosecution plans to introduce at trial.[179] They also require disclosure of exculpatory information or information that would go to the credibility of the prosecution's case or tend to mitigate the accused's guilt.[180] The ICTY Appeals Chamber has emphasized the importance of disclosing exculpatory information, ruling that the prosecution must disclose such evidence unless reasonably accessible to the accused.[181] The ICTY statute stipulates that states must cooperate with the tribunal "in the investigation and prosecution of persons accused of committing serious violations of international humanitarian law."[182] The ICTY's rules also empower judges to issue warrants, subpoenas, and other orders as necessary for purposes of an investigation or the conduct of a trial.[183]

But despite recognizing the accused's right to secure evidence, the ICTY's rules limit disclosure of information not only to the public, but to the accused as well. These limits, moreover, have increased over time. The rules, for example, allow states to oppose disclosure where it would purportedly prejudice their national security interests[184] and to seek an immediate appeal of an interlocutory decision that directly affects those interests.[185] The rules place additional restrictions on disclosure to encourage states to cooperate with investigations and prosecutions.[186] They authorize the prosecution to request that the trial chamber protect from disclosure information where revealing that information is contrary to the public interest or would affect the security interests of a state.[187] They also permit prosecutors to withhold from disclosure evidence submitted by a state on a confidential basis where that evidence is used to generate new (or "lead") evidence[188] and to restrict the ability of defense counsel or the tribunal itself to probe such evidence when a state consents to its use in court. Judges, for example, cannot order a party to produce additional evidence received from the person or entity that provided the initial confidential lead information and cannot compel a witness called to introduce confidential information from answering any questions related to that information or its origin if the witness declines to answer on grounds of confidentiality.[189] Importantly, the rules allow the prosecutor to apply to the Trial Chamber sitting *in camera* (in private) to be relieved from his or her obligation to disclose potentially exculpatory evidence in the prosecutor's possession where such disclosure may prejudice a further or ongoing investigation or for any other reason that may be contrary to the public interest or affect the security interests of any state.[190] This provision is in tension with a basic principle of due process under many national legal systems and international law: that prosecutors must share with a defendant any information suggesting his actual innocence.[191]

The ICTY's rules limiting disclosure reflect the reality that international criminal prosecutions depend heavily on state cooperation to obtain key witnesses and evidence.[192] The United States, for example, urged that the ICTY's rules protect a state's right to ensure that sensitive intelligence information provided to the tribunal's prosecutor remains confidential. It made this demand over the strong objection of the American Bar Association that such nondisclosure would threaten the credibility and integrity of the proceedings and, for example, insisted on strict conditions before permitting high-level US officials to testify at the trial of Slobodan Milošević.[193] Other powerful western nations have voiced similar concerns about the need to protect sensitive information.[194]

While limits on disclosure may reflect the practical challenges of prosecuting international crimes, they can jeopardize a defendant's fair trial rights, as the case of

Tihomir Blaškić shows. As noted above, Blaškić, a former Colonel and then-General in the Bosnian Croat army, was prosecuted under a theory of command responsibility for international crimes related to the ethnic cleansing of Muslim civilians in Bosnia. The Trial Chamber issued subpoenas to Croatia and several Croatian officials ordering them to produce documents sought by the prosecutor relating to military command structures and plans of action.[195] The Appeals Chamber, on an interlocutory appeal, ruled to quash the subpoenas. It determined that although the ICTY could issue binding orders to states, it could not issue such orders to individual state officials acting in their official capacity.[196] Further, it said, the ICTY had only limited power to enforce its rulings against states by reporting a state's noncompliance to the UN Security Council.[197] After the Trial Chamber convicted and sentenced Blaškić – and following the death of Croatia's former President, Franjo Tuđman and the election of a new government – documents came to light minimizing Blaškić's responsibility. This new evidence led to a reversal of Blaškić's conviction on most charges and a significant reduction in his sentence.[198] *Blaškić* illustrates the ICTY's limited capacity to ensure state compliance and the potential impact on a defendant's due process rights.[199]

Defense counsel also have repeatedly accused prosecutors at the ICTY and other tribunals of not adhering to disclosure deadlines and judges have expended significant time and resources resolving disclosure disputes.[200] Defense attorneys have complained, for example, about the prosecution's continual disclosure of new evidence and changing of its witness lists, thus keeping the defense off-balance and making it difficult to develop and maintain an effective defense plan.[201] Additionally, the ICTY and ICTR have been criticized for inconsistently imposing sanctions on the prosecution for noncompliance with its disclosure obligations[202] and for allowing such noncompliance to extend unduly the length of proceedings.[203]

***

Another area of controversy concerns the provisional release of defendants.[204] Provisional release – more commonly known as bail – rests on two fundamental criminal law safeguards: the presumption of innocence and the right to trial without undue delay. The two are closely related as the longer a suspect is detained pending trial, the greater the infringement on the presumption of innocence.[205] These safeguards are a cornerstone of human rights law, which also embraces the principle of *in dubio pro libertate* (if in doubt favor liberty).[206] The presumption of innocence, moreover, applies categorically, regardless of the severity of the alleged offense, and should require strict justifications to detain accused individuals.[207] In international criminal tribunals, however, the presumption of innocence is often marginalized, with detention being the norm and provisional release the exception.[208]

Several factors explain this variance from human rights standards. ICL's more restrictive approach to provisional release reflects not only the gravity of the crimes, but also the relative lack of enforcement power of international tribunals, which makes it more difficult both to apprehend suspects and to ensure their presence at trial if provisionally released. A defendant's provisional release in areas destabilized by armed conflict and political and social upheaval heightens the risk that the defendant could abscond or intimidate witnesses. For the ICTY, which is situated at The Hague, a defendant's lack of family and community ties in the Netherlands initially proved a significant obstacle to provisional release there.[209]

The duration of international criminal trials exacerbates limits on provisional release, frequently causing defendants to spend years in detention before their cases are tried.[210] In one case before the ICTY, nine years elapsed between the transfer of the accused individuals to the tribunal and the tribunal's issuance of its judgment.[211] Concerns about undue delays include not only the time taken in bringing an accused person to trial, but also, in some instances, the time between the close of trial and issuance of the judgment.[212] Delays at the ICTY – and the implications for the rights of the accused – prompted greater use of measures intended to expedite trials. Judges, for example, made more use of status and pretrial conferences to maintain control over the progression of cases and increased their reliance on written statements.[213]

The evolution of the ICTY's approach to provisional release highlights the tribunal's struggle to implement this protection for defendants.[214] The ICTY statute mandates arrest and detention once an indictment has been confirmed, and there is no right to be released when pretrial detention lasts beyond a reasonable time, as is the case under some human rights treaties.[215] Rule 65 originally provided for provisional release pending trial only in exceptional circumstances, which the accused had the burden of proving, leading to a highly restrictive approach.[216] ICTY trial chambers routinely denied provisional release.[217] A 1999 amendment to this rule eliminated the exceptional circumstances requirement, partly due to increased cooperation by relevant state authorities in the territory of the former Yugoslavia.[218] This change led to the first provisional release of a defendant not on medical grounds.[219] In ordering the provisional release of two individuals after an extended period of pretrial detention, the Trial Chamber cited the tribunal's obligation to respect internationally recognized human rights standards.[220] Yet, some judges cautioned against placing too much emphasis on those standards, explaining that they must consider the context in which international criminal tribunals operate in determining reasonable limits on pretrial detention.[221] In a controversial 2008 decision, the Appeals Chamber tightened the requirement for provisional release, ruling that the accused had to demonstrate "compelling humanitarian grounds" to justify release at later stages of trial proceedings, in addition to fulfilling the general requirements of Rule 65.[222] A 2011 amendment eliminated that additional requirement, thus again strengthening the presumption of innocence.[223]

The 2011 amendment led to the ICTY's pretrial release of defendants who would not otherwise have been freed. It brought the ICTY's rules closer in line with human rights standards on provisional release from pretrial detention and strengthened protections for the accused in this area.[224] The rise in voluntary surrenders by defendants and the natural aging of defendants at the ICTY, which has been in existence for more than two decades, also helped lead to an increase in provisional release.[225] Additionally, the willingness of countries in the former Yugoslavia to host and supervise defendants for the duration of the respective bail period while assuring their return to the tribunal facilitated provisional release in multiple cases.[226] Discrepancies with human rights standards nonetheless remain with respect to the length of time an accused is detained prior to trial and an accused's general ability to obtain provisional release. Accused individuals who did not benefit from a guarantee by a Balkan state were far more likely to be denied pretrial release as the absence of a state guarantee weighed heavily against such release.[227] Also, although in practice several ICTY trial chambers implicitly assigned the prosecution the burden of establishing that the accused poses a danger to victims or witnesses, the dominant view is that the burden still remains on the defendant to prove both that he will appear for trial and that he does not pose a danger to any victim, witness, or other person.[228] Human rights law, by contrast, expressly places that burden on the prosecution.[229] Thus, despite a gradual evolution at the ICTY in favor of protecting a defendant's ability to obtain provisional release, the presumption of innocence in this regard has remained more an aspiration than a hard rule.[230] At the ICTR, provisional release was nonexistent, and the ICTR's decisions did not seriously consider whether the defendants, who were accused of horrific acts of genocide, could be safely released while awaiting trial.[231]

Many domestic jurisdictions impose a presumption of dangerousness or flight risk when a defendant is accused of serious crimes.[232] Additionally, some jurisdictions consider the strength of the prosecution's case as a factor in the provisional release analysis.[233] Thus, international criminal tribunals are not alone in falling short of human rights standards on provisional release, at least where serious crimes are alleged. Limits on provisional release in ICL nonetheless pose particular concerns because international criminal courts are expected to model fair trial standards and because the trials are typically long. The ICTY, moreover, historically prosecuted a number of low-level offenders, whose detention is more difficult to justify on grounds of the severity of the alleged offense. And even where defendants obtain provisional release, delays can still prejudice their right to a fair trial by undermining their ability to present an effective defense, particularly given the degree to which memories of witnesses fade over time.[234]

***

Defense counsel issues represent another area of vulnerability in ICL's treatment of the accused. Nuremberg provided the ICTY and ICTR with an important model in its firm recognition of a defendant's right to counsel. Nuremberg, however, also foreshadowed some of the obstacles international criminal tribunals face both in ensuring an effective defense and achieving equality of arms between the prosecution and defense.[235]

The principle of equality of arms, as developed by modern human rights tribunals, dictates that a suspect not be placed in a procedurally disadvantaged position compared to the prosecutor and that both parties be treated equally.[236] The principle of equality of arms serves as an umbrella for other safeguards. It includes access not only to procedural mechanisms, but also to defense counsel who can effectively gather and present evidence and challenge the prosecution's case.[237]

The ICTY statute addresses defense issues in several places, providing for a defendant's right to the assistance of counsel, including counsel of his own choosing; to assigned legal counsel if the defendant cannot afford it; to self-representation; and to adequate time and facilities to mount a defense.[238] The ICTR statute contains the same provisions.[239] The ICTY Appeals Chamber acknowledged early on that "[t]he principle of equality of arms between the prosecutor and the accused in a criminal trial goes to the heart of the fair trial guarantee."[240] The ICTY insisted that, in conformance with this principle, both parties be afforded procedural equality, which includes adequate time and facilities for the preparation of a defense at trial, and looked to human rights decisions to interpret the content of these requirements.[241] The ICTY further explained that it would give the principle of equality of arms a more liberal interpretation than that ordinarily provided in domestic courts.[242] However, because the ICTY and ICTR's statutes do not describe these provisions in detail, and because of the absence of a prior body of ICL jurisprudence, these tribunals had to flesh out the commitment to securing equality of arms through adequate and effective defense representation in individual cases.

Defense issues initially garnered less attention at the ICTY and ICTR than other fair trial safeguards. However, they gained greater traction over time, leading to increased remuneration, resources, training, and other support for defense counsel.[243] The development of a more experienced defense bar and increased regulation by the tribunals themselves also elevated the quality of defense representation.[244] The ICTY, for example, raised the qualifications for defense counsel it assigned to represent indigent defendants and created a Code of Conduct for defense counsel, which included a disciplinary mechanism for resolving complaints of violations of ethics.[245] It also imposed stricter conflict-of-interest rules for defense counsel.[246] (By contrast, the ICTY Office of the Prosecutor's code of conduct is brief and consists mainly of vague and abstract language, making it more difficult to address claims of prosecutorial misconduct.)[247] While some of these measures may constrain the freedom of defendants to select counsel, they have contributed to a more professionalized defense bar.[248] The developments in defense representation implemented over time by the ICTY, ICTR, and successor tribunals demonstrate their recognition that the entire accountability enterprise – as understood since Nuremberg – depends on the zealous and effective legal representation of defendants.[249]

Yet, despite the increased resources and attention given to defense issues, international criminal tribunals have not accepted the proposition that equality of arms requires equality of means and resources between the prosecution and defense.[250] Instead, the principle of equality of arms is understood merely to require equality of treatment.[251] The ICTY and the SCSL, for example, have cited the prosecution's higher burden of proof at trial as a justification for disparate resources.[252] As the ICTY Appeals Chamber noted, the prosecution "has the burden of telling an entire story, of putting together a coherent narrative and proving every necessary element of the crimes charged beyond a reasonable doubt," whereas the defense's strategy "often focuses on poking specifically targeted holes in the Prosecution's case."[253] Formal equality, in short, has proven insufficient to level the playing field, and international and hybrid tribunals have struggled, with mixed success, to address continued resource imbalances between the prosecution and defense.[254]

One inherent structural problem is that the ICTY, the ICTR, and most hybrid tribunals did not establish the defense as a separate organ within the court. Instead, defense counsel are subsumed within the Registry, which makes the defense external contractors and reliant on the Registry for funding and decision-making approval, including approval for resources needed to gather information, thereby impeding true equality of arms.[255] (The Special Tribunal for Lebanon, the hybrid tribunal established following the assassination of Lebanon's former Prime Minister Rafik Hariri, is an exception in this area, as it has a fully independent defense office within the tribunal, although the defense office still depends on the Registry to determine its overall budget.)[256] Funding constraints pose another major obstacle for the defense and can hinder the adequacy of the defendant's representation by counsel.[257] Despite improvements, imbalances between the prosecution and defense remain, including in their ability to obtain proper facilities, trained investigators, and sufficient remuneration to provide for quality legal representation.[258] While some defendants have received excellent representation, others have had counsel whose representation suffered due to lack of experience, insufficient substantive knowledge of ICL, and lack of familiarity with a tribunal's procedures.[259]

In addition to addressing structural disparities, more rigorous application of the principle of equality of arms requires greater attention to actual inequality, including the parties' respective ability to access relevant evidence. Defense counsel, for example, have faced obstacles in gaining access to evidence and locating witnesses in countries where crimes are being investigated, and may require the tribunal's assistance in carrying out this essential function.[260] In Rwanda, the Rwandan government hindered defense counsel from conducting investigations there, including through the denial of permission to visit sites referenced in the indictment, interference with defense witnesses, and threats to and actual arrests of defense investigators and defense counsel,[261] including American lawyer Peter Erlinder, who was arrested for allegedly violating Rwanda's genocide denial laws.[262] Erlinder had previously won an acquittal for a former military commander charged with conspiracy to commit genocide and was in the country to defend an opposition leader on charges of genocide denial.[263] Concerns about Rwanda's unwillingness to cooperate surfaced in other cases as well.[264] The prosecution, to be sure, can face similar challenges in accessing evidence without state cooperation, and such non-cooperation may be beyond a tribunal's power to address. The barriers nevertheless are typically greater for the defense, and the ICTY and ICTR did not initially provide defense lawyers with the same protections as prosecutors and did not always do all within their power to mitigate the barriers facing the defense.[265] Additionally, the ICTY and ICTR's increased emphasis on judicial management to expedite proceedings prompted efforts to limit defense counsel's latitude to present its case, such as by excluding some documents and barring some defense witnesses.[266]

One of the thorniest defense issues concerns the accused's right to self-representa-tion.[267] Although this issue has arisen sporadically at other tribunals, it has bedeviled the ICTY.[268] The right to self-representation triggered controversy in several high-profile cases before the ICTY.[269] Competing views on a defendant's right to self-representation highlight divergent approaches between common law systems, which recognize the right, and civil law systems, which generally do not. This issue also reflects some challenges of applying human rights standards in the context of international criminal trials. Over time, the ICTY imposed greater limits on this right in response to the practical demands of completing trials in a timely manner and achieving its other goals.

The ICTY statute provides that the accused can conduct his defense in person or through legal assistance of his own choosing, and can have legal assistance provided to him without payment by him when he cannot afford it.[270] The text of the ICTY's self-representation provision was taken from an identical provision in the ICCPR.[271]

There are several reasons why an accused person might want to represent himself. Some are universal to all criminal defendants, others are more particular to defen-dants in international criminal proceedings. A defendant may wish to represent himself because he feels his attorney is not capable of providing effective representa-tion. Relatedly, a defendant might want to exert more control over the proceedings. This latter motive is more common among defendants who formerly occupied high-level positions in the government or military.[272] Another reason a defendant might wish to represent himself – and one particularly prevalent in international criminal proceedings – is to have more latitude to pursue goals that fall outside the traditional parameters of a criminal trial. A defendant who believes that the tribunal itself is politicized – for example, because it focuses exclusively or disproportionately on the crimes committed by one side of a conflict – might want to highlight this point and contextualize historical events.[273] This message, moreover, might be directed not principally at the judges in the defendant's case, but rather externally at constitu-encies back home.[274] A defendant may also distrust the counsel assigned by the same court that was created to try him. Additionally, some defendants may wish to combine self-representation with representation by counsel for complex legal issues, a practice the ICTY has permitted.[275]

Competing interests, however, suggest the need to limit or qualify the right to self-representation. Those interests – often captured under the label "interests of justice" – include ensuring that proceedings are conducted in a timely and coherent manner. When an accused person seeks to hijack a trial for political purposes, it can derail proceedings and threaten their legitimacy. In those instances, it may become necessary to restrict a defendant's right to self-representation, not only so that the trial may proceed in an orderly fashion, but also to ensure that an adequate defense to the charges is presented to the tribunal before it renders judgment.

Trial judges initially construed the ICTY's self-representation provisions broadly. But it became evident, particularly during the Slobodan Milošević and Vojislav Šešelj trials, that the accused was exploiting the right to self-representation to disrupt, prolong, and undermine the proceedings, turning them into political theater and prompting concerns about the capacity of international tribunals to bring nationalist and racialist leaders to justice.[276]

In *Milošević*, judges allowed the defendant to represent himself but appointed *amici curiae* counsel to help the court protect the accused's rights. Milošević obstructed judicial proceedings from the outset, refusing to answer questions, launching into prolonged, legally irrelevant speeches, and disparaging witnesses and the court. Milošević's severe health issues exacerbated these problems, forcing the tribunal to operate on a reduced schedule.[277] After numerous delays, the Trial Chamber appointed counsel for Milošević, over Milošević's strenuous objections, because of the risk to the trial's integrity and timely completion. On an interlocutory appeal, the Appeals Chamber agreed with the Trial Chamber that the right to defend oneself was not absolute, but held that "the right to self-representation [was] an indispensable cornerstone of justice," and that any restrictions on it "must be limited to the minimum extent necessary to protect the Tribunal's interest in assuring a reasonably expeditious trial."[278] The Appeals Chamber thus affirmed the Trial Chamber's ruling to impose counsel, but eliminated restrictions on Milošević's role to enable him to remain in charge of presenting his case when he was physically able to do so.[279] Delays continued both because Milošević persisted in flouting procedural rules and because of his medical condition.[280] The Trial Chamber never delivered a verdict because Milošević suffered an untimely death before the trial concluded.

The most extreme clash between a defendant's right to self-representation and the orderly conduct of proceedings occurred in the case of Vojislav Šešelj, leader of the far-right Radical Party in Serbia. From the outset, Šešelj flouted the ICTY's rules and attempted to undermine the proceedings by using them as a political platform. The Trial Chamber responded initially by appointing standby counsel (to take over in case Šešelj was removed), and eventually by imposing counsel on Šešelj. The

Appeals Chamber, however, repeatedly reversed and undercut the Trial Chamber's efforts to restrict Šešelj's self-representation. It initially found that Šešelj had not received adequate notice before the appointment of counsel and subsequently acquiesced in Šešelj's opposition to the appointment of standby counsel in the face of a highly publicized hunger strike by Šešelj that left him in critical medical condition.[281] Šešelj's obstructionist tactics continued, leading to several contempt proceedings against Šešelj for the disclosure of confidential information about protected prosecution witnesses, but the Trial Chamber nevertheless declined to impose counsel.[282] Critics have assailed the ICTY's continued capitulation to Šešelj.[283] Among other failings, the tribunal failed to provide clarity about what type of obstructionist behavior would warrant the imposition of counsel.[284] In 2014, the ICTY granted Šešelj provisional release because of his declining health, and in 2016, the Trial Chamber acquitted Šešelj of war crimes and crimes against human-ity, igniting celebrations by his supporters and outrage among victims and their families.[285] The MICT Appeals Chamber will decide the prosecutor's appeal of Šešelj's acquittal in 2018. Šešelj continues to represent himself.

The ICTY took a more restrictive approach to an accused's right of self-represen-tation in the case of former Bosnian Serb leader Radovan Karadžić, who was convicted in 2016 of genocide and other international crimes. Shortly after Karadžić's arrest, the ICTY adopted Rule 45 *ter*, enabling a trial chamber, in the interests of justice, to instruct the Registrar to assign counsel to represent the interests of the accused.[286] This rule gave a trial chamber a stronger legal basis to act early on to impose standby counsel if circumstances required it.[287] In Karadžić's case, the Trial Chamber imposed a strict schedule on the defendant, which the Appeals Chamber upheld, explaining that in electing to represent himself, Karadžić neces-sarily forfeited some of the advantages of having trial counsel to handle trial preparation.[288] When Karadžić subsequently refused to appear at trial, the Trial Chamber, relying on Rule 45 *ter*, ordered the Registrar to appoint standby counsel who would take over as assigned counsel if the accused continued to absent himself from the proceedings or engaged in conduct that impeded the proper and expedi-tious conduct of the trial. The Appeals Chamber upheld the appointment of standby counsel, confining its prior ruling in *Šešelj* to its facts.[289] On appeal, Karadžić opted to be represented by counsel, namely the person who served as his legal advisor at trial.

The trajectory of the ICTY's jurisprudence suggests a continued acknowledgment of an accused's right of self-representation, but also an increased recognition that this right is not absolute and must be balanced against other considerations that may require imposing limitations on it.[290] The ICTY's adoption of a more restrictive approach to the right of self-representation reflects both experience gained over time and increased confidence in its own legitimacy. The tribunal's later decisions suggest it no longer felt the same need to "ben[d] over backwards" to accommodate an accused's desire to represent himself at the expense of orderly and expeditious proceedings in order to counteract perceptions of unfairness or political justice.[291] While the ICTR and hybrid tribunals, such as the SCSL and STL, have only rarely had occasion to address issues surrounding self-representation, they have authority to impose restrictions on the defendant's exercise of this right and appear willing to impose such restrictions.[292]

The ICTY has also struggled to ensure that defendants who exercise their right to self-representation can do so in a meaningful way through adequate access to office facilities, the translation of materials, and legal assistance. The ICTY, for example, has provided for payment of legal advisors for defendants. Milošević, the first defendant to represent himself before the tribunal, received three legal advisors; Karadžić received the most assistance, including multiple advisors, case managers, and investigators.[293] Access to resources and legal assistance implicates the principle of equality of arms as well as a defendant's ability to follow and participate in proceedings. The ICTY has indicated, however, that a defendant who elects to represent himself will not have the same level of funding for legal assistance as one who is assigned counsel because he cannot afford it.[294] The degree to which tribunals are willing to provide assistance, such as support staff, turns on whether they conceptualize the right to self-representation as a waiver of legal assistance or of legal representation. Viewing it as the latter, as the ICTY has generally done, can contribute to fairer and more expeditious proceedings by helping ensure that an adequate defense is presented.[295]

The ICTY's approach to self-representation does not diverge significantly from, and in some instances exceeds, human rights standards and the protections provided by national courts. The Human Rights Committee, the body of independent experts that monitors compliance with the ICCPR, has recognized an accused's right to self-representation,[296] but it has found that this right is not absolute.[297] The European Convention on Human Rights, a leading regional human rights treaty, requires a similar balancing of an accused's right to self-representation against the interests of justice, which includes concerns about the expeditiousness and integrity of the proceedings.[298] The European Court of Human Rights, moreover, has not mandated a high threshold for imposing counsel over the objection of the accused. Additionally, national systems that recognize a right to self-representation, such as the United States, still allow judges to restrict, if not terminate, this right when defendants engage in seriously obstructive behavior to ensure order and prevent delay.[299] In the United States, trial courts also have discretion to deny requests for hybrid representation, which combines self-representation with representation by counsel, and, in some cases, prohibit hybrid representation altogether.[300]

International criminal tribunals should have the latitude to approach the right of self-representation pragmatically given the gravity of the alleged crimes and the various challenges international prosecutions face. The most significant flaw in the ICTY's jurisprudence has thus not been its attempt to balance a defendant's right of self-representation against other goals, but rather its inconsistency in applying this right.[301]

***

The two *ad hoc* tribunals established in the mid-1990s represent a critical stage in the development of ICL and made lasting contributions on matters of procedure and substance. The ICTY and ICTR addressed, with varying degrees of success, the obstacles faced by international courts tasked with prosecuting mass atrocities while protecting the rights of the accused. The ICTY, in particular, helped pave the way for a permanent international criminal court by expanding and refining the template established at Nuremberg. Both tribunals also illustrate, however, the continuing barriers to achieving the goals of accountability and fairness, several of which, such as an international court's limited enforcement power and dependence on state cooperation, stem from the nature of ICL itself.

NOTES

1. S.C. Res. 827, preamble, U.N. Doc. S/RES/827 (May 25, 1993).
2. S.C. Res. 955, S/RES/955 (November 8, 1994).
3. U.N. Charter, June 26, 1945, art. 39, 59 Stat. 1031, T.S. No. 933 (entered into force on October 24, 1945).
4. U.N. Secretary-General, Report of the Secretary-General Pursuant to Paragraph 2 of Security Council Resolution 808, para. 106, U.N. Doc. S/25704 (May 3, 1993) (U.N. Secretary General, Report).
5. Secretary-General's Report on Aspects of Establishing an International Tribunal for the Prosecution of Persons Responsible for the Serious Violations of International Humanitarian Law Committed in the Territory of the Former Yugoslavia, Annex, art. 21, U.N. Doc. S/25704 (1993), reprinted in 32 I.L.M. 1159, 1192 (1993) (ICTY Statute); Statute of the International Criminal Tribunal for the Prosecution of Persons Responsible for Genocide and Other Serious Violations of International Humanitarian Law Committed in the Territory of Rwanda and Rwandan Citizens Responsible for Genocide and other such Violations Committed in the Territory of Neighboring States, between January 1, 1994, and December 31, 1994, art. 20, S.C. Res. 955, U.N. SCOR, 49th Sess., Annex, 3453d mtg., U.N. Doc. S/RES/955 (1994) reprinted in 33 I.L.M. 1598, 1602 (1994) (ICTR Statute).
6. Salvatore Zappalà, *Human Rights in International Criminal Proceedings* (Oxford, England: Oxford University Press, 2003), 105.
7. Gregory S. Gordon, "Toward an International Criminal Procedure: Due Process Aspirations and Limitations," *Columbia Journal of Transnational Law* 46 (2007), 635, 655–58.
8. Lily O'Neill and Göran Sluiter, "The Right to Appeal a Judgment of the Extraordinary Chambers in the Courts of Cambodia," *Melbourne Journal of International Law* 10 (2009), 596, 617.
9. Jens David Ohlin, "A Meta-Theory of International Criminal Procedure: Vindicating the Rule of Law," *UCLA Journal of International Law and Foreign Affairs* 14 (2009), 77.
10. UN ICTY Website, Key Figures of the Cases, www.icty.org/en/cases/key-figures-cases.

11. S.C. Res. 1503, U.N. Doc. S/RES/1503 (August 28, 2003); S.C. Res. 1534, U.N. Doc. S/RES/1534 (March 26, 2004).
12. Assessment and report of Judge Theodor Meron, President of the International Criminal Tribunal for the Former Yugoslavia, provided to the Security Council pursuant to paragraph 6 of Security Council resolution 1534 (2004) and covering the period from May 24 to November 18, 2013, transmitted by letter to President of the Security Council, U.N. Doc. S/2013/678, at 39 (November 18, 2013).
13. ICTR, Key Figures of Cases, www.unictr.org/en/cases/key-figures-cases.
14. Statute of the International Residual Mechanism for Criminal Tribunals, S.C. Res. 1966, Annex 1, U.N. Doc. S/RES/1966 (December 22, 2010).
15. Jenia Iontcheva Turner, "Legal Ethics in International Criminal Defense," *Chicago Journal of International Law* 10 (2010), 685, 698.
16. Jessica Peake, "A Spectrum of International Criminal Procedure: Shifting Patterns of Power Distribution in International Criminal Courts and Tribunals," *Pace International Law Review* 26 (2014), 182, 198–99.
17. Zappalà, *Human Rights in International Criminal Proceedings*, 23.
18. John Jackson, "Finding the Best Epistemic Fit for International Criminal Tribunals: Beyond the Adversarial Inquisitorial Dichotomy," *Journal of International Criminal Justice* 7 (2009), 20.
19. See, for example, Stephanos Bibas and William W. Burke-White, "International Idealism Meets Domestic-Criminal-Procedure Realism," *Duke Law Journal* 59 (2010), 637, 693; The Human Rights Center and the International Human Rights Law Clinic, University of California, Berkeley, and the Centre for Human Rights, University of Sarajevo, "Accountability and Social Reconstructions: An Interview Study of Bosnian Judges and Prosecutors," *Berkeley Journal of International Law* 18 (2000), 102, 136–37.
20. Bibas and Burke-White, "International Idealism Meets Domestic-Criminal-Procedure Realism," 693–94.
21. Gordon, "Toward an International Criminal Procedure," 687–88. The United Kingdom, also a common law system, does, however, allow the prosecution to appeal acquittals in some cases. See Crown Prosecution Service, *Retrial of Serious Offenses*, www.cps.gov.uk/legal/p_to_r/retrial_of_serious_offences/.
22. Zappalà, *Human Rights in International Criminal Proceedings*, 176–77.
23. John A. E. Vervaele, *"Ne Bis In Idem*: Towards a Transnational Constitutional Principle in the EU?" *Utrecht Law Review* 9(4) (2013), 211, 213.
24. Albin Eser, "Procedural Structure and Features of International Criminal Justice: Lessons from the ICTY," in Bert Swart, Alexander Zahar, and Göran Sluiter eds., *The Legacy of the International Criminal Tribunal for the Former Yugoslavia* (Oxford: Oxford University Press, 2011), 120–21.
25. Mirjan Damaška, "What Is the Point of International Criminal Justice?" *Chicago-Kent Law Review* 83 (2008), 329, 331; Jenia Iontcheva Turner, "Policing International Prosecutors," *New York University Journal of International Law and Politics* 45 (2012), 175, 204–09; Jens David Ohlin, "A Meta-Theory of International Criminal Procedure," 84–85.
26. Darryl Robinson, "The Identity Crisis of International Criminal Law," *Leiden Journal of International Law* 21 (2008), 925, 933–34.
27. Ibid., 930.
28. Damaška, "What Is the Point of International Criminal Justice?" 359–60.

29. Mirjan Damaška, "The Competing Visions of Fairness: The Basic Choice for International Criminal Tribunals," *North Carolina Journal of International Law and Commercial Regulation* 36 (2011), 365.

30. International Covenant on Civil and Political Rights, art. 14, adopted December 16, 1966, 999 U.N.T.S. 171 (entered into force March 23, 1976) (ICCPR).

31. ICTY Statute, art. 21(1).

32. *Prosecutor v. Alekovski*, Case No. IT-95–14/1-AR73, ICTY Appeals Chamber, Decision on Prosecutor's Appeal on Admissibility of Evidence, para. 25 (February 16, 1999) (*Alekovski* Appeals Chamber Decision on Admissibility); See also *Prosecutor v. Milutinović*, Case No. IT-05–87-T, ICTY Trial Chamber III, Decision Denying Prosecution's Request for Certification of Rule 73 *bis* Issue for Appeal, para. 10 (August 30, 2006).

33. *Prosecutor v. Haradinaj*, Case No. IT-04–84-A, ICTY Appeals Chamber, Judgment, para. 377 (July 19, 2010); Yvonne, McDermott, "Rights in Reverse: A Critical Analysis of Fair Trial Rights under International Criminal Law," in William A. Schabas, Yvonne McDermott, and Niamh Hayes eds., *The Ashgate Research Companion to Civil International Criminal Law: Critical Perspectives* (United Kingdom: Ashgate, 2013).

34. Yvonne McDermott, *Fairness in International Criminal Trials* (Oxford: Oxford University Press, 2016), 109–110, 116.

35. ICTR Statute, art. 20; Statute of the Special Court for Sierra Leone, annexed to the Agreement between the United Nations and the Government of Sierra Leone on the Establishment of the Special Court for Sierra Leone, signed on January 16, 2002, art. 20.

36. *Prosecutor v. Norman*, Case No. SCSL-2003–09-PT-64, SCSL Appeals Chamber, Decision on the Applications for a Stay of Proceedings and Denial of Right to Appeal, para. 8 (November 4, 2003).

37. Jelena Pejic, "The Tribunal and the ICC: Do Precedents Matter?" *Albany Law Review* 60 (1997), 841, 852–53.

38. Jacob Katz Cogan, "International Criminal Courts and Fair Trials: Difficulties and Prospects," *Yale Journal of International Law* 27 (2002), 111, 115–16.

39. See, for example, Kai Ambos, "Joint Criminal Enterprise and Command Responsibility," *Journal of International Criminal Justice* 5 (2007), 159; Allison Marston Danner and Jenny S. Martinez, "Guilty Associations: Joint Criminal Enterprise, Command Responsibility, and the Development of International Law," *California Law Review* 93 (2005), 75; Neha Jain, *Perpetrators and Accessories in International Criminal Law: Individual Modes of Responsibility for Collective Crimes* (Oxford: Hart, 2014); Jens David Ohlin, "Joint Intentions to Commit International Crimes," *Chicago Journal of International Law* 11 (2011), 693; Mark Osiel, *Making Sense of Mass Atrocity* (Cambridge: Cambridge University Press, 2009); Elies van Sliedregt, *Individual Criminal Responsibility in International Criminal Law* (Oxford: Oxford University Press, 2012).

40. Antonio Cassese, *International Criminal Law* (Oxford: Oxford University Press, 2nd ed., 2008), 189–90.

41. *Prosecutor v. Tadić*, Case No. IT-94–1-T, ICTY Trial Chamber, Judgment, para. 373 (May 7, 1997).

42. *Prosecutor v. Tadić*, Case No. IT-94–1-A, ICTY Appeals Chamber, Judgment, para. 233 (July 15, 1999) (*Tadić* Appeals Judgment).

43. Ibid., paras. 195–204.

44. Ohlin, "Joint Intentions to Commit International Crimes," 693, 696.

45. *Tadić*, Appeals Judgment, paras. 189–90.

46. Ibid., paras. 201–10.

47. Danner and Martinez, "Guilty Associations," 110–12.

48. Ibid.
49. *Pinkerton v. United States*, 328 U.S. 640 (1946). For discussions of the link between JCE III and conspiracy, see, for example, Danner and Martinez, "Guilty Associations," 140–41, and Ohlin, "Joint Intentions to Commit International Crimes," 703.
50. Danner and Martinez, "Guilty Associations," 140–41.
51. Ibid., 104; Mark Noferi, "Towards Attenuation: A 'New' Due Process Limit on *Pinkerton* Conspiracy Liability," *American Journal of Criminal Law* 33 (2006), 91, 92, 128–33.
52. Secretary General's Report Pursuant to Paragraph 2 of S.C. Res. 808, paras 34–35, U.N. Doc. No. S/25704 (May 3, 1993).
53. *Restatement (Third) of Foreign Relations Law of the United States* § 102(2) (1987).
54. Robinson, "The Identity Crisis of International Criminal Law," 939–40.
55. *Prosecutor v. Kvocka*, Case No. IT-98–30/1-T, ICTY Trial Chamber, Judgment, para. 307, (November 2, 2001).
56. Martinez and Danner, "Guilty Associations," 135.
57. *Prosecutor v. Vasiljevic*, Case IT-98–32-A, ICTY Appeals Chamber, Judgment, para. 111, (February 25, 2004).
58. George P. Fletcher and Jens David Ohlin, "Reclaiming Fundamental Principles of Criminal Law in the Darfur Case," *Journal of International Criminal Justice* 3 (2005), 550.
59. *Prosecutor v. Brđanin*, Case No. IT-99–36-A, ICTY Appeals Chamber, Judgment, para. 430 (April 3, 2007); *Prosecutor v. Kvocka*, Case No. IT-98030/I-A, Appeals Chamber, Judgment, para. 97 (February 28, 2005); Robinson, "The Identity Crisis of International Criminal Law," 939.
60. Robinson, "The Identity Crisis of International Criminal Law," 940.
61. Jenia Iontcheva Turner, "Defense Perspectives on Law and Politics in International Criminal Trials," *Virginia Journal of International Law* 48 (2008), 529, 561.
62. Fletcher and Ohlin, "Reclaiming Fundamental Principles of Criminal Law," 550.
63. *Prosecutor v. Karadžić*, Case No. IT-95–5/18-AR72.4, ICTY Appeals Chamber, Decision on Prosecution's Motion Appealing Trial Chamber's Decision on JCE III Foreseeability, paras. 13–19 (June 25, 2009).
64. Michael G. Karnavas, "The ICTY Legacy: A Defense Counsel's Perspective," *Goettingen Journal of International Law* 3 (2011), 1053, 1073; Turner, "Defense Perspectives on Law and Politics in International Criminal Trials," 561–62.
65. Fausto Pocar, "Notes on Joint Criminal Enterprise before the International Criminal Tribunal for the former Yugoslavia," *University of the Pacific Law Review* 48 (2017), 189, 193, and n. 37.
66. Turner, "Defense Perspectives on Law and Politics in International Criminal Trials," 561–62.
67. *Prosecutor v. Sesay*, Case No. SCSL-04–15-A, SCSL Appeals Chamber, Judgment, para. 99 (October 26, 2009).
68. David Scheffer and Anthony Dinh, "The Pre-Trial Chambers Significant Decision on Joint Criminal Enterprise for Individual Responsibility," *Cambodia Tribunal Monitor*, at 2, June 3, 2010, www.cambodiatribunal.org/assets/pdf/court-filings/ctm_scheffer_dinh_jce_commentary_3_june_2010.pdf; Lachezer Yanev, "The Theory of Joint Criminal Enterprise Liability at the ECCC: A Difficult Relationship," in Simon M. Meisenberg and Ignaz Segmiller eds., *The Extraordinary Chambers in the Courts of Cambodia: Assessing their Contribution to International Criminal Law* (The Hague: T.M.C. Asser Press, 2016), 203, 205.

69. *Case of Nuon Chea*, Case No. 002/19–09-2007-ECCC-D97/15/9, ECCC Pre-Trial Chamber, Decision on the Appeals Against the Co-Investigative Judges Order on Joint Criminal Enterprise (JCE), paras. 79–83 (May 20, 2010).

70. *Case of Nuon Chea*, Case No. 002/19–09-2007-ECCC-E100/6, ECCC Trial Chamber, Decision on the Applicability of Joint Criminal Enterprise, paras. 32–35 (September 12, 2011).

71. *Prosecutor v. Simić*, Case No. IT-95-9-T, ICTY Trial Chamber II, Judgment, Separate and Partly Dissenting Opinion of Judge Per-Johan Lindholm, paras. 2, 5 (October 17, 2003).

72. See, for example, Mohamed Elewa Badar, "'Just Convict Everyone!'—Joint Perpetration: From Tadić to Stakić and Back Again," *International Criminal Law Review* 6 (2006), 293, 302; Shane Darcy, "An Effective Measure of Bringing Justice?: The Joint Criminal Enterprise Doctrine of the International Criminal Tribunal for the Former Yugoslavia," *American University Law Review* 20 (2004), 153, 184–88; Fletcher and Ohlin, "Reclaiming Fundamental Principles of Criminal Law," 550; Michael G. Karnavas, "The fiction of JCE III in customary international law," *michaelgkarnavas.net/Blog*, January 1, 2015, http://michaelgkarnavas.net/blog/2015/01/26/the-fiction-of-jce-iii/; William A. Schabas, "*Mens Rea* and the International Criminal Tribunal for the Former Yugoslavia," *New England Law Review* 37 (2003), 1015, 1034.

73. ICTY Achievements, http://www.icty.org/sid/324.

74. Cassese, *International Criminal Law*, 193–94.

75. Schabas, "*Mens Rea* and the International Criminal Tribunal for the Former Yugoslavia," 1034.

76. *Prosecutor v. Karadžić*, Case No. IT-95-5/18-T, ICTY Trial Chamber, Judgment (March 24, 2016). The Karadžić case is currently on appeal.

77. Cassese, *International Criminal Law*, 191.

78. *Prosecutor v. Krnojelac*, Case No. IT-97-25-A, ICTY Appeals Chamber, Judgment, para. 116 (September 17, 2003).

79. See, for example, Mark Osiel, "Modes of Participation in Mass Atrocities," *Cornell International Law Journal* 38 (2004), 793.

80. Richard H. Minear, *Victor's Justice: The Tokyo War Crimes Trial* (Princeton: Princeton University Press, 1971), 67.

81. Richard L. Lael, *The Yamashita Precedent: War Crimes and Command Responsibility* (Wilmington: Scholarly Resources, 1982), 94–95.

82. Sean D. Murphy, "Doctrine of Command Responsibility in U.S. Human Rights Cases," *American Journal of International Law* 96 (2002), 719, 721–22; Roger S. Clark and Ved P. Nanda, "An Introduction: Symposium on International Criminal Law," *Transnational Law and Contemporary Problems* 5 (1995), i, xiii.

83. Darryl Robinson, "How Command Responsibility Got So Complicated: A Culpability Contradiction, Its Obfuscation, and a Simple Solution," *Melbourne Journal of International Law* 13 (2012), 1, 9.

84. Danner and Martinez, "Guilty Associations," 123–24; Jason Senghesier, "Command Responsibility for Omissions and Detainee Abuse in the 'War on Terror,'" *Thomas Jefferson Law Review* 30 (2008), 693, 709.

85. *In re Yamashita*, 327 U.S. 1, 35 (1946) (Murphy, J., dissenting).

86. ICTY Statute, art. 7(1).

87. Ibid., art. 7(3); *Prosecutor v. Kordic*, Case No. IT-95-14/2-A, ICTY Appeals Chamber, Judgment, para. 839 (December 17, 2004).

88. Danner and Martinez, "Guilty Associations," 120–21.

89. U.N. Secretary General, Report, S/25704, para. 56.
90. Karen R. Michaeli and Uval Shany, "The Case against Ariel Sharon: Revisiting the Doctrine of Command Responsibility," *New York University Journal of International Law and Politics* 34 (2002), 797, 827.
91. Ibid., 834; Greg R. Vetter, "Command Responsibility of Non-Military Superiors in the International Criminal Court," *Yale Journal of International Law* 25 (2000), 89, 92–93.
92. Damaška, "What Is the Point of International Criminal Justice?" 350.
93. Robinson, "The Identity Crisis of International Criminal Law," 927, 950–52.
94. Ibid., 953–55.
95. *Prosecutor v. Akayesu*, Case No. ICTR-96–4-T, ICTR Trial Chamber, Judgment, para. 489 (September 2, 1998).
96. *Prosecutor v. Delalić*, Case No. IT-96–21-T, ICTY Trial Chamber, Judgment, para. 387 (November 16, 1998).
97. *Prosecutor v. Delalić*, Case No. IT 96–21-A, ICTY Appeals Chamber, Judgment, para. 241 (February 20, 2001) (*Delalić* Appeals Chamber Judgment). See also Sherrie L. Russell-Brown, "The Last Line of Defense: The Doctrine of Command Responsibility and Gender Crimes in Armed Conflict," *Wisconsin International Law Journal* 22 (2004), 125, 154–55.
98. *Delalić*, Appeals Chamber Judgment, paras. 294–309. The Appeals Chamber, however, affirmed the conviction of the commandant for his own commission of the war crimes of rape and torture. See Richard P. Barrett and Laurie E. Little, "Lessons for Yugoslav Rape Trials: A Role for Conspiracy Law in International Tribunals," *Minnesota Law Review* 88 (2003), 30, 48.
99. *Prosecutor v. Blaškić*, Case No. IT-95–14-T, ICTY Trial Chamber, Judgment, para. 332 (March 3, 2000).
100. *Prosecutor v. Blaškić*, Case No. IT-95–14-A, ICTY Appeals Chamber, Judgment, paras. 62–64, 257–58 (July 29, 2004).
101. Elies van Sliedregt, "Command Responsibility at the ICTY—Three Generations of Case-law and Still Ambiguity," in Swart et al. eds., *The Legacy of the International Criminal Tribunal for the Former Yugoslavia*, 381.
102. *Prosecutor v. Perišić*, Case No. IT-04–81-A, ICTY Appeals Chamber, Judgment (September 28, 2013) (*Perišić* Appeals Judgment).
103. *Prosecutor v. Perišić*, Case No. IT-04–81-T, ICTY Trial Chamber, Judgment (September 6, 2011).
104. Leila Nadya Sadat, "Can the ICTY's *Perišić* and *Šainović* Cases Be Reconciled," *American Journal of International Law* 108 (2014), 475, 475–76.
105. *Perišić* Appeals Judgment, paras. 71–73.
106. *Prosecutor v. Šainović*, Case No. IT-05–87-A, ICTY Appeals Chamber, Judgment (January 23, 2014).
107. Ibid., para. 1642.
108. *Prosecutor v. Taylor*, Case No. SCSL-03–01-A, SCSL Appeals Chamber, Judgment (September 26, 2012).
109. Ibid., para. 438.
110. Rome Statute of the International Criminal Court, art. 25(c)(3), July 17, 1998, 2187 U.N. T.S. 90; Mark A. Summers, "Prosecuting Generals for War Crimes: The Shifting Sands of Accomplice Liability in International Criminal Law," *Cardozo Journal of International and Comparative Law* 23 (2015), 519, 521.
111. Summers, "Prosecuting Generals for War Crimes," 545.

112. James G. Stewart, "The ICTY Loses Its Way on Complicity—Part I," *Opinio Juris*, April 3, 2013, http://opiniojuris.org/2013/04/03/guest-post-the-icty-loses-its-way-on-complicity-part-1/; Jennifer Trahan and Erin K. Lovall, "The ICTY Appellate Chamber's Acquittal of Momčilo Perišić: The Specific Direction Element of Aiding and Abetting Should Be Rejected or Modified to Explicitly Include a 'Reasonable Person' Due Diligence Standard," *Brooklyn Journal of International Law* 40 (2014), 171, 196.

113. Jens David Ohlin, "Why Did the ICTY Acquit Stanisic and Simatovic," *Lieber Code*, June 1, 2013, www.liebercode.org/2013/06/why-did-icty-acquit-stanisic-and.html.

114. Stewart, "The ICTY Loses Its Way on Complicity—Part I"; Trahan and Lovall, "The ICTY Appellate Chamber's Acquittal of Momčilo Perišić," 206; Marko Milanovic, "The Limits of Aiding and Abetting Liability: The ICTY Appeals Chamber Acquits Momcilo Perisic," *EJIL: Talk!*, March 11, 2013, www.ejiltalk.org/the-limits-of-aiding-and-abetting-liability-the-icty-appeals-chamber-acquits-momcilo-perisic/; Summers, "Prosecuting Generals for War Crimes," 544.

115. Kevin Jon Heller, "Why the ICTY's 'Specifically Directed' Requirement Is Justified," *Opinio Juris*, June 2, 2013, http://opiniojuris.org/2013/06/02/why-the-ictys-specifically-directed-requirement-is-justified/.

116. Ibid.

117. Alexander K. A. Greenawalt, "Foreign Assistance Complicity," *Columbia Journal of Transnational Law* 54 (2016), 531, 541–42.

118. Milanovic, "The Limits of Aiding and Abetting Liability."

119. Ibid.

120. Greenawalt, "Foreign Assistance Complicity," 598.

121. Ibid., 599.

122. Trahan and Lovall, "The ICTY Appellate Chamber's Acquittal of Momčilo Perišić," 204.

123. Greenawalt, "Foreign Assistance Complicity," 543.

124. Ibid., 599–601.

125. ICTY Statute, art. 21.

126. ICTR Statute, art. 20.

127. ICTY Statute, art. 15; ICTR Statute, art. 14.

128. Rules of Procedure and Evidence, International Tribunal for the Prosecution of Persons Responsible for Serious Violations of International Humanitarian Law Committed in the Territory of the Former Yugoslavia Since 1991, U.N. Doc. IT/32/Rev. 49 (February 11, 1994) (ICTY RPE); International Criminal Tribunal for Rwanda, Rules of Procedure and Evidence, U.N. Doc. ITR/3/REV.1 (June 29, 1995) (ICTR RPE).

129. Mark A. Drumbl and Kenneth S. Gallant, "Appeals in the *Ad Hoc* International Criminal Tribunals: Structure, Procedure, and Recent Cases," *Journal of Appellate Practice and Process* 3 (2001), 589, 613–14.

130. Damaška, "What Is the Point of International Criminal Justice?" 340; McDermott, *Fairness in International Criminal Trials*, 12–14; Megan A. Fairlie, "Rule-Making from the Bench: A Place for Minimalism at the ICTY," *Texas International Law Journal* 39 (2004), 257 262–63.

131. Máximo Langer, "The Rise of Managerial Judging in International Criminal Law," *American Journal of Comparative Law* 53 (2005), 835; Daryl A. Mundis, "From 'Common Law' Towards 'Civil Law': The Evolution of the ICTY Rules of Procedure and Evidence," *Leiden Journal of International Law* 14(2) (2001), 367, 368.

132. McDermott, *Fairness in International Criminal Trials*, 14.

133. Sanja Kutnjak Ivkovic, "Justice by the International Criminal Tribunal for the former Yugoslavia," *Stanford Journal of International Law* 37 (2001), 255, 274–75 (quoting remarks of ICTY Judge Richard May).

134. Geert-Jan Alexander Knoops, "The Dichotomy between Judicial Economy and Equality of Arms within International and Internationalized Criminal Trials: A Defense Perspective," *Fordham International Law Journal*. 28 (2005), 1566, 1580; Jenia Iontcheva Turner, "Defense Perspectives on Fairness and Efficiency at the International Criminal Court," in Kevin Jon Heller, Jens Ohlin, and Sarah Nouwen et al. eds., *Oxford Handbook on International Criminal Law* (Oxford: Oxford University Press, 2017) (forthcoming), SMU Deadman School of Law Legal Studies Research Paper No. 349, at 6, http://dx.doi.org/10.2139/ssrn.2940483.

135. *Prosecutor v. Tadić*, Case No. IT-94-I-T, ICTY Trial Chamber, Decision on the Prosecutor's Motion Requesting Protective Measures for Victims and Witnesses (August 10, 1995).

136. Ibid., para. 26 (citing ICTY Statute, art. 22).

137. Ibid., para. 28.

138. Ibid., Separate Opinion of Judge Ninian Stephen.

139. Natasha A. Affolder *"Tadić*, The Anonymous Witness and the Sources of International Procedural Law," *Michigan Journal of International Law* 19 (1998), 445, 46.

140. Gordon, "Toward an International Criminal Procedure," 695.

141. ICTY RPE, Rule 89(C)-(D). The ICTR rules do not contain the same express provision, but the same principle is applied as a matter of jurisprudence. See Christopher Gosnell, "Admissibility of Evidence," in Karim A. A. Khan, Caroline Buisman, and Chris Gosnell eds., *Principles of Evidence in International Criminal Justice* (Oxford: Oxford University Press, 2010), 378.

142. *Prosecutor v. Tadić*, Case No. IT-94-1-T, ICTY Trial Chamber II, Decision on Defense Motion on Hearsay, para. 16 (August 5, 1996) (*Tadić* Decision on Defense Motion on Hearsay). See also *Alekovski* Appeals Chamber Decision on Admissibility, para. 15.

143. *Tadić* Decision on Defense Motion on Hearsay, paras. 14, 19.

144. *Prosecutor v. Brđanin*, Case No. IT-99–36-T, ICTY Trial Chamber II, Decision on the Defence "Objection to Intercept Evidence," para. 63 (October 3, 2003).

145. Ibid.

146. Alex Whiting, "The ICTY as a Laboratory of International Criminal Procedure," in Swart, et al. eds., *The Legacy of the International Criminal Tribunal for the Former Yugoslavia*, 93–94

147. The rule stated originally that "Witnesses shall, in principle, be heard directly by the Chambers." ICTY RPE, Rule 90(A) (March 14, 1994).

148. ICTY RPE, Rule 71(C); Megan A. Fairlie, "The Abiding Problem of Witness Statements in International Criminal Trials," *New York University Journal of International Law and Politics* 50 (forthcoming), Florida International University Legal Studies Research Paper No. 17-08 (April 2017), 10, https://ssrn.com/abstract=2956413.

149. Whiting, "The ICTY as a Laboratory," 97–100.

150. ICTY RPE, Rule 92.

151. Ibid., Rule 89(F).

152. Ibid., Rule 92 *bis*.

153. Patrick Robinson, "The Interaction of Legal Systems in the Work of the International Criminal Tribunal for the Former Yugoslavia," *ILSA Journal of International and Comparative Law* 16 (2009), 5, 9–10.

154. Patricia M. Wald, "Rules of Evidence in the Yugoslav War Tribunal," *Quinnipiac Law Review* 21 (2003), 761, 769; Gordon, "Toward an International Criminal Procedure," 684–85.

155. Gideon Boas, "Developments in the Law of Procedure and Evidence at the International Criminal Tribunal for the Former Yugoslavia and the International Criminal Court," *Criminal Law Forum* 12 (2001), 167, 176; Fairlie, "The Abiding Problem of Witness Statements," 41.

156. ICTY RPE, Rule 92 *bis*; Fairlie, "The Abiding Problem of Witness Statements," 15.

157. Fairlie, "The Abiding Problem of Witness Statements," 26–30.

158. Ibid., 25–26.

159. ICTY RPE, Rule 92 *ter*; Whiting, "The ICTY as a Laboratory," 98–99.

160. ICTY RPE, Rule 92 *quater*.

161. Ibid., Rule 92 *quinquies*.

162. Fairlie, "The Abiding Problem of Witness Statements," 57.

163. Michele Caianiello, "Law of Evidence at the International Criminal Court: Blending Accusatorial and Inquisitorial Models," *North Carolina Journal of International Law and Commercial Regulation* 36 (2011), 287, 315–16.

164. Goran Sluiter, Hakan Friman, and Suzannah Linton et al., eds., *International Criminal Procedure: Principles and Rules* (Oxford: Oxford University Press, 2013), 1049.

165. Beth Van Schaack, "The Building Blocks of Hybrid Justice," *Denver Journal of International Law and Policy* 44 (2016), 169, 264; Patrick Matthew Hassan-Morlai, "Evidence in International Criminal Trials: Lessons and Contributions from the Special Court for Sierra Leone," *African Journal Legal Studies* 3 (2009), 96, 112.

166. Hassan-Morlai, "Evidence in International Criminal Trials," 113–14.

167. Whiting, The ICTY as a Laboratory," 99–100.

168. Fairlie, "The Abiding Problem of Witness Statements," 35. As critics note, however, the rule itself does not require the accused's participation in the witness intimidation. Ibid., 36.

169. Ibid., 37–38; Michele Caianiello, "First Decisions on the Admission of Evidence at ICC Trials: A Blending of Accusatorial and Inquisitorial Models," *Journal of International Criminal Justice* 9 (2011), 385, 407–08.

170. Gosnell, "Admissibility of Evidence," in Khan et al., eds., *Principles of Evidence*, 375.

171. Turner, "Defense Perspectives on Law and Politics in International Criminal Trials," 558–59.

172. Patricia M. Wald, "To 'Establish Incredible Events by Credible Evidence': The Use of Affidavit Testimony in Yugoslavia War Crimes Tribunal Proceedings," *Harvard International Law Journal* 42 (2001), 535, 548–49.

173. ICTY RPE, Rule 94(B); ICTR RPE, Rule 94(B).

174. *Prosecutor v. Hadžihasanović*, Case No. IT-01-47-T, ICTY Trial Chamber II, Decision on Judicial Notice of Adjudicated Facts (April 20, 2004).

175. McDermott, *Fairness in International Criminal Trials*, 44–45.

176. Ibid., 45.

177. Ibid.

178. Ibid.

179. ICTY RPE, Rule 66(A).

180. Ibid., Rule 68.

181. *Prosecutor v. Blaškić*, Case No. IT-95-14, ICTY Trial Chamber, Decision on the Production of Discovery Materials, para. 47 (January 27, 1997).

182. ICTY Statute, art. 29.

183. ICTY RPE, Rule 54.
184. Ibid., Rule 54 *bis* (F).
185. Ibid., Rule 108 *bis*; Drumbl and Gallant, "Appeals in the *Ad Hoc* International Criminal Tribunals," 589, 614–15.
186. *Prosecutor v. Milošević*, Case No. IT-02–54-A, ICTY Appeals Chamber, Public Version of the Confidential Decision on the Interpretation and Application of Rule 70, para. 19 (October 23, 2002).
187. ICTY RPE, Rule 66(C).
188. Ibid., Rule 70(B).
189. Ibid., Rule 70(C)-(D).
190. Ibid., Rule 68.
191. Laura Moranchek, "Protecting National Security Evidence While Prosecuting War Crimes: Problems and Lessons for International Criminal Justice from the ICTY," *Yale Journal of International Law* 31 (2006), 477, 487–89.
192. Ibid., 485.
193. Ibid., 481–85.
194. Ibid., 485.
195. *Prosecutor v. Blaškić*, Case No. IT-95–14-PT, ICTY Trial Chamber II, Decision on the Objection of the Republic of Croatia to the Issuance of Subpoenae Duces Tecum, para. 131 (July 18, 1997).
196. *Prosecutor v. Blaškić*, Case No. IT-95–14-AR108 *bis*, ICTY Appeals Chamber, Judgment on the Request of the Republic of Croatia for Review of the Decision of Trial Chamber II of 18 July 1997, paras. 38–45 (October 29, 1997).
197. Ibid., paras. 33–37.
198. Gordon, "Towards an International Criminal Procedure," 678–79.
199. Ibid; Cogan, "International Criminal Courts and Fair Trials," 122–24.
200. Milan Markovic, "The ICC Prosecutor's Missing Code of Conduct," *Texas International Law Journal* 47 (2011) 201, 217.
201. Jarinde Temminck Tuinstra, "Defending the Defenders: The Role of Defense Counsel in International Criminal Trials," *Journal of International Criminal Justice* 8 (2010), 463, 479.
202. Zappalá, *Human Rights in International Criminal Proceedings*, 145–46; Charles Chernor Jalloh and Amy DiBella, "Equality of Arms in International Criminal Law: Continuing Challenges," in Schabas et al., *The Ashgate Research Companion to International Criminal Law*, 252, 285.
203. McDermott, *Fairness in International Criminal Trials*, 84.
204. Megan A. Fairlie, "The Precedent of Pretrial Release at the ICTY: A Road Better Left Less Traveled," *Fordham International Law Journal* 33 (2011), 1101; Patrick L. Robinson, "Ensuring Fair and Expeditious Trials at the International Criminal Tribunal for the Former Yugoslavia," *European Journal of International Law* 11 (2000), 586–88.
205. Daniel J. Rearick, "Innocent Until Alleged Guilty: Provisional Release at the ICTR," *Harvard International Law Journal* 44 (2003), 577.
206. Stefan Treschel, "Rights in Criminal Proceedings under the ECHR and the ICTY Statute—A Precarious Comparison," in Swart et al. eds., *The Legacy of the International Criminal Tribunal for the Former Yugoslavia*, 165.
207. Caroline Davidson, "No Shortcuts on Human Rights: Bail and the International Criminal Trial," *American University Law Review* 60 (2010), 1, 16.
208. Zappalá, *Human Rights in International Criminal Proceedings*, 70.
209. Davidson, "No Shortcuts on Human Rights," 5.

210. Wolfgang Schomberg, "The Role of International Criminal Tribunals in Promoting Respect for Fair Trial Rights," *Northwestern University Journal of International Human Rights* 8 (2009), 1, 22, 42–46; James Meernik and Rosa Aloisi, "Is Justice Delayed at the International Criminal Tribunals," *Judicature* 91 (2008), 276, 281.

211. McDermott, *Fairness in International Criminal Trials*, 57

212. Ibid.

213. Zappalá, *Human Rights in International Criminal Proceedings*, 118.

214. Raphael Sznajder, "Provisional Release at the ICTY: Rights of the Accused and the Debate that Amended a Rule," *Northwestern University Journal of International Human Rights* 11 (2013), 3.

215. Treschel, "Rights in Criminal Proceedings under the ECHR and the ICTY Statute," 164.

216. Zappalá, *Human Rights in International Criminal Proceedings*, 70, 95–96.

217. Patricia Wald and Jenny Martinez, "Provisional Release at the ICTY: A Work in Progress," in Richard May, David Tolbert, John Hocking, Ken Roberts, Bing Bing Jia, Daryl Mundis, and Gabriel Oosthuizen eds., *Essays on ICTY Procedure and Evidence in Honour of Gabrielle Kirk McDonald* (The Hague: Kluwer, 2001), 231, 233.

218. Zappalá, *Human Rights in International Criminal Proceedings*, 70.

219. Ibid., 96.

220. Wald and Martinez, "Provisional Release at the ICTY," 243–44 and n. 58.

221. *Prosecutor v. Brđanin*, Case No. IT-99-36-PT, ICTY Trial Chamber II, Decision on Motion by Radoslav Brđanin for Provisional Release, para. 26 (July 25, 2000).

222. *Prosecutor v. Prlić*, IT-04-74-AR.65.7, ICTY Appeals Chamber, Decision on Prosecution's Appeal from Décision Relative à la Demande de Mise en Liberté Provisoire de l'Accusé Petković dated March 31, 2008, para. 15 (April 21, 2008); Sznajder, "Provisional Release at the ICTY," 11.

223. ICTY RPE, Rule 65(B), U.N. Doc IT/32/Rev. 46 (October 21, 2011).

224. McDermott, *Fairness in International Criminal Trials*, 43.

225. Davidson, "No Shortcuts on Human Rights," 5, 35.

226. McDermott, *Fairness in International Criminal Trials*, 43.

227. Fairlie, "The Precedent of Pretrial Release," 1165–67.

228. Ibid., 1153–54.

229. Sznajder, "Provisional Release at the ICTY," 127; *Ilijkov v. Bulgaria*, 2001-IV Eur. Ct. H. R. Para. 85 (2001).

230. Sznajder, "Provisional Release at the ICTY," 128.

231. Daniel J. Rearick, "Innocent Until Alleged Guilty: Provisional Release at the ICTR," *Harvard International Law Journal*, 44 (2003), 577, 578; Davidson, "No Shortcuts on Human Rights," 3.

232. Wald and Martinez, "Provisional Release at the ICTY," 234 and n. 11.

233. Davidson, "No Shortcuts on Human Rights," 17–18.

234. McDermott, *Fairness in International Criminal Trials*, 59–61.

235. Jalloh and DiBella, "Equality of Arms in International Criminal Law," 265.

236. Geert-Jan Alexander Knoops and Robert R. Amsterdam, "The Duality of State Cooperation within International and National Criminal Cases," *Fordham International Law Journal* 30 (2007), 260, 265.

237. Jalloh and DiBella, "Equality of Arms in International Criminal Law," 257–59; Stefania Negri, "The Principle of 'Equality of Arms' and the Evolving Law of International Criminal Procedure," *International Criminal Law Review* 5 (2005), 513, 522, 543.

238. ICTY Statute, arts. 18(3), 21(4)(b), 21(4)(d).

239. ICTR Statute, arts. 17(3), 20(4)(b), 20(4)(d); Michael P. Scharf and Ahran Kang, "Errors and Missteps: Key Lessons the Iraqi Special Tribunal Can Learn from the ICTY, ICTR, and SCSL," *Cornell International Law Journal* 38 (2005), 911, 925.
240. *Tadić* Appeals Judgment, para. 44.
241. Gabrielle McIntyre, "Equality of Arms—Defining Human Rights in the Jurisprudence of the International Criminal Tribunal for the former Yugoslavia," *Leiden Journal of International Law* 16 (2003), 269, 271–74.
242. *Tadić* Appeals Judgment, paras. 50–52.
243. Nancy Amoury Combs, "Regulation of Defense Counsel: An Evolution towards Restriction and Legitimacy," in Swart et al. eds., *The Legacy of the International Criminal Tribunal for the Former Yugoslavia*, 296.
244. Michael A. Newton, "Evolving Equality—The Development of the International Defense Bar," *Stanford Journal of International Law* 47 (2011), 379, 381–83.
245. ICTY Code of Professional Conduct for Defense Counsel Appearing before the International Tribunal, U.N. Doc. IT/125/Rev. 3 (July 22, 2009).
246. Ibid., art. 14.
247. Markovic, "The ICC Prosecutor's Missing Code of Conduct," 210–11, 217.
248. Combs, "Regulation of Defense Counsel," 298–301.
249. Newton, "Evolving Equality," 384.
250. *Prosecutor v. Kayishema and Ruzindana*, Case No. ICTR 95–1-A, ICTR Appeals Chamber, Judgment, paras. 63–71 (June 1, 2001); Knoops, "The Dichotomy between Judicial Economy and Equality of Arms," 1568.
251. Ndiva Kofele-Kale, "Presumed Guilty: Balancing Competing Rights and Interests in Combating Economic Crimes," *International Lawyer* 40 (2006), 909, 938.
252. Jalloh and DiBella, "Equality of Arms in International Criminal Law," 274–75.
253. *Prosecutor v Oric*, Case No. IT–03–68-AR73.2, ICTY Appeals Chamber, Interlocutory Decision on Length of Defence Case, para. 7 (July 20, 2005). See also *Prosecutor v Sesay*, Case No. SCSL-04–15-T, SCSL Trial Chamber I, Decision on the Sesay Defence Team's Application for Judicial Review of the Registrar's Refusal to Provide Additional Funds for an Additional Counsel as Part of the Implementation of the Arbitration Agreement of the 26th of April 2007, para. 39 (February 12, 2008).
254. Negri, "The Principle of 'Equality of Arms,'" 552–53, 570.
255. Richard J. Wilson, "'Emaciated' Defense or a Trend to Independence and Equality of Arms in Internationalized Criminal Tribunals?" *Human Rights Brief* 15 (Winter, 2008), 6, 8; James Meernik, "Equality of Arms? The Individual vs. The International Community in War Crimes Tribunals," *Judicature* 86 (2003) 312, 316; Kenneth S. Gallant, "Politics, Theory, and Institutions: Three Reasons Why International Criminal Defense Is Hard, and What Might Be Done about One of Them," *Criminal Law Forum* 14 (2003), 317.
256. Charles Chernor Jalloh, "The Special Tribunal for Lebanon: A Defense Perspective," *Vanderbilt Journal of Transnational Law* 47 (2014), 765, 796–97.
257. Bibas and Burke-White, "International Idealism Meets Domestic-Criminal-Procedure Realism," 678–79.
258. Jackson, "Finding the Best Epistemic Fit for International Criminal Tribunals Beyond the Adversarial-Inquisitorial Dichotomy," 17, 26–27; Jalloh and Dibella, "Equality of Arms in International Criminal Law," 251; Negri, "The Principle of 'Equality of Arms,'" 552.

259. Sonja B. Starr, "Ensuring Defense Counsel Competence at International Criminal Tribunals," *UCLA Journal of International Law and Foreign Affairs* 14 (2009), 169, 171–72.

260. McDermott, *Fairness in International Criminal Trials*, 87.

261. Turner, "Defense Perspectives on Law and Politics in International Criminal Trials," 591–92.

262. Lindsay Roberts, "International Criminal Court for Rwanda," *Human Rights Brief* 18(1) (2010), 43.

263. Jennifer Wren Morris, Note, "The Trouble with Transfers: An Analysis of the Referral of Uwinkindi to the Republic of Rwanda for Trial," *Washington University Law Review* (2012), 505, 526–27.

264. *Prosecutor v. Nahimana*, Case No. ICTR-99–52-T, ICTR Trial Chamber I, Decision on Motion to Stay the Proceedings in the Trial of Ferdinand Nahimana, paras. 1–2 (June 5, 2003).

265. McIntyre, "Equality of Arms," 275; Jalloh and Dibella, "Equality of Arms in International Criminal Law," 269–71.

266. Knoops, "The Dichotomy between Judicial Economy and Equality of Arms," 1578–81.

267. Yuval Shany, "The Legitimacy Paradox of Self-Representation," in Timothy Waters ed., *The Milošević Trial: An Autopsy* (Oxford: Oxford University Press, 2014); Alexander Zahar, "Legal Aid, Self-Representation, and the Crisis at the Hague Tribunal," *Criminal Law Forum* 19 (2008), 241, 242–44, 254–62.

268. Jarinde Temminck Tuinstra, "The ICTY's Continuing Struggle with the Right to Self-representation," in Swart et al. eds., *The Legacy of the International Criminal Tribunal for the Former Yugoslavia*, 345–46.

269. Göran Sluiter, "Fairness and the Interests of Justice: Illusive Concepts in the *Milošević* Case," *Journal of International Criminal Justice* 3 (2005), 9, 10–11, 19.

270. ICTY Statute, art. 21(4)(d).

271. ICCPR, art. 14(3)(d).

272. Tuinstra, "The ICTY's Continuing Struggle with the Right to Self-Representation," 353.

273. Martti Koskenniemi, "Between Impunity and Show Trials," *Max Planck Yearbook of United Nations Law* 6, (2002), 1, 13–17.

274. Michael P. Scharf, "The Perils of Permitting Self-Representation in International War Crimes Trials," *Journal of Human Rights* 4 (2005), 513, 514.

275. *Prosecutor v. Krajišnik*, Case No. IT-00–39-A, ICTY Appeals Chamber, Decision on Momčilo Krajišnik's Motion to Reschedule Status Conference and Permit Alan Dershowitz to Appear, paras. 8–9 (February 28, 2008).

276. Whiting, "The ICTY as a Laboratory," 102.

277. Combs, "Regulation of Defense Counsel," 306–08.

278. *Milošević v. Prosecutor*, Case No. IT-02–54-AR73.7, ICTY Appeals Chamber, Decision on Interlocutory Appeal of the Trial Chamber's Decision on the Assignment of Defense Counsel, paras. 11, 17 (November 1, 2004).

279. Schomberg, "The Role of International Criminal Trials," 53–54.

280. Combs, "Regulation of Defense Counsel," 307–08.

281. Ibid., 308–10.

282. *Prosecutor v. Šešelj*, Case No. IT-03–67-T, ICTY Trial Chamber III, Public Version of the "Consolidated Decision on Assignment of Counsel, Adjournment and Prosecution Motion for Additional Time with Separate Opinion of Presiding Judge Antonetti in Annex," paras. 67, 73 (November 24, 2009).

283. Göran Sluiter, "Compromising the Authority of International Criminal Justice," *Journal of International Criminal Justice* 5 (2007), 529, 534–36; Combs, "Regulation of Defense Counsel," 310–11.
284. Tuinstra, "The ICTY's Continuing Struggle with the Right to Self-Representation," 360–62.
285. Marlise Simons, "Vojislav Seselj, Serbian Nationalist, Is Acquitted of War Crimes by Hague Tribunal," *New York Times*, March 31, 2016.
286. ICTY RPE, Rule 45 *ter*.
287. Whiting, "The ICTY as a Laboratory," 104.
288. *Prosecutor v. Karadžić*, Case No. IT-95–5/18-AR73.5, Decision on Radovan Karadžić's Appeal of the Decision on Commencement of Trial, para. 24, October 13, 2009.
289. Whiting, "The ICTY as a Laboratory," 104 Combs, "Regulation of Defense Counsel," 313–14.
290. Nina H.B. Jørgensen, "The Problem of Self-Representation at the International Criminal Tribunals," *Journal of International Criminal Justice* 4 (2006), 64, 64–66.
291. Combs, "Regulation of Defense Counsel," 306, 316–17, 320.
292. Nancy Amoury Combs, "Legitimizing International Criminal Justice: The Importance of Process Control," *Michigan Journal of International Law* 33 (2012), 321, 357.
293. Tuinstra, "The ICTY's Continuing Struggle with the Right to Self-Representation," 365, 369.
294. Ibid., 368–69.
295. Ibid., 365.
296. *Michael and Brian Hill v. Spain*, Communication No. 526/1993, U.N. Doc. CCPR/C/59/D/526/1993 (April 2, 1997).
297. Michael P. Scharf and Christopher M. Rassi, "Do Former Leaders Have an International Right to Self-Representation in War Crimes Trials," *Ohio Journal on Dispute Resolution* 20 (2005), 3, 16–18.
298. Treschel, "Rights in Criminal Proceedings under the ECHR and the ICTY Statute," 176–79.
299. *Faretta v. California*, 422 U.S. 806, 834, n. 46 (1975).
300. Joseph A. Colquitt, "Hybrid Representation: Standing the Two Sided Coin on Its Edge," *Wake Forest Law Review* 38 (2003), 55, 100.
301. Ibid., 373.

3

The Creation of a Permanent International Criminal Court

The concept of a permanent international criminal court dates back at least to the 1920s, following the failed war crimes prosecutions after World War I.[1] After World War II, a committee of the International Law Commission (ILC), established by the UN General Assembly to promote the development of international law, drafted statutes for a permanent court and adopted a draft code of offenses, building on the legacy of the Nuremberg prosecutions.[2] But geopolitical tensions prevented the creation of a permanent court for decades. Eventually, the conclusion of the Cold War and the establishment of the *ad hoc* tribunals for the former Yugoslavia and for Rwanda helped spur the creation of a permanent court. A multiyear drafting and negotiating process culminated in July 1998, when state delegations met in Rome to finalize and adopt the treaty that would serve as the statute for the new International Criminal Court (ICC).[3] The treaty entered into force in 2002. Today, more than 120 countries are States Parties to the Rome Statute, although that list excludes several leading global powers, including the United States, China, and Russia.

The Rome Statute established genocide, crimes against humanity, and war crimes as core international crimes.[4] It also included the crime of aggression, but deferred providing a substantive definition of or jurisdictional triggers for that offense.[5] Amendments to the Rome Statute adopted in 2010 at the Review Conference in Kampala, Uganda, defined the crime of aggression and provided the conditions and timetable for activating the ICC's exercise of jurisdiction over it.

The Rome Statute provides that States Parties accept the jurisdiction of the Court over the three core international crimes and that the Court may exercise this jurisdiction where the crime occurs on the territory of a State Party (or the State's vessel or aircraft) or is committed by a State Party's national.[6] It additionally permits a non-State Party to accept the Court's jurisdiction over a particular crime on an *ad hoc* basis.[7] The Rome Statute provides the following three triggers for the Court's jurisdiction: referral to the ICC Prosecutor by the UN Security Council acting under its Chapter VII powers;[8] referral by a State Party for crimes committed on its territory;[9] or an investigation by the ICC Prosecutor *proprio motu* (on his or her own initiative).[10] The crime of aggression is subject to a special jurisdictional framework.[11] Only a UN Security Council referral is not subject to the territorial and nationality limitations on the Court's jurisdiction described above. Additionally, the Security Council can, by adopting a resolution under Chapter VII of the UN Charter, request that the ICC defer any investigation or prosecution for renewable periods of twelve months.[12] Of the jurisdictional triggers, a *proprio motu* investigation by the ICC Prosecutor is the most controversial, as it creates a mechanism for international criminal prosecutions without state consent and outside the Security Council framework.

The Rome Statute further requires that the crimes be of sufficient gravity to be admissible.[13] Also, under the Rome Statute's complementarity regime, a case is not admissible before the ICC if it is being investigated or prosecuted by a state with jurisdiction over that crime (unless the state is unwilling or unable to carry out the investigation or prosecution).[14]

The ICC commits to safeguarding the rights of the accused even as it seeks to hold the most serious perpetrators accountable for the worst atrocities. The Rome Statute provides that the ICC Prosecutor must "[f]ully respect the rights of persons arising under th[e] Statute."[15] It further states that the ICC is bound by "principles and rules of international law" and that its application of law must be "consistent with internationally recognized human rights."[16] On paper, the ICC provides defendants with the most extensive fair trial rights of any international criminal tribunal to date. The Rome Statute and the ICC's Rules of Procedure and Evidence (RPE): expand the rights of individuals during investigations, including through protections against arbitrary arrest and coercive interrogation; supply an enforceable right to compensation for suspects who suffer unlawful arrest or detention; strengthen provisions to facilitate the provisional release of defendants; afford suspects the right to participate with counsel in indictment confirmation hearings; expressly incorporate the right to a fair hearing conducted impartially and provide a detailed set of rules to help ensure judicial competence and independence; specify a broad and categorical protection of the right not to testify (as opposed to other tribunals which protect only the right not to testify against oneself or to confess guilt); and reinforce the presumption of innocence by explicitly placing the burden of proof on the prosecution.[17]

These developments reflect the continued influence of international human rights law, whose universality demands its application regardless of the nature of the proceedings. They also suggest an awareness among states that the procedures established for international criminal tribunals might one day be applied against their own citizens.[18] The ICC's provisions safeguarding the rights of the accused thus demonstrate the Court's broader aim of promoting respect for fair trials while seeking accountability for grave crimes.[19] The ICC, moreover, has issued rulings to help implement these safeguards. In the prosecution of Congolese rebel leader Jean-Pierre Bemba, for example, the ICC reinforced the presumption of innocence by rejecting the admission of the totality of prosecution witness statements into evidence, which would have forced the defense to disprove their admissibility.[20] In the prosecution of Uhuru Kenyatta, the President of Kenya, for his role in the 2013 postelection violence in Kenya, the ICC refused to grant the prosecution's request for an indefinite adjournment, citing the defendant's right to be tried without undue delay.[21]

At the same time, the ICC faces various obstacles in upholding fair trial protections. Even more than prior tribunals, the ICC embraces the ambitious, but sometimes conflicting, goals of international criminal justice. The ICC's stated purpose is "to put an end to impunity for the perpetrators" of the crimes within its jurisdiction and "thus contribute to the prevention of such crimes."[22] The ICC, moreover, seeks to honor the rights and concerns of victims. It not only provides for reparations, but also expands the ability of victims to participate in proceedings.[23] Further, the ICC strives to establish a historical record of the crimes it adjudicates.[24] While the pursuit of these goals can advance human rights norms, it can also clash with the presumption of innocence and the principle of individual criminal responsibility.

The most significant obstacles to the ICC's implementation of fair trial rights are the type of practical challenges commonly faced by international criminal tribunals, such as gathering evidence from conflict zones and a heavy reliance on state cooperation. These obstacles, moreover, tend to be greater at the ICC because of its global focus. Unlike the ICTY and ICTR, for example, the ICC cannot concentrate on crimes committed within a particular country or region during a specific time period.

The Rome Statute includes more detailed procedural requirements than the respective statutes for the ICTY and ICTR, which were sparse by comparison. But it also provides that the ICC's RPE can be amended only by a two-thirds majority of States Parties.[25] While the Rome Statute's more extensive delineation of procedural rules may increase predictability, it reduces the ICC's ability to adapt the RPE in response to challenges the Court confronts on the ground.[26] ICC judges have instead sought to find the necessary procedural flexibility by other means. They have amended the Regulations of the Court, intended to address matters "necessary for [the Court's] routine functioning,"[27] for such purposes as authorizing trial judges to modify the legal characterization of the facts underlying the charges.[28] Judges have also relied on broad interpretations of the Rome Statute for such powers as ordering witnesses to appear and provide testimony.[29] Even so, judges still have no way of forcing a State Party to fulfill this legal obligation other than by reporting its noncompliance to the Assembly of States Parties or, in the case of a UN Security Council referral, to the Security Council.[30] The Rome Statute also introduces a level of political involvement in trial procedures at odds with the notion of the ICC as a politically neutral and independent court by restricting the adoption of amendments to the RPE to States Parties.[31] The Rome Statute, moreover, permits proposals to amend the RPE only from a State Party, judges acting by absolute majority, or the prosecutor.[32] Defense counsel thus cannot propose amendments to the ICC's RPE, in contrast to the practice of the ICTY and ICTR. The lack of a provision for proposals of rule changes by defense counsel narrows opportunities for the presentation of defense perspectives and can adversely affect the defense function.[33]

***

Like prior tribunals, the ICC must steer between the collective nature of international criminality and the individualized judgments of criminal law.[34] The ICC's focus on prosecuting the most serious offenders heightens the importance of doctrines of collective criminality in fulfilling its mission. The Court must, therefore, articulate doctrines nimble enough to capture the various ways that individuals may jointly commit international crimes without destabilizing the principle of individual responsibility fundamental to criminal law.

The Rome Statute provides several ways to hold individuals responsible for crimes physically perpetrated by others. The Rome Statute, for example, codifies the doctrine of command responsibility.[35] It provides that a military commander, or a person effectively acting as one, may be prosecuted where he knew or should have known that a subordinate was committing or was about to commit a crime, and "failed to take all necessary and reasonable measures" within his power to stop it or "to submit the matter to the competent authorities for investigation and prosecution."[36] The Rome Statute also authorizes command responsibility for nonmilitary commanders, although it articulates a different standard for such officials. A civilian superior may be held criminally responsible where he either "knew, or consciously disregarded information which clearly indicated" that his subordinates were committing or were about to commit crimes.[37] One justification for a stricter *mens rea* standard for civilian superiors is that military commanders are in charge of an inherently lethal force and thus necessarily bear greater responsibility for the conduct of their subordinates.[38] But civilian superiors may be equally responsible for the commission of grave crimes,[39] and the distinction is thus in tension with the Rome Statute's broader goal of accountability. While subjecting civilian superiors to a stricter standard could make it more difficult to prosecute them,[40] in practice the challenge of establishing that civilian superiors exercise effective command and control over the perpetrators often presents the more significant challenge for the prosecution.[41]

The Rome Statute also provides that individuals may be held criminally responsible as principals for direct perpetration (commission of a crime by that person) as well as for co-perpetration (commission of a crime together with another person) and indirect perpetration (commission of a crime through another person).[42] The Rome Statute further specifies various forms of accomplice liability, whether under express provisions, such as those addressing solicitation and aiding and abetting,[43] or under a residual (catchall) provision.[44] The distinction between principals and accomplices can have significant implications for sentencing. The former generally receive higher sentences,[45] although recent sentences imposed by the ICC against

Jean-Pierre Bemba (based on command responsibility for crimes of sexual violence committed by his soldiers in the Central African Republic)[46] and by the Special Court for Sierra Leone (SCSL) against Charles Taylor (for aiding and abetting atrocities committed in Sierra Leone during its civil war in the 1990s)[47] suggest that is not necessarily the case. The distinction is also important for the principle of fair labelling – the obligation to identify properly defendants for their respective criminal conduct.[48] Fair labelling requires that doctrines of criminal responsibility reflect the reality that the main perpetrators may be distant from the crime and may not be identical to those who physically execute it.

In its first case, the ICC moved away from the controversial doctrine of Joint Criminal Enterprise (JCE), which is not specifically referred to in the Rome Statute. The ICC Prosecutor had charged former Congolese warlord Thomas Lubanga Dyilo with conscripting and enlisting child soldiers in the Democratic Republic of Congo (DRC). Since Lubanga had no direct involvement in recruiting child soldiers, his responsibility was based on his essential role in a common plan involving leaders of the Forces Patriotiques pour Libération du Congo (FPLC), the military wing of the political group in the DRC that Lubanga founded and led.[49] In place of JCE, the Pre-Trial Chamber, the division of the ICC responsible for handling initial judicial proceedings and confirming the charges against the accused, employed the doctrines of co-perpetration and indirect perpetration, which condition criminal responsibility on the defendant's control over the relevant crime he is accused of committing rather than his physical commission of it (direct perpetration).[50] If a defendant is in control of the criminal act, for example, by means of his ordering or soliciting a murder, he is an indirect perpetrator even if he does not physically carry out the crime (such as by pulling the trigger in a murder); if a defendant acts in conjunction at a leadership level with others, he and the other leaders are classified as co-perpetrators because they share control over the commission of the crime.[51] Co-perpetration requires the existence of a common plan among the participants and an essential contribution to that plan by the defendant.[52] A defendant's contribution is essential where he could frustrate the plan by not carrying out his task, thereby demonstrating his joint control.[53] Application of a control theory, a distinguishing feature of co-perpetration, thus turns on whether the mastermind (or person in the background) can exercise effective control over the direct perpetrators by means of the organizational apparatus that he created and dominates.[54] Since Lubanga and others exercised joint control over the crime, the Pre-Trial Chamber concluded, Lubanga's participation was best understood as a form of co-perpetration.[55] The Trial Chamber I subsequently upheld the Pre-Trial Chamber's adoption of a control theory of liability.[56]

Co-perpetration and indirect perpetration provide a means of distinguishing between principals and accessories when crimes are committed by a plurality of individuals.[57] Unlike co-perpetration and indirect perpetration, which regard defendants as principals, accessorial liability under the Rome Statute does not require an essential contribution by the accused but rather, the ICC has suggested, only a substantial or significant contribution.[58]

The ICC extended the control theory of criminal responsibility in the case of Germain Katanga and Mathieu Ngudjolo Chui, militia leaders accused of war crimes and crimes against humanity in the DRC. In its decision confirming the charges, the Pre-Trial Chamber rejected the defense argument that the phrase in the Rome Statute "jointly with another person" could include co-perpetration or indirect perpetration, but not indirect co-perpetration.[59] It ruled that a co-perpetrator could be held responsible for crimes committed not only by his culpable subordinates, but also by the subordinates of his co-perpetrator based on mutual attribution (joint indirect perpetration).[60] In *Katanga* and *Chui*, it permitted the Pre-Trial Chamber to attribute crimes to Katanga and Chui that were committed by each other's respective ethnic militias implementing Katanga and Chui's common plan to attack and take over a village.[61] The Pre-Trial Chamber utilized the doctrine of indirect co-perpetration because the subordinates of one defendant's ethnic militia were unlikely to have taken orders from the commander of the other defendant's ethnic militia, which constituted a distinct entity, thus resulting in the commission of crimes by subordinates beyond the control of one of the two defendants.[62] In reaching this result, the Court relied heavily on a controversial German legal doctrine known as *Organisationsherrschaft*, which bases a person's control over an act on his position within a hierarchical organization.[63] Indirect co-perpetration creates greater opportunities to bring charges against superiors under expanded notions of direct liability,[64] and the ICC has subsequently relied on the doctrine in other cases.[65]

Because of their focus on control and their requirement of an essential contribution (as opposed to a substantial contribution under JCE), co-perpetration and indirect perpetration could help the ICC avoid JCE's excesses, particularly those associated with JCE III.[66] The ICC's adoption of doctrines of co-perpetration and indirect perpetration have nevertheless been criticized for exaggerating the importance of control at the expense of the respective and distinct mental states of the participants in joint criminal endeavors.[67] These doctrines could, for example, permit convictions for acts outside the common plan, including where the goal itself was not criminal but created a substantial risk of criminal consequences, based on a theory of recklessness.[68] In that respect, criminal responsibility under a control theory could end up resembling JCE III, which allows tribunals to impose criminal responsibility on individuals for foreseeable crimes not within the common plan.[69] Such a result would circumvent the will of the Rome Statute's drafters, who deliberately excluded conspiracy liability.[70] The necessity of this type of control theory in ensuring accountability is also subject to question since the ICC still might prosecute participation short of the essential contribution required for co-perpetration under accessory theories of liability, such as aiding or abetting or indirect assistance, since they require only a significant or substantial contribution.[71] Indeed, indirect assistance does not even require that the accused intended to facilitate the commission of the crime (as aiding and abetting does), but only that he made his contribution knowing the intention of the group acting with a common purpose.[72]

Doctrines of collective criminal responsibility will remain critical tools for the ICC as it pursues its goal of prosecuting those most responsible for grave crimes. The indictment against the President of Sudan, Omar Hassan Ahmad al-Bashir, for genocide, crimes against humanity, and war crimes, for example, relies on the doctrine of indirect participation, alleging that al-Bashir mobilized the state apparatus as part of a plan to destroy entire ethnic groups.[73] Al-Bashir is the first sitting head of state indicted by the ICC. Should proceedings move forward – a highly uncertain prospect given al-Bashir's opposition and the political controversy his indictment has triggered – it will provide a window into the Court's effort to maintain the principle of individual responsibility while addressing the role of senior officials in the commission of international crimes.

***

In the area of procedure, the ICC faces various challenges in maintaining its commitment to the rights of the accused. The nondisclosure of evidence is one of the main areas of contention. In some instances, the prosecution opposes disclosure because third parties have provided information on condition of confidentiality. In other instances, states or nongovernment organizations may refuse to provide information that they deem sensitive to the Court. Common reasons for nondisclosure include ensuring the safety of witnesses and victims (as well as victims' families) and protecting a state's national security interests.[74]

While nondisclosure of evidence to the public can undermine the transparency of and public confidence in judicial proceedings, nondisclosure to the accused poses particular fair trial concerns. Nondisclosure is in tension with human rights norms, which require providing the accused with access to documents and other evidence that the accused requires to prepare his case,[75] and with provisions of the Rome Statute. The Rome Statute requires, for example, the disclosure of prior statements by prosecution witnesses sufficiently in advance of trial.[76] Article 67(2) of the Rome Statute contains a broad requirement for the disclosure of exculpatory material, mandating that the prosecutor "disclose to the defence evidence in [his or her] possession or control which he or she believes shows or tends to show the innocence of the accused, or to mitigate the guilt of the accused, or which may affect the credibility of prosecution evidence," and that this evidence be disclosed "as soon as practicable."[77] Rule 77 of the RPE further requires that the prosecution allow the defense to inspect written or photographic evidence in its control that is material to the preparation of the defense or intended for use by the prosecution as evidence at the hearing to confirm the charges or at trial.[78] These disclosure obligations reflect the ICC's commitment to upholding protections under international human rights law, which treats the disclosure of evidence to the defense, particularly exculpatory evidence, as a fair trial safeguard.[79]

Yet, the Rome Statute also contains confidentiality provisions that can conflict with the Prosecutor's disclosure obligations. Article 54(3)(e) provides that the Prosecutor may "[a]gree not to disclose, at any stage of the proceedings, documents or information that the Prosecutor obtains on the condition of confidentiality and solely for the purpose of generating new evidence, unless the provider of the information consents."[80] Further, Rule 82 states that where the prosecution has in its possession material covered by Article 54(3)(e), it may not introduce that material into evidence without the prior consent of the information provider.[81] Additionally, Article 72 outlines various measures to protect from disclosure information that a state believes would prejudice its national security interests.[82]

While Rome Statute's disclosure provisions recognize the ICC's commitment to ensuring the fair trial rights of the accused, its confidentiality provisions acknowledge the practical obstacles the ICC Prosecutor faces in investigating mass atrocities and the Prosecutor's reliance on third parties for information. The prosecution has accordingly explained that the power to enter into such agreements lies at "the core of [its] ability to fulfill its mandate."[83]

The prosecution's competing disclosure and confidentiality obligations clashed in *Lubanga*.[84] Previously, the ICC had entered into a Relationship Agreement with the United Nations that created a framework for the disclosure of confidential information and provided for the nondisclosure of information given by the UN to the ICC Prosecutor.[85] In *Lubanga*, the prosecution entered into confidentiality agreements with the United Nations and nongovernment organizations in the DRC pursuant to Article 54(3) of the Rome Statute to obtain thousands of documents connected to the case. Those agreements promised to keep documents from both the defense and the Court. Some of the documents contained potentially exculpatory information, including that Lubanga suffered from a medical condition, had acted under duress or in self-defense, and had insufficient command over those who committed the crimes with which he was charged. The prosecution eventually brought the matter to the Court's attention. After the Trial Chamber ordered the prosecution to negotiate with the providers of the information to allow for its disclosure, which the prosecution was unable to do, the prosecution began taking inconsistent positions regarding the exculpatory nature of the material.[86] The information providers, which included the United Nations and other international organizations, maintained that confidentiality was important to protecting their operations on the ground, safeguarding their personnel from retaliation, and ensuring the lives and safety of their sources.[87] In 2008, the Trial Chamber imposed an indefinite stay of the proceedings and ordered the defendant's release from custody.[88] It justified this measure based on violations of the defendant's right to a fair trial. In light of those violations, the Trial Chamber reasoned, "the need to sustain the efficacy of the judicial process" trumped "the interest of the world community to put persons accused of the most heinous crimes against humanity on trial, great as it is."[89] The Trial Chamber criticized the prosecution not only for failing to disclose the information, but also for misusing confidentiality agreements to obtain evidence it would present at trial rather than for the limited purpose of obtaining lead evidence that would never be presented in the courtroom.[90]

The Appeals Chamber agreed that the prosecution's withholding of potentially exculpatory information obtained through confidentiality agreements would violate Lubanga's fair trial rights and maintained the stay.[91] The Appeals Chamber did not order the Prosecutor to disclose the potentially exculpatory documents to the defense, but instead ruled that the Prosecutor had to disclose the documents to the Trial Chamber so that it could evaluate whether the documents had to be provided to the defense.[92] The Appeals Chamber, however, reversed the Trial Chamber's order to release Lubanga, noting that the prosecution had received permission from the UN to disclose certain documents to the Court while the appeal was pending.[93] The prosecution eventually obtained permission to disclose the potentially exculpatory material to the defense and the stay was lifted.[94]

Resolution of this particular dispute did not, however, resolve the tension between Articles 54(3)(e) and 67(2). The Appeals Chamber did not, for example, determine what counterbalancing measures it would impose if the prosecution failed to receive permission to disclose the documents to the Court or what would happen if the prosecution disclosed exculpatory evidence to the Court that the Court found was relevant but could not be provided to the defense. The latter scenario – similar to situations encountered in domestic proceedings concerning terrorism or other crimes that involve classified or other sensitive information – can potentially be addressed by providing summaries of the information or substitute materials,[95] although the adequacy of such measures remains open to question. The Trial Chamber and Appeals Chamber in *Lubanga* did, however, assert their authority to resolve any conflicts between the need to preserve the confidentiality of lead evidence and the Rome Statute's disclosure requirements, rather than leave resolution of such conflicts to the prosecution.[96]

Similar tensions surfaced during the confirmation of charge proceedings in *Katanga*, prompting the Pre-Trial Chamber to threaten to declare certain confidentiality clauses null and void.[97] The Pre-Trial Chamber ultimately concluded that the prosecution could satisfy its disclosure obligations in the confirmation of charge context by providing the defense analogous information to that contained in documents covered by Article 54(3)(e).[98]

These tensions are likely to persist even where the prosecution applies a more circumscribed approach and does not use the lead evidence provision to obtain evidence for use at trial, as it did in *Lubanga*. The ICC Prosecutor often faces significant challenges in accessing and obtaining evidence. Unlike the ICC Prosecutor, Nuremberg prosecutors had access to crime sites, significant documentation of the defendants' roles in the commission of crimes, and the cooperation of the major powers. Prosecutors at the ICTY and ICTR, while sometimes lacking these advantages, could nevertheless focus on a single conflict, developing access to crime sites and experience in the region over time.[99] The ICTY, however, became increasingly cautious following the Kosovo War about disclosing evidence, such as military and intelligence information it received from NATO countries that the provider states insisted be withheld from both the defense and the court.[100] To address state concerns, the ICTY amended its Rules of Procedure and Evidence to make the disclosure of exculpatory evidence obtained by the prosecution from third parties subject to the ICTY's provisions on confidentiality agreements.[101] The Special Tribunal for Lebanon (STL) has similarly prioritized confidentiality over disclosure, although other courts, such as the ICTR, SCSL, and Extraordinary Chambers in the Courts of Cambodia (ECCC), have not.[102]

The ICC thus faces substantial, if not unique, challenges surrounding the collection and disclosure of evidence. It often must rely on the cooperation of nongovernment entities on the ground to investigate mass atrocities given its own lack of enforcement power, global focus, and resource limitations.[103] Those entities can provide an excellent source of information about mass crimes. They may, however, be more reluctant to share information with the prosecution without assurances of confidentiality. A negotiated resolution was reached in *Lubanga*, as the Office of the Prosecutor and the United Nations entered into a subsequent arrangement that gave ICC judges access to confidential material provided by the UN to the prosecution.[104] But that arrangement was applicable only to that case, and future information providers could refuse to allow information to be disclosed. In the case of such continued opposition to disclosure based on Article 54(3)(e), the ICC would need to consider counterbalancing measures, including potentially directing that the charges in relation to which there was exculpatory material be withdrawn.[105] *Lubanga* does, nevertheless, offer several lessons for helping to mitigate the tension between disclosure and confidentiality, including: the need for more judicious use of confidentiality agreements by the prosecution so that such agreements cover only a limited number of documents and are used only in exceptional circumstances; the need for more exacting treatment by the UN and other information providers about which documents genuinely demand confidential treatment; and the value of supplementary agreements between the Office of the Prosecutor and information providers that allow for judicial access to the confidential material.[106]

A related issue concerns the identity of intermediaries. In 2010, the ICC Trial Chamber imposed a second indefinite stay in *Lubanga* when the prosecution refused to comply with its order to release the identity of an intermediary whom the prosecution had used to contact witnesses against Lubanga in the DRC.[107] Defense witnesses had indicated that certain intermediaries had sought to coach them and influence their testimony, supporting the need for disclosure of the intermediary's identity. The prosecution argued, however, that disclosing the intermediary's identity could hinder the prosecution's ability to gather information from dangerous locations and endanger the intermediary's safety, thus violating the prosecution's duty under the Rome Statute to protect witnesses. The Trial Chamber subsequently ordered Lubanga's release on the ground that his fair trial rights had been compromised and he could not remain in preventive custody on the supposition that the trial would resume again.[108] It emphasized that the fair trial rights of the accused could not be guaranteed if the Court could not ensure compliance with its orders.[109]

The Appeals Chamber, in turn, criticized the prosecution for its noncompliance, explaining that no criminal court can operate when the prosecution believes it has the power to disregard the Court's binding rulings, even where the prosecution believes those rulings conflict with its obligations to nonparties.[110] The Appeals Chamber nonetheless reversed the imposition of a stay, explaining that the Trial Chamber had not first imposed sanctions on the Prosecutor to ensure compliance with its order.[111] It also reversed the Trial Chamber's order of release, which had been predicated on the stay.[112] In instructing the Trial Chamber to seek less drastic remedies, the Appeals Chamber highlighted how an indefinite stay could undercut the ICC's ability to ensure justice is done on behalf of victims and to protect the accused's interest in a final decision on the alleged crimes themselves.[113] The two stays entered in *Lubanga* as a result of prosecutorial nondisclosure – the first over potentially exculpatory evidence and the second over the identity of an intermediary – further prolonged the proceedings, which lasted more than eight years.[114] Eventually, the identities of the intermediaries were provided to the defense, either because the prosecution disclosed them or called the intermediaries to testify.[115] In its final judgment finding Lubanga guilty of war crimes, the Trial Chamber found that several intermediaries had improperly influenced the trial proceedings.[116] The Trial Chamber also found, however, that it had taken sufficient measures to protect the defendant's rights during the trial, including by addressing any potential prejudice resulting from incomplete or late disclosure.[117]

Similar tensions surround state opposition to the disclosure of information the state deems harmful to its national security interests pursuant to Article 72 of the Rome Statute.[118] At the *ad hoc* tribunals, UN member states had to provide requested evidence to the court; judges then evaluated whether national security interests existed and, if so, whether they outweighed the interests of international justice in the evidence. The ICTY Appeals Chamber concluded that the tribunal was not precluded from examining documents raising national security considerations.[119] The Rome Statute similarly empowers the ICC to determine issues arising out of motions for nondisclosure, but also places greater emphasis on the right of states to deny access to information by making states the final arbiter where documents are not already in the control of the Court.[120] Article 72 sets forth a detailed procedural framework in which ICC judges and prosecutors work directly with states to devise solutions, such as narrowing or clarifying the request for information, using redactions or summaries, conducting *in camera* proceedings, or obtaining comparable information from another source, before determining whether justice requires the disclosure of the materials.[121] Increasing judicial authority to review and require the disclosure of sensitive information, based on the type of scheme employed in *Lubanga*, could lessen the willingness of states to cooperate with the ICC.[122] On the other hand, overbroad protection of information possessed by states undermines a defendant's ability to challenge the prosecution's case and to prepare an effective defense, especially where that information is exculpatory. States, moreover, tend to articulate their national security interests in expansive terms, thus jeopardizing the effective functioning of the Court and the fair trial rights of defendants.[123]

Defense counsel have raised other disclosure concerns. They point to frequent delays by the Office of the Prosecutor, explaining how its disclosure of a significant amount of information on the eve, if not the day, of a final deadline can compromise the preparation of an effective defense.[124] Witness protection, however, remains a significant concern at the ICC.[125] ICC judges have accordingly determined that the timing of disclosure by the prosecution must also take into consideration the need to protect witnesses and that such disclosure may be delayed as long as evidence to be used at the confirmation hearing or at trial is provided sufficiently in advance to allow the defendant to prepare his case.[126]

Defense counsel also cite the redaction of information by the prosecution. Redactions may be necessary to protect witnesses and families, and thus redactions to protect at-risk individuals may remain in effect for a period before the trial starts or the witness testifies. Such redactions can, however, make it difficult for defense counsel to understand the meaning and significance of important documents.[127] Imposing or maintaining redactions therefore requires demonstration of an objectively justifiable risk in disclosing the information to the defense. Redactions also must not be prejudicial to or inconsistent with the right of the accused to a fair and impartial trial.[128] Despite these protections, in practice redactions are often imposed reflexively, leading to what two experienced defense counsel describe as a "bureaucratic, overbroad, and resource-draining redaction regime" that undermines the presentation of a defense and risks miscarriages of justice.[129] During the ICC's effort to prosecute postelectoral violence in Kenya, for example, crimes against humanity charges against at least one prominent official were likely wrongly confirmed for trial (and only later withdrawn) based on the redaction of important information about a key prosecution witness that undermined the prosecution's case against the defendant.[130]

Prosecutorial investigations of witness tampering have also raised concerns. Former Congolese rebel commander Bosco Ntaganda requested that the ICC stay his trial for war crimes and crimes against humanity, claiming that the prosecution abused the Court's process by inappropriately accessing critical defense information during its investigation of alleged witness tampering by Ntaganda.[131] The prosecution had initiated its witness tampering investigation pursuant to Article 70 of the Rome Statute, which addresses offenses against the administration of justice.[132]

Ntaganda claimed that the Office of the Prosecutor obtained thousands of recordings of his nonprivileged conversations, including those concerning defense strategy and his personal knowledge of the case, thus undermining the fairness and integrity of the principal proceedings against him.[133] In response, the Office of the Prosecutor maintained that Ntaganda suffered no prejudice from the prosecution's "uncovering a scheme of witness interference and coaching that [Ntaganda] directed."[134] While ICC judges have yet to rule on Ntaganda's request, the controversy suggests the potential value in the Office of the Prosecutor's utilizing prophylactic measures to safeguard a defendant's fair trial rights, such as cordoning off the main prosecution team from the Article 70 investigation, while still vigorously pursuing allegations such as witness tampering that critically undermine the administration of justice. The Office of the Prosecutor has recognized witness tampering as an increasing threat to the ICC's mission, and it previously obtained a conviction of Congolese rebel leader Jean-Pierre Bemba and four associates for corruptly influencing fourteen witnesses.[135]

Another significant issue centers on the ICC's use of evidence not subject to cross-examination. Under a revision to Rule 68, which initially made the introduction of prior recorded testimony dependent on cross-examination, the ICC now allows the use of such testimony against defendants without cross-examination, subject to several conditions.[136] The Assembly of States Parties adopted this provision in 2013 to reduce the length of trial proceedings and streamline the presentation of evidence.[137] The following year, the Appeals Chamber ruled that the revision to Rule 68 could not be applied retroactively to allow the admission of recorded statements of five prosecution witnesses against Kenya's Deputy President, William Ruto, and his codefendant, Joshua Sang, because of the adverse effect on the defendants' rights, a ruling that ultimately helped cause the case to collapse.[138] In 2016, the ICC terminated crimes against humanity charges against the two defendants.[139]

Rule 68 has nevertheless prompted concerns about diluting the fair trial rights of defendants in other cases – concerns similar to those previously expressed about ICTY provisions facilitating the use of written evidence.[140] In particular, commentators have cautioned that the ICC could use Rule 68 to loosen further limitations on evidence not subject to cross-examination in order to expedite proceedings.[141] For example, while Rule 68 does not permit the use of prior recorded statements that go to the acts and conduct of the accused, its use for crime-base evidence – to establish what crimes occurred rather than who committed them – could still undermine a defendant's ability to contest his ultimate guilt, including by hindering his ability to challenge that a widespread or systematic attack occurred, one of the required elements of a crime against humanity.[142]

A further area of controversy concerns Regulation 55, which a majority of judges adopted in 2004.[143] Regulation 55 allows a Trial Chamber, in its discretion, to amend the legal characterization of the facts underlying the charges at trial. The Trial Chamber's amendments may not, however, exceed the facts and circumstances described in the charges or amend the charges themselves.[144] The regulation requires that the Trial Chamber give the participants notice of the potential amendment and an opportunity to make written and oral submissions regarding it.[145] The judges adopted the regulation to help foster judicial efficiency and to avoid impunity by preventing a defendant's acquittal where evidence clearly establishes his guilt under a different legal characterization than that contained in the charges.[146] In *Lubanga*, the Appeals Chamber overturned the Trial Chamber's determination that it could potentially recharacterize the facts to include charges related to sexual violence, regardless of the stage of the trial.[147] In the prosecution of Jean-Pierre Bemba for crimes against humanity and war crimes in the Central African Republic, the Pre-Trial Chamber refused to confirm certain charges, finding them cumulative and citing the burden that excessive charging placed on the defense.[148] It confirmed charges only on the basis that Bemba knew crimes were being committed. The Trial Chamber, however, subsequently notified the parties and participants after the defense had begun presenting its case that it would also consider the alternative form of knowledge – that Bemba, a former military commander, should have known that his forces were committing or about to commit crimes.[149] In convicting Bemba, the Trial Chamber found that Bemba knew in fact that his soldiers were engaged, or were about to engage, in the murder, rape, and pillage of civilians.[150] Although the ICC's judgment in *Bemba* earned praise for advancing accountability through the use of command responsibility,[151] the case also highlights concerns about the ICC's legal recharacterization of facts in pursuit of this goal.

Some critics maintain that Regulation 55 is *ultra vires* because it exceeds the authority of judges to adopt regulations for the "routine functioning" of the Court.[152] The most significant controversy surrounding Regulation 55, however, concerns its potential impact on the fair trial rights of accused persons. The ICC's reliance on Regulation 55 in *Katanga* and *Chui* is instructive. The original indictment in *Katanga* and *Chui* charged crimes against humanity and war crimes based on a theory of indirect co-perpetration. After the close of trial and before judgment, the Trial Chamber recharacterized Katanga's mode of liability as common purpose liability, which merely requires that the defendant contribute to the charged crimes.[153] (Shortly thereafter it acquitted Chui, whose case had been severed from Katanga's.)[154] The change was significant because Katanga had admitted that he had known about and potentially indirectly contributed to crimes of his (unidentified) former subordinates, but denied that he had intended to commit the crimes charged or that he had control over them, both material elements of indirect co-perpetration.[155] The Trial Chamber stressed its authority under the Rome Statute to determine the truth and consider the guilt of the accused based on the evidence, without necessarily being confined to the prosecution's legal characterization of the facts.[156] But in a sharp dissent, Judge Christine Van den Wyngaert maintained that the reframed charges exceeded the nature and scope of the original charges, thus undermining the rights of the accused.[157] She argued, moreover, that the recharacterization of the facts weakened the legal and moral authority of the judgment even if other aspects of the trial were fair.[158] Several commentators have underscored the risk such recharacterization poses to a defendant's right to be informed of the charges, right against self-incrimination, and, most importantly, right to prepare an effective defense by undermining trial strategy.[159] As Kevin Jon Heller notes, trial strategy can encompass challenges not just to the prosecution's factual allegations, but also to how those facts are framed.[160] Although Regulation 55 contains safeguards for defendants,[161] the considerable authority it gives judges to change the legal characterization of the facts, coupled with the general pressure on judges to accommodate the interests of the prosecution and victims in obtaining accountability for grave crimes, risks weakening protections for the accused.[162]

The increased pressure on the ICC to expedite proceedings has generated additional concerns about limiting procedural safeguards. The Assembly of States Parties, for example, has stressed the need to make the Court more efficient, and judicial study groups have proposed various initiatives to achieve this end.[163] These measures typically focus on greater use of case management tools by judges, including increased monitoring and regulation of disclosures, requiring the prosecution (and in some instances the defense) to produce summaries of the evidence to be disclosed, and rejecting or reshaping charges.[164] Measures designed to increase efficiency can undermine the defense's case strategy and the equality of arms through restrictions on defense investigations and resources, thus exacerbating existing structural disparities between the defense and prosecution.[165]

Increased efficiency is not, however, necessarily at odds with defendants' interests. Survey data suggests that defense attorneys believe that some case management tools can positively impact the defense. Judges, for example, can use these tools to resist the Court's administrative arm from restricting defense investigations and staffing.[166] Judges also can utilize case management tools to help address persistent defense concerns about the prosecution's failure to adhere to the substance and timing of its disclosure obligations, as well as the prosecution's excessive use of redactions.[167] Thus, while case management tools pose risks, they have the potential to strengthen the operation of defense procedural protections on the ground.

***

Another recurring area of controversy involves the ICC's effort to serve the interests of victims, including by maximizing their participation in proceedings in their own capacity and not merely in their traditional role as witnesses. Nuremberg and other World War II-era criminal tribunals did not recognize the right of victims to participate in proceedings. The *ad hoc* tribunals established for the former Yugoslavia and for Rwanda did not allow victims to participate personally in the proceedings, except as witnesses, and did not provide victims any entitlement to receive reparations or compensation for damages suffered from the atrocities perpetrated against them.[168] Justice for victims in these prior international tribunals thus largely remained symbolic. The Rome Statute provides victims unprecedented rights to participate in international criminal proceedings.[169] The ICC's robust approach to victim's rights reflects an effort to combine goals of restorative justice, which focuses on repairing the harm from criminal behavior, with criminal law's retributive goal of punishing offenders.[170] The ICC's Victims and Witnesses Unit offers protective measures and security arrangements for victims and witnesses who come before the Court. The ICC also recognizes the right of victims to reparations and other redress, including rehabilitation – even if they did not participate in the criminal prosecution – and has established the Trust Fund for Victims to achieve this goal.[171] By 2014, 12,000 individuals had sought to participate as victims in proceedings before the ICC, and more than 5,000 had obtained victim status and participated in some manner before the Court.[172]

The ICTY and ICTR's more restrictive approach to victim participation reflects the influence of Anglo-American common law systems, in which a victim's role is generally confined to providing witness testimony when called by the prosecution, defense, or court, or at the sentencing phase following the conviction of the accused.[173] Civil law systems of Continental Europe, however, have traditionally allowed a greater role for victims, either as civil claimants who intervene and participate in criminal proceedings brought by the state or as private prosecutors who can directly summon the accused to court and demonstrate the accused's culpability without action by public prosecutors.[174]

The ICC's emphasis on victims reflects the Court's ambitious goals, which extend beyond adjudicating the guilt or innocence of individual defendants. Its elevation of the role of victims is buoyed by international human rights norms, which stress the importance of providing redress to victims as well as prosecuting perpetrators of grave crimes,[175] and by theories of transitional justice that emphasize the perspective and interests of victims in societies seeking to recover from widespread violence and atrocities.[176] The ICC's framework for more robust victim participation responds to past criticisms of the ICTY and ICTR for creating a disconnect between the prosecutor's office and the individuals and communities that suffered directly from the crimes. It also reflects an awareness of the need for an international criminal court – especially one, like the ICC, located far from where the atrocities occurred – to connect with the people and communities most impacted.[177] Enabling victims to participate directly and providing mechanisms for redress is thus important to the ICC's overall mission and legitimacy.

The Rome Statute provides that where "the personal interests of the victims are affected, the Court shall permit their views and concerns to be presented and considered at stages of the proceedings determined to be appropriate by the Court."[178] Victims may participate, in varying degrees, from the initial investigation of a situation, where the Prosecutor contemplates bringing charges, through the trial and sentencing of individual defendants.[179] Opportunity for victim participation starts when a prosecutor concludes that there is a reasonable basis to proceed with an investigation.[180] During the preliminary investigation in the Congo, for example, six alleged victims were granted the right to participate before the first suspect, Thomas Lubanga Dyilo, was even in ICC custody.[181] The Appeals Chamber subsequently ruled, however, that victims may participate only in proceedings before the Court, and have no general right to participate in the investigation itself.[182] When, for example, a prosecutor seeks the Pre-Trial Chamber's authorization for an investigation, victims may make representations to the Pre-Trial Chamber to determine whether a situation warrants action by the Court.[183] While victims may offer information to the prosecution, they have no right to demand particular investigative measures or to request reviews of prosecutorial decisions not to investigate.[184]

Victims also have the right to participate at the case stage, after a warrant or summons to appear has been issued. At that point, the focus shifts from investigating a situation to determining the specific crimes committed by particular individuals. To participate at this stage, victims must demonstrate a personal interest. This requires more than a generalized interest in the outcome of a prosecution, although the ICC case law suggests that this showing can be made in various ways.[185] At the pretrial stage, victims are granted permission to present their views and concerns at hearings to confirm charges against the accused and to determine whether the accused should be provisionally released.[186] At trial, victim participation can take different forms. Victims can potentially obtain court records and filings; gain access to hearings, status conferences, and other proceedings; file written submissions; make opening and closing statements; and offer and examine evidence where it assists in determining the truth or at the Court's request.[187] Victims can, for example, apply to be heard as witnesses, independent of the prosecution or defense, as occurred in the *Katanga* trial with the presentation of a "victim's case" after the prosecution's case.[188] As the Appeals Chamber noted, for victim participation to be meaningful, victims must have at least the potential to submit evidence addressing the culpability of the accused and to challenge the admissibility and relevance of evidence.[189]

The Rome Statute also provides, however, that the presentation and consideration of victims' views and concerns must be conducted in "a manner which is not prejudicial to or inconsistent with the rights of the accused and a fair and impartial trial."[190] In general, the greater the emphasis a court places on protecting the interests of victims, the greater the potential for conflict with the interests of defendants.[191] The Rome Statute not only recognizes the potential for victim participation to infringe a defendant's fair trial rights, but also suggests that in case of a conflict between the two, the latter should prevail.[192]

A defendant's rights may be affected by victim participation in various ways. Allowing victims to participate during the investigation stage can potentially influence the impartiality of the Prosecutor who may feel pressure to pursue charges or disregard other factors, such as the crime's gravity.[193] Victim participation at trial poses the most significant concerns. Such participation, to be sure, can help connect victims to the proceedings and provide an outlet for the expression of their views. But it also can create an atmosphere of anger and outrage that leads judges more easily to attribute blame to defendants, even if subconsciously, and prejudices a defendant's right to a fair trial.[194] Victim participation at trial, moreover, means that defendants must now counter the accusations of multiple accusers, thus undermining the principle of equality of arms.[195] Unlike the Prosecutor, participating victims do not have a duty to disclose exculpatory material to the defense, including, for example, information that might undermine the reliability of a witness whom a victim calls to testify about the guilt of the accused.[196] Additionally, concerns may arise where victims who provide testimony also serve as witnesses since victims necessarily have a personal interest in the outcome.[197] Victim participation, moreover, can delay what are already lengthy proceedings by requiring the Court to address a range of additional issues, from deciding victim applications to participate at the investigation stage to managing victim presentation of testimony at trial.[198] The potential for delay is increased because victims must demonstrate a personal interest at each stage of the proceedings in which they seek to participate and show how that interest will be affected.[199]

The ICC has accordingly imposed restrictions on victim participation both to protect defendants' rights and to accommodate prosecution concerns about victim interference with its investigation and trial strategy. The Pre-Trial Chamber has restricted the scope of victim participation during investigations and clarified that permission to participate at that stage does not guarantee participation once charges have been entered; at that point, victims must show a causal link between harms suffered and crimes specified in the arrest warrant.[200] Restrictions have been placed on the ability of victims to introduce evidence during charge confirmation hearings.[201] In the courtroom, victims have been permitted to participate through their legal representatives, but have not been allowed to make personal statements.[202] The Appeals Chamber has also imposed limits on the introduction of evidence by victims at trial and on victim challenges to the admissibility and relevance of evidence.[203]

The ability of victims to present evidence at trial thus depends on several factors, including their personal interests, the relevance of the evidence, and the potential infringement of a defendant's rights.[204] Mediation between the interests of victims and the fair trial rights of accused individuals is left largely to the discretion of the Court, which makes determinations on a case-by-case basis.[205] Notwithstanding the limits that the ICC has placed on victim participation, some commentators maintain that victim participation should be restricted entirely to sentencing (if allowed at all), after the accused's guilt has already been established.[206]

While the ICC's elevation of victims' rights can adversely impact protections for defendants, the Court has also disappointed victims and their advocates in its implementation of the victim participation regime. The sheer number of victims seeking participation, coupled with the inability of most victims to retain their own lawyers, has required the use of common legal representation. But grouping large numbers of victims together raises concerns about the adequacy of the representation and the marginalization of the victims themselves, who may believe their interests are being ignored.[207] The recent reorganization under the Court's ReVision project, which consolidates all ICC victim-related functions in a single office within the Registry, seeks to improve the delivery of services and assistance to victims. Victims' organizations have nevertheless raised concerns about the impact on victims' representation, including limits on the choice of counsel and the management of potential conflicts of interest.[208] Many victims in situation countries where the ICC is conducting investigations are ineligible to participate because they cannot meet the required showing that they were affected by the specific crimes charged by the Prosecutor, and only a few victims who are granted participant status appear in trial proceedings. Other victim-centered critiques include a lack of victim input into the crimes charged, inadequate outreach by the prosecution to victims and communities, and an overall lack of coordination with victims' groups.[209] One result is that victims tend to be amalgamated into an abstract entity, with few individuals actually being represented in legal proceedings.[210] Organizations that support an expanded role for victims at the ICC reject the proposition that increasing victim participation unduly delays proceedings and drains judicial resources.[211] They emphasize the positive features of victim participation, whether by contributing to truth-finding or identifying facts or legal issues overlooked by prosecutors and defense counsel.[212] Yet, the risks to the rights of defendants – as well as the potential for delay – remain significant in any framework of criminal adjudication that places such strong emphasis on the participatory rights and interests of victims.

***

The ICC's selection of the situations it investigates and the cases it prosecutes also implicates fairness concerns. The term situation refers to the time and place where crimes within the Court's jurisdiction have been committed, while cases describe the particular defendant (or defendants) alleged to have committed those crimes. When the ICTY and ICTR were established, their constitutive documents set forth the parameters of their authority, and each tribunal was confined to selecting cases within those parameters (crimes committed in the territory of the former Yugoslavia for the ICTY or crimes committed in Rwanda, or by Rwandan nationals in neighboring states, in 1994, for the ICTR). The Rome Statute lacks any such limits on the ICC's potential reach.[213] The ICC was instead envisioned as a global court created to punish the gravest crimes wherever and whenever they occur. Yet, this vision has always been in tension with limits on the ICC's jurisdiction due to the Court's design and the practical obstacles the ICC faces.

Selectivity may be understood horizontally (which situations from a particular time period are chosen for investigation and prosecution) and vertically (which individuals within that situation are singled out for prosecution). Selectivity considerations are implicated not only across situations, but also within a given situation when less responsible – typically lower level – officials are targeted instead of more responsible – typically higher level – officials. Recurring patterns in the selection of situations and cases reinforce realist critiques of ICL as merely another means by which power is exercised, with the strongest states continuing to assert their control and influence on the international stage.[214]

One of the ICC's animating goals was to push back against such theories of international relations and respond to demands for a more depoliticized system of international criminal justice. Crucial to this goal was the creation of an independent prosecutor. At the Rome Conference, some states, including the US, sought to confine the ICC's jurisdiction to referrals by the Security Council or self-referrals by member states.[215] States advocating this position not only wanted to maintain the prerogatives of the Security Council, but also feared that prosecutorial discretion could result in reckless or politicized prosecutions.[216] The United States, for example, cautioned that an independent prosecutor would pursue politically motivated prosecutions that targeted US military actions.[217] However, a group of like-minded states, supported by various nongovernment organizations that played an important role in setting the agenda, insisted on the inclusion of an independent prosecutor to counterbalance the Security Council and to enhance the overall fairness and legitimacy of an international criminal court.[218] Those favoring a stronger prosecutor thought that making Security Council referral obligatory would diminish the Court's credibility and moral authority, narrowly constrict its role, and overly politicize the institution.[219] Supporters of an independent prosecutor eventually prevailed, leading to the creation of a prosecutor with the ability to initiate cases without a referral from a State Party or the Security Council.[220] The prosecutor, moreover, could initiate an investigation based on information from any reliable source he or she deems appropriate,[221] making the prosecutor receptive to input from – and pressure by – nongovernment organizations, victims groups, and norm entrepreneurs.

At the time, an independent prosecutor was viewed as one of the Rome Statute's most important achievements by allowing cases to be brought based on considerations of law and justice rather than on the self-interest or sheer power of a particular state.[222] Proponents thus envisioned that an independent prosecutor could bring international criminal justice "a further step down the road from partiality to impartiality" and strengthen human rights protections by making prosecutions for atrocities less dependent on decisions by dominant states.[223]

Yet, prosecutorial independence has proven a double-edged sword, raising expectations that the ICC has been unable to fulfill. Perhaps the most significant challenge to achieving this goal is embedded in the Rome Statute itself. The Rome Statute's territorial and nationality restrictions on the ICC's jurisdiction make it difficult to prosecute individuals from non-States Parties, particularly individuals from the three permanent members of the UN Security Council – China, Russia, and the United States – that have refused to join the Court. The ICC not only lacks jurisdiction over crimes committed within the territory or by nationals of nonmember states, but any of these three countries can block the alternative path to ICC jurisdiction of Security Council referral under Chapter VII through exercise of their respective veto power.[224] Consequently, officials from three of the world's leading powers are, for practical purposes, potentially subject to ICC prosecution only for crimes committed on the territory of States Parties (or other states that consent to the Court's jurisdiction).

The ICC Prosecutor also remains subject to additional constraints under the Rome Statute. To proceed with an investigation, the Prosecutor must first determine that there is a reasonable basis to believe a crime within the Court's jurisdiction is being (or has been) committed; that the situation involves cases of sufficient gravity; and that national courts are not already investigating or prosecuting in good faith.[225] The Prosecutor may also decline to initiate an investigation or pursue a prosecution if he or she finds that it would not be "in the interests of justice."[226] The decision to commence an investigation through the exercise of the Prosecutor's *proprio motu* power is subject to judicial review by the Pre-Trial Chamber.[227] The Prosecutor's decision to decline to open a formal investigation in a referred situation is likewise subject to review by the Pre-Trial Chamber, although the nature of that review varies based on the ground cited by the Prosecutor. If, for example, the Prosecutor declines to open a formal investigation into a situation or pursue a prosecution against certain individuals based on the interests of justice, the Pre-Trial Chamber can demand that the Prosecutor reconsider the decision; if the Prosecutor's decision is based on a different ground, the Pre-Trial Chamber can only request that the Prosecutor reconsider it.[228]

Practical considerations have a significant effect on the ICC's selection of cases and serve as a further constraint on the Prosecutor's power. Lacking any law enforcement authority of its own, the ICC relies heavily on states, especially those with powerful militaries, for such essential tasks as arresting suspects, gathering evidence, securing the production of witnesses, and enforcing its judgments.[229] The Court also depends on states for continued financial support. The ICC's budget permits only a handful of prosecutions annually, thus forcing the Prosecutor to choose a few cases from among many.[230]

These practical considerations limit the ICC's ability to fulfill its goal of combatting impunity for grave crimes, particularly those committed by senior government officials.[231] The Security Council, for example, did not fund its referral to the ICC for Libya or the Darfur, Sudan, placing the full cost on the ICC, and has done little to support the ICC's investigations in either country.[232] To the contrary, the Security Council, as well as various member states, failed to act in the face of flagrant noncompliance by Sudan's President, Omar Hassan al-Bashir, who has traveled the globe in defiance of international arrest warrants issued by the Court.[233] In 2014, the ICC Prosecutor suspended the investigation into the situation in the Darfur following a lack of support by the Security Council, which, among other things, failed to implement economic sanctions or take other action against States Parties that hosted visits by al-Bashir.[234] In 2017, the ICC Pre-Trial Chamber II ruled that South Africa had a duty to arrest al-Bashir when al-Bashir was in South Africa attending an African Union summit in 2015 and surrender him to the Court, but refused to refer South Africa to the Assembly of States Parties or to the UN Security Council for noncompliance with its legal obligations.[235] In exercising their discretion against a referral to external organs, the ICC judges explained that such referral would not be an effective means of obtaining South Africa's cooperation.[236] While the ICC's ruling might be viewed as a pragmatic solution to ensure South Africa's continued support for the Court, it nevertheless sends a message to States Parties that noncompliance has no consequences.[237]

The ICC Prosecutor blamed the collapse in 2014 of its case against Uhuru Kenyatta, the former finance minister who was elected president of Kenya in 2013, on Kenya's lack of cooperation.[238] An ICC Trial Chamber subsequently ruled that the government of Kenya had breached its obligation to cooperate with the ICC by failing to provide evidence in the case against Kenyatta and referred the matter to the Assembly of States Parties.[239] Such referral is the sole mechanism available to a trial chamber in non-Security Council referred cases, and its enforcement remains essentially political.[240]

The United States' ability to exert influence over the ICC has been noteworthy. The United States has not only refused to ratify the Rome Statute, but has also sought to insulate its officials from possible ICC prosecution by negotiating a series of bilateral agreements with other countries.[241] The United States has supported the ICC in some ways, including by backing UN Security Council referrals to the Court of the situations in the Darfur and in Libya. But it has also sought to immunize any US person from potential exposure to criminal responsibility by the ICC. The Security Council resolutions for the Darfur and Libya, for example, prevent any possible exercise of jurisdiction over nationals of nonmember states (and thus over US nationals).[242] The United States has also influenced the ICC's protracted preliminary examination in Colombia, an important US ally, by working within the rubric of complementarity. In what one scholar describes as a strategy of "calculated engagement," Colombia has, with US assistance, designed a transitional justice process intended to prevent a formal ICC investigation or prosecution by addressing crimes within the ICC's jurisdiction while also protecting politically powerful actors and reducing and mitigating sentences for middle- and lower-level members of government or aligned forces.[243] Although US cooperation with the ICC increased under the Obama administration,[244] the United States' selective engagement with Court has arguably hurt the Court's relations with other states, especially in Africa.[245]

The ICC has thus generally sought to accommodate the concerns of major powers.[246] Despite the Rome Statute's creation of an independent prosecutor, situations and cases before the ICC largely track realist models of international relations, with stronger states generally supporting prosecutions against defendants from weaker states because of the lower international relations costs.[247]

Implementation of the ICC's specialized jurisdiction over the crime of aggression could further entrench this pattern. The Rome Statute initially placed the crime of aggression within the ICC's jurisdiction but did not define aggression or supply jurisdictional triggers over it until the 2010 Kampala agreement.[248] The resulting amendments to the Rome Statute define acts of aggression as the use of armed force by one state against the sovereignty, territorial integrity, or political independence of another state whose character, gravity, and scale constitute a manifest violation of the UN Charter, and list various acts that would so qualify.[249] The amendments limit criminal responsibility to individuals who are in a position to exercise effective control over or to direct a state's political or military action, and who plan, prepare, initiate, or execute acts of aggression.[250] The ICC's jurisdiction over the crime of aggression is set to take effect after January 1, 2017, once thirty States Parties have ratified the amendments and the Assembly of States Parties votes by a two-thirds majority to activate the ICC's jurisdiction.[251] Once this jurisdiction is activated, the ICC will become the first international tribunal since Nuremberg and Tokyo empowered to prosecute the crime of aggression. The ICC, however, may exercise jurisdiction only over crimes of aggression committed one year after the ratification or acceptance of the amendments by thirty States Parties.[252]

Supporters hail this development as an important, albeit partial, step towards fulfilling the legacy of Nuremberg, which treated aggression as the supreme international crime.[253] The amendments, however, both face significant obstacles in achieving this goal and pose concerns about how jurisdiction over crimes of aggression might eventually be exercised.

The amendments' potential impact on the Security Council's authority to determine acts of aggression by virtue of its exclusive responsibility for maintaining international peace and security under the UN Charter proved particularly controversial at Kampala.[254] The amendments outline different roles for the Security Council, depending on the trigger mechanism.[255] In cases referred by States Parties or in investigations *proprio motu*, the Prosecutor must first ascertain whether the Security Council has made a determination of an act of aggression.[256] Where the Security Council has made such a determination, the Prosecutor may proceed with the investigation; where the Security Council has not done so within six months after the date of notification of the situation before the Court by the Prosecutor to the UN Secretary-General, a Pre-Trial Chamber of the ICC may authorize the investigation to commence.[257] In either circumstance, the Security Council's determination is not binding on the ICC's own assessment of whether an act of aggression has occurred.[258] These provisions help carve out a role for the ICC in determining acts of aggression.[259] The ICC, however, cannot exercise jurisdiction over crimes of aggression committed by nationals or on the territory of non-States Parties or nonconsenting State Parties absent Security Council referral.[260] This limitation is the result of pressure exerted by the United States and other major powers at Kampala.[261] The United States had warned that ICC jurisdiction over the crime of aggression could discourage states from intervening to prevent humanitarian catastrophes because such intervention would carry a risk of international criminal prosecution and had proposed (unsuccessfully) language that would have expressly excluded from crimes of aggression the use of force to prevent genocide, crimes against humanity, and war crimes.[262] The Security Council also can defer any investigation or prosecution for renewable twelve-month periods.[263] Additionally, State Parties may opt out of the Court's jurisdiction over the crime of aggression by lodging a declaration with the ICC Registrar prior to any act of aggression otherwise subject to ICC jurisdiction.[264] While it remains uncertain how the ICC would pursue crimes of aggression once its jurisdiction is activated, the restrictions on its exercise of that jurisdiction could exacerbate existing perceptions of major power influence over the Court.

Critics frequently point to the ICC's disproportionate focus on countries in Africa.[265] According to one scholar, this focus threatens to transform the ICC "into a Western court to try African crimes against humanity."[266] The ICC has experienced significant strains in its relationship with the African Union.[267] In October 2016, South Africa, Burundi, and Gambia announced their intention to withdraw from the Court.[268] South Africa subsequently revoked its decision to withdraw from the ICC, citing a ruling by a South African court declaring the withdrawal unconstitutional and invalid, and Gambia similarly reversed its decision to withdraw from the Court.[269] Yet, such signs of resistance, particularly by influential states like South Africa, have prompted fears of a coordinated exodus by African leaders that could undermine the Court's legitimacy and survival.[270]

The ICC has also faced criticism for its selection of cases within a given situation by targeting one side of a conflict despite evidence that all sides committed international crimes.[271] The ICC, for example, has practiced such selectivity in Uganda by prosecuting only members of the Lord's Resistance Army and excluding Ugandan government and military officials; in the Côte D'Ivoire by prosecuting only the deposed Laurent Gbagbo and his supporters and excluding supporters of the victorious Alassane Ouattara; and in the Ituri region of the Democratic Republic of Congo by prosecuting only rebel and militia leaders.[272] In Uganda, for example, the ICC charged Lubanga with the crimes of conscripting and enlisting child soldiers even though virtually every party to the conflict there engaged in that practice.[273] Such intra-situational selectivity, moreover, tends to shield government forces, thus reinforcing the "classic impunity paradigm" of the state sheltering its own forces and undercutting the ICC's goal of bringing the most responsible individuals to justice.[274]

These criticisms, however, must be viewed in context. The initial situations before the ICC have typically been referred by either the individual governments on whose territory the crimes occurred (Uganda, the DRC, the Central African Republic, and Mali) or the Security Council (the Darfur and Libya). The ICC, for example, was invited by the government to review the situation in northern Uganda, and its involvement received broad support both in Europe and Africa.[275] In these situations, moreover, prosecutions of only one side of a conflict appeared to be the price of self-referral by the African states.[276] The two exceptions are the Pre-Trial Chamber II's March 2010 decision authorizing the prosecution's request to open an investigation *proprio motu* in the situation of Kenya and the Pre-Trial Chamber III's October 2011 decision authorizing the prosecution's request to open an investigation *proprio motu* in the situation of Côte d'Ivoir.[277] And in Kenya, the ICC initiated its investigation because of nonaction by Kenya.[278] Specifically, the ICC Prosecutor sought authorization to investigate *proprio motu* crimes committed during the postelection violence in Kenya only after Kenya had refused to approve the locally sponsored accountability mechanism proposed by the Commission of Inquiry into Post-Election Violence, which had advocated establishing a hybrid tribunal, consisting of national and international judges and staff, to prosecute alleged crimes.[279] African leaders, moreover, have leveraged self-referrals to insulate themselves and their supporters from prosecution. This opportunistic use of the Rome Statute's self-referral mechanism suggests how a simplistic framing that pits a Eurocentric court against states in the developing world – and equates ICL with colonialism – obscures a more nuanced postcolonial reality in which local power structures interact with international organizations to target weaker domestic communities.[280]

But while the reality is more nuanced than it first appears, it is difficult to deny that the ICC's docket contributes to a perception of universal justice as "universal in name only."[281] Further, the ICC's selection decisions have helped enable political and military elites in Africa (and elsewhere) to seize upon historical grievances and paint the Court – even if unfairly – as a pro-western institution biased against Africa and other developing nations in order to avoid accountability for their own crimes.[282] In Kenya, for example, political leaders called for the country's withdrawal from the ICC after the Court opened an investigation there.[283] And the ICC's decision to issue an arrest warrant for al-Bashir prompted substantial resistance, including by the African Union, which adopted a nonbinding resolution condemning the action and declining assistance,[284] although several important African states entered formal reservations to the resolution.[285]

The ICC's selection decisions thus highlight another dimension of fairness that has long plagued ICL. Even if the ICC rigorously protects the procedural rights of the accused individuals before it, the Court's failure to widen its reach to include international crimes committed by powerful countries or state forces more generally will undermine the principle that no person is above the law and weaken the Court's legitimacy in the long run.

NOTES

1. J. Holmes Armstead, Jr., "The International Criminal Court: History, Development, and Status," *Santa Clara Law Review* 38 (1998), 745, 747. The International Law Association first proposed a permanent court in 1926.
2. Leila Sadat, "The Proposed International Criminal Court: An Appraisal," *Cornell International Law Journal* 29 (1996), 665, 676–85.
3. Rome Statute of the International Criminal Court, July 17, 1998, 2187 U.N.T.S. 90 (Rome Statute).
4. Ibid., art. 5.
5. Ibid., art. 5(2).
6. Ibid., art. 12(1)–(2).
7. Ibid., art. 12(3).
8. Ibid., art. 13.
9. Ibid., arts. 13–14.
10. Ibid., art. 13(1).
11. Ibid., arts. 15 *bis*, 15 *ter*.
12. Ibid., art. 16.
13. Ibid., art. 17(1)(d).
14. Ibid., art. 17(1)(a)–(b).
15. Ibid., art. 54(c).
16. Ibid., art. 21.
17. Angela Walker, Comment, "The ICC Versus Libya: How to End the Cycle of Impunity for Atrocity Crimes by Protecting Due Process," *UCLA Journal of International Law and Foreign Affairs* 18 (2014), 303, 336–37; Gregory S. Gordon, "Toward an International Criminal Procedure: Due Process Aspirations and Limitations," *Columbia Journal of Transnational Law* 45 (2007), 635, 669–70; Salvatore Zappalà, *Human Rights in International Criminal Proceedings* (Oxford: Oxford University Press, 2001), 94; Yvonne McDermott, *Fairness in International Criminal Trials* (Oxford: Oxford University Press, 2016), 43–44, 46–47, 61.
18. Zappalà, *Human Rights in International Criminal Proceedings*, 48.
19. Jenia Iontcheva Turner, "Policing International Prosecutors," *New York University Journal of International Law and Politics* 45 (2012), 175, 205.
20. *Prosecutor v. Bemba*, Case No. ICC-01/05–01/08–1386, Appeals Chamber, Judgment on the appeals of Mr. Jean-Pierre Bemba Gombo and the Prosecutor against the decision of Trial Chamber III entitled "Decision on the admission into evidence of materials contained in the prosecution's list of evidence," para. 73 (May 3, 2011).
21. *Prosecutor v. Kenyatta*, Case No. ICC-01/09–02/11, Trial Chamber V(b), Decision on Prosecution's application for further adjournment, para. 31, Dec. 3, 2014.
22. Rome Statute, preamble.
23. Ibid., art. 68(3).
24. Turner, "Policing International Prosecutors," 207–08; Stuart Ford, "A Social Psychology Model of the Perceived Legitimacy of International Criminal Courts: Implications for the Success of Transitional Justice Mechanisms," *Vanderbilt Journal of Transnational Law* 45 (2012), 405, 472–75.
25. Rome Statute, arts. 51(2), 123(3).
26. Alex Whiting, "The ICTY as a Laboratory of International Criminal Procedure," in Bert Swart, Alexander Zahar, and Göran Sluiter eds., *The Legacy of the International Criminal Tribunal for the Former Yugoslavia* (Oxford, England: Oxford University Press, 2011), 107.

27. Rome Statute, art. 52.
28. Margaux Dastugue, Note, "The Faults in 'Fair' Trials: An Evaluation of Regulation 55 at the International Criminal Court," *Vanderbilt Journal of Transnational Law* 48 (2015), 273, 280–82; McDermott, *Fairness in International Criminal Trials*, 14.
29. *Prosecutor v. Ruto*, Case No. ICC-01/09–01/11 OA 7 OA 8, Appeals Chamber, Judgment on the Appeals of William Samoei Ruto and Mr. Joshua Arap Sang against the Decision of Trial Chamber V(A) of 17 April 2014 Entitled "Decision on Prosecutor's Application for Witness Summonses and Resulting Request for State Party Cooperation," paras. 112–13, 132–33 (October 9, 2014).
30. Charles Chenor Jalloh, "Prosecutor v. Ruto, Case No. ICC-01/09–01/11, Appeals Judgment on Witnesses Summons," *American Journal of International Law* 109 (2015), 610, 616.
31. Dominic Kennedy and Isabel Düsterhöft, "The Proper Role for International Defense Counsel Organizations," in Colleen Rohan and Gentian Zyberi eds., *Defense Perspectives on International Criminal Justice* (Cambridge: Cambridge University Press, 2017), 157.
32. Rome Statute, art. 51(2).
33. Kennedy and Düsterhöft, "The Proper Role for International Defense Counsel Organizations," 157.
34. Jens David Ohlin, "Joint Intentions to Commit International Crimes," *Chicago Journal of International Law* 11 (2011), 693, 720. See also James G. Stewart, "The End of 'Modes of Liability' for International Crimes," *Leiden Journal of International Law* 25 (2012), 1, 4.
35. Rome Statute, art. 28.
36. Ibid., art. 28(a).
37. Ibid., art. 28(b).
38. Yaël Ronen, "Superior Responsibility of Civilians for International Crimes Committed in Civilian Settings," *Vanderbilt Journal of Transnational Law* 43 (2010), 313, 351–52.
39. Ibid., 352.
40. Jamie Allan Williamson, "Some Considerations on Command Responsibility and Criminal Liability," *International Review of the Red Cross* 90 (2008), 303, 308–09; Greg R. Vetter, "Command Responsibility of Non-Military Superiors in the International Criminal Court (ICC)," *Yale Journal of International Law* 25 (2000), 89, 95–97.
41. Ronen, "Superior Responsibility of Civilians," 354.
42. Rome Statute, art. 25(3)(a).
43. Ibid., art. 25(3)(b)–(c).
44. Ibid., art. 25(3)(d).
45. Jocelyn Courtney and Christodoulos Kaoutzanis, "Protective Gatekeepers: The Jurisprudence of the ICC's Pre-Trial Chambers," *Chicago Journal of International Law* 15 (2015), 518, 530–31.
46. Jason Burke, "John Pierre Bemba sentenced to 18 years in prison by international criminal court," *The Guardian*, June 21, 2016. See also Houston John Goodell, "The Greatest Measure of Deterrence: A Conviction for John Pierre Bemba Gombo," *UC Davis Journal of International Law and Policy* 18 (2011), 191, 193.
47. Marlise Simons and J. David Goodman, "Ex-Liberian Leader Gets 50 Years for War Crimes," *New York Times*, May 30, 2012.
48. Ohlin, "Joint Intentions to Commit International Crimes," 751.
49. *Prosecutor v. Lubanga Dyilo*, Case No. ICC-01/04–01/06, Pre-Trial Chamber I, Decision on the confirmation of charges, paras. 538–39 (January 29, 2007) (*Lubanga*, Decision on the confirmation of charges).

50. Ibid., para. 330; Courtney and Kaoutzanis, "Protective Gatekeepers," 529–30.

51. Ohlin, "Joint Intentions to Commit International Crimes," 723.

52. *Lubanga*, Decision on the confirmation of charges, paras. 342–43.

53. Ibid., para. 347.

54. Kai Ambos, "Joint Criminal Enterprise and Command Responsibility," *Journal of International Criminal Justice* 5 (2007), 159, 181–82; Jens David Ohlin, "The One or the Many," *Criminal Law and Philosophy* 9 (2015), 285, 294.

55. *Lubanga*, Decision on the confirmation of charges, para. 341.

56. *Prosecutor v. Lubanga Dyilo*, Case No. ICC-01/04–01/06, Trial Chamber I, Judgment pursuant to Article 74 of the Statute, para. 994 (March 14, 2012) (*Lubanga* Judgment)

57. *Lubanga*, Decision on the confirmation of charges, para. 327; Hiromi Sato, "The Separate Crime of Conspiracy and Core Crimes in International Criminal Law," *Connecticut Journal of International Law* 32 (2016), 73, 105–06.

58. Alexandra Link, Note, "Trying Terrorism, Joint Criminal Enterprise, Material Support, and the Paradox of International Criminal Law," *Michigan Journal of International Law* 34 (2013), 439, 463–64; Alexander K. A. Greenawalt, "Foreign Assistance Complicity," *Columbia Journal of Transnational Law* 54 (2016), 531, 584–85, and n. 195; Mark A. Summers, "Prosecuting Generals for War Crimes: The Shifting Sands of Accomplice Liability in International Criminal Law," *Cardozo Journal of International and Comparative Law* 23 (2013), 519, 538–39.

59. *Prosecutor v. Katanga and Chui*, Case No. ICC-01/04–01/07, Pre-Trial Chamber I, Decision on the confirmation of charges, paras. 490–93 (September 30, 2008) (*Katanga* Decision on the confirmation of charges).

60. Ibid, paras. 519–20; Neha Jain, "The Control Theory of Perpetration in International Criminal Law," *Chicago Journal of International Law* 12 (2011), 159, 186.

61. *Katanga* Decision on the confirmation of charges, paras. 5–7, 11, 492–93.

62. Shachar Eldar, "Indirect Co-Perpetration," *Criminal Law and Philosophy* 8 (2014), 605, 607.

63. Jain, "The Control Theory," 183–84; Pamela J. Stephens, "Collective Criminality and Individual Responsibility: The Constraints of Interpretation," *Fordham International Law Journal* 37 (2014), 501, 523–24.

64. Courtney and Kaoutzanis, "Protective Gatekeepers," 530–31.

65. Eldar, "Indirect Co-Perpetration," 607.

66. Ohlin, "Joint Intentions to Commit International Crimes," 706; Courtney and Kaoutzanis, "Protective Gatekeepers," 533–34.

67. Ohlin, "Joint Intentions to Commit International Crimes," 721.

68. *Lubanga* Decision on the confirmation of charges, paras. 352–56; Ohlin, "Joint Intentions to Commit International Crimes," 732.

69. Ohlin, "Joint Intentions to Commit International Crimes," 723–24. But see Jain, "The Control Theory," 187–93 (challenging Professor Ohlin's critique of the ICC's control theory).

70. Ambos, "Joint Criminal Enterprise and Command Responsibility," 172–73.

71. Rome Statute, art. 25(3)(d); Courtney and Kaoutzanis, "Protective Gatekeepers," 533–34.

72. Rome Statute, arts. 25(3)(c), (d); Greenawalt, "Foreign Assistance Complicity," 584–85; Link, "Trying Terrorism," 464.

73. Office of the Prosecutor, *Situation in Darfur, The Sudan*, Summary of the Case; Prosecutor's Application for Warrant of Arrest under Article 58 against Omar Hassan Ahmad Al Bashir, at 1 (July 14, 2008), www.icc-cpi.int/NR/rdonlyres/64FA6B33 -05C3-4E9C-A672-3FA2B58CB2C9/277758/ICCOTPSummary20081704ENG.pdf;

Florian Jessberger and Julia Geneuss, "On Application of a Theory of Indirect Perpetration in Al Bashir: German Doctrine at The Hague?" *Journal of International Criminal Justice* 6 (2009), 853, 854–55.

74. Sabine Swoboda, "Confidentiality for the Protection of National Security Interests," *International Review of Penal Law* 81 (2010), 209, 211.

75. Human Rights Committee, General Comment No. 13, U.N. Doc. CCPR/C/21/Rev.1/ Add.6, para. 9 (November 11, 1994).

76. Rome Statute, art. 64(3)(c); ICC Rules of Procedure and Evidence (RPE), Rule 76.

77. Rome Statute, art. 67(2).

78. ICC RPE, Rule 77.

79. Christodoulos Kaoutzanis, "A Turbulent Adolescence Ahead: The ICC's Insistence on Disclosure in the Lubanga Trial," *Washington University Global Studies Law Review* 12 (2013), 263, 271.

80. Rome Statute, art. 54(3).

81. ICC RPE, Rule 82.

82. Rome Statute, art. 72.

83. *Prosecutor v. Lubanga Dyilo*, Case No. ICC-01/04–01/06 OA 13, Appeals Chamber, Judgment on the appeal of the Prosecutor against the decision of Trial Chamber I entitled "Decision on the consequences of non-disclosure of exculpatory materials covered by Article 54(3)(e) agreements and the application to stay the prosecution of the accused, together with certain other issues raised at the Status Conference on 10 June 2008," para. 25 (October 21, 2008) (*Lubanga* Judgment on appeal of decision on nondisclosure of exculpatory materials).

84. Larry D. Johnson, "The *Lubanga* Case and Cooperation between the UN and the ICC," *Journal of International Criminal Justice* 10 (2012), 887, 887–88.

85. Negotiated Relationship Agreement between the International Criminal Court and the United Nations, ICC-ASP/3/Res.1, art. 18, entered into force October 4, 2004.

86. Turner, "Policing International Prosecutors," 185–86; Milan Markovic, "The ICC Prosecutor's Missing Code of Conduct," *Texas International Law Journal* 47 (2011), 201, 213.

87. Kaoutzanis, "A Turbulent Adolescence Ahead," 277.

88. *Prosecutor v. Lubanga Dyilo*, Case No. ICC-01/04–01/06, Trial Chamber I, Decision on the consequences of nondisclosure of exculpatory materials covered by Article 54(3)(e) agreements and the application to stay the prosecution of the accused, together with certain other issues raised at the Status Conference on June 10, 2008, para. 94 (June 13, 2008).

89. Ibid., para. 90.

90. Ibid., paras. 71–75.

91. *Lubanga* Judgment on appeal of decision on nondisclosure of exculpatory materials, para. 95.

92. Ibid., paras. 3, 48.

93. *Prosecutor v. Lubanga Dyilo*, Case No. ICC-01/04–01/06 OA 12, Appeals Chamber, Judgment on the appeal of the Prosecutor against the decision of Trial Chamber I entitled "Decision on the release of Thomas Lubanga Dyilo," paras. 39–42 (October 21, 2008).

94. Milan Markovic, "The ICC Prosecutor's Missing Code of Conduct," 214.

95. Alex Whiting, "Lead Evidence and Discovery before the International Criminal Court: The Lubanga Case," *UCLA Journal of International Law and Foreign Affairs*, (2009), 207, 221–22.

96. Ibid., 222–25.

97. *Prosecutor v. Katanga and Chui*, Case No. ICC-01/04–01/07–621, Pre-Trial Chamber I, Decision on Article 54(3)(e) Documents Identified as Potentially Exculpatory or Otherwise Material to the Defence's Preparation for the Confirmation Hearing, para. 63 (June 20, 2008).

98. Ibid., paras. 77–86; Johnson, "The *Lubanga* Case," 893–94.

99. Whiting, "Lead Evidence and Discovery before the International Criminal Court," 229–30; Mark B. Harmon and Fergal Gaynor, "Prosecuting Massive Crimes with Primitive Tools: Three Difficulties Encountered by Prosecutors in International Criminal Proceedings," *Journal of International Criminal Justice* 2 (2004), 403, 404.

100. Kaoutzanis, "A Turbulent Adolescence Ahead," 272–73.

101. ICTY Rules of Procedure and Evidence, Rule 68, U.N. Doc. IT/32/REV.44 (December 10, 2009); Kaoutzanis, "A Turbulent Adolescence Ahead," 272–73.

102. Kaoutzanis, "A Turbulent Adolescence Ahead," 272–73.

103. Ellen Baylis, "Outsourcing Investigations," *UCLA Journal of International Law and Foreign Affairs* 14 (2009), 121, 122.

104. Johnson, "The *Lubanga* Case," 895.

105. *Lubanga* Judgment on appeal of decision on nondisclosure of exculpatory materials, para. 48, and Separate Opinion of Judge Georghios M. Pikis, para. 8; Kaoutzanis, "A Turbulent Adolescence Ahead," 297.

106. Johnson, "The *Lubanga* Case," 901–02.

107. *Prosecutor v. Lubanga Dyilo*, Case No. ICC-01/04–01/06, Trial Chamber I, Decision on Prosecution's Urgent Request for Variation of Time-Limit to Disclose the Identity of Intermediary 143 or Alternatively to Stay Proceedings Pending Further Consultations with the VWU, paras. 12, 31 (July 8, 2010) (*Lubanga* Trial Chamber I Decision on Time-Limit to Disclose the Identity of Intermediary)

108. Markovic, "The ICC Prosecutor's Missing Code of Conduct," 222–23.

109. *Lubanga*, Trial Chamber I Decision on Time-Limit to Disclose the Identity of Intermediary, para. 31.

110. *Prosecutor v. Lubanga Dyilo*, Case No. ICC-01/04–01/06 OA 18, Appeals Chamber, Judgment on appeal of the Prosecutor against the decision of Trial Chamber I of 8 July 2010 entitled "Decision on the Prosecution's Urgent Request for Variation of the Time-Limit to Disclose the Identity of Intermediary 143 or Alternatively to Stay Proceedings Pending Further Consultations with the VWU," para. 42 (October 8, 2010) (*Lubanga* Judgment on appeal of Decision on Time-Limit to Disclose the Identity of Intermediary).

111. Ibid., para. 59.

112. *Prosecutor v. Lubanga Dyilo*, Case No. ICC-01/04–01/06 OA 17, Appeals Chamber, Judgment on appeal of Prosecutor against the oral decision of Trial Chamber I of 15 July 2010 to release Thomas Lubanga Dyilo, para. 1 (October 8, 2010).

113. *Lubanga* Judgment on appeal of Decision on Time-Limit to Disclose the Identity of Intermediary, para. 60.

114. McDermott, *Fairness in International Criminal Trials*, 55–56.

115. Kaoutzanis, "A Turbulent Adolescence Ahead," 294–95.

116. *Lubanga* Judgment, paras. 291, 373, 450.

117. Ibid., paras. 120–21.

118. Rome Statute, art. 72.

119. *Prosecutor v. Blaškić*, Case No. IT-95–14-T, Appeals Chamber, Judgment on the Request of the Republic of Croatia for Review of the Decision of the Trial Chamber II of July 18, 1997, paras. 61–66 (October 29, 1997).

120. Swoboda, "Confidentiality for the Protection of National Security Interests," 214–15; Mirjan Damaška, "The International Criminal Court Between Aspiration and Achievement," *UCLA Journal of International Law and Foreign Affairs* 14 (2009), 19, 24.
121. Rome Statute, art. 72(5)–(7); Laura Moranchek, "Protecting National Security Evidence While Prosecuting War Crimes: Problems and Lessons for International Criminal Justice from the ICTY," *Yale Journal of International Law* 31 (2006), 477, 499.
122. Kaoutzanis, "A Turbulent Adolescence Ahead," 301.
123. Swoboda, "Confidentiality for the Protection of National Security Interests," 216–17.
124. Karim A. A. Khan and Anand A. Shah, "Defensive Practices: Representing Clients before the International Criminal Court," *Law and Contemporary Problems* 76 (2013), 191, 201–05.
125. Alex Whiting, "Dynamic Investigative Practice at the International Criminal Court," *Law and Contemporary Problems* 76 (2013), 163, 179–82.
126. *Prosecutor v. Katanga and Chui*, Case No. ICC-01/04/07, Trial Chamber II, Public redacted version of the Decision on the Protection of Prosecution Witnesses 267 and 353 of 20 May 2009, para. 31 (May 28, 2009).
127. Khan and Shah, "Defensive Practices," 206–07.
128. ICC RPE, Rule 81(4); *Prosecutor v. Katanga*, Case No. ICC-01/04–01/07, Appeals Chamber, Judgment on the appeal of the Prosecutor against the decision of Pre-Trial Chamber I entitled "First Decision on the Prosecution Request for Authorisation to Redact Witness Statements," paras. 64, 71 (May 13, 2008).
129. Khan and Shah, "Defensive Practices," 212.
130. Ibid., 210.
131. Wairagala Wakabi, "Ntaganda Wants Trial Stopped after Prosecution Accessed 'Critical Defense Information,'" *International Justice Monitor*, April 17, 2017, www.ijmonitor.org/2017/04/ntaganda-wants-trial-stopped-after-prosecution-accessed-critical-defense-information/.
132. Rome Statute, art. 70.
133. *Prosecutor v. Ntaganda*, Case No. ICC-01/04–02/06, Trial Chamber VI, Defence Request for stay of proceedings with prejudice to the Prosecutor, para. 6 (March 21, 2017).
134. *Prosecutor v. Ntaganda*, Case No. ICC-01/04–02/06, Trial Chamber VI, Prosecution's response to the "Defence Request for stay of proceedings with prejudice to the Prosecution," paras. 5, 9 (April 6, 2017).
135. Wairagala Wakabi, "Bemba and Four Associates Convicted for Witness Tampering," *International Justice Monitor*, October 19, 2016, www.ijmonitor.org/2016/10/bemba-and-four-associates-convicted-for-witness-tampering/.
136. ICC RPE, Rule 68(2)(c)(ii).
137. Study Group on Governance, *Working Group on Lessons Learnt: Second Report of the Court to the Assembly of States Parties*, para. 19 (October 12, 2013), https://asp.icc-cpi.int/iccdocs/asp_docs/ASP12/ICC-ASP-12–37-Add1-ENG.pdf.
138. *Prosecutor v. Ruto and Sang*, Case No. ICC-01/09–01/11–2024, Appeals Chamber, Judgment on the appeals of Mr. William Samoei Ruto and Mr. Joshua Arap Sang against the decision of Trial Chamber V(A) of August 19, 2015 entitled "Decision on Prosecution Request for Admission of Prior Recorded Testimony," para. 78 (February 12, 2016).
139. International Justice Resource Center, "ICC Dismisses Case against Kenya's Deputy President William Ruto," April 11, 2016, www.ijrcenter.org/2016/04/11/icc-dismisses-case-against-kenyas-deputy-president-william-ruto/.

140. Megan A. Fairlie, "The Abiding Problem of Witness Statements in International Criminal Trials," *New York University Journal of International Law and Politics* 50 (forthcoming), Florida International University Legal Studies Research Paper No. 17-08 (April 2017), 1–2, 38–40, https://papers.ssrn.com/sol3/papers.cfm?abstract_id=2956413.

141. Ibid.

142. Rome Statute, art. 7; McDermott, *Fairness in International Criminal Trials*, 91.

143. McDermott, *Fairness in International Criminal Trials*, 64–65.

144. International Criminal Court, Regulations of the Court, Doc. No. ICC-BD/01-01-04 (adopted 26 May 2004), Regulation 55(1).

145. Ibid., Regulation 55(2).

146. Sophie Rigney, Case Note, "'The Words Don't Fit You': Recharacterization of the Charges, Trial Fairness, and *Katanga*," *Melbourne Journal of International Law* 15 (2014), 515, 518.

147. *Prosecutor v. Lubanga*, Case No. ICC-01/04–01-91/06, Appeals Chamber, Judgment on the Appeals of Mr. Lubanga Dyilo and the Prosecutor against the Decision of the Trial Chamber I of 14, July 2009 entitled "Decision Giving Notice to the Parties and Participants that the Legal Characterization of the Facts May Be Subject to Change in Accordance with Regulation 55(2) of the Regulations of the Court," para. 93 (December 8, 2009).

148. *Prosecutor v Bemba*, Case No. ICC-01/05–01/08–424, Pre-Trial Chamber II, Decision Pursuant to Articles 61(7)(a) and (b) of the Rome Statute on the Charges of the Prosecutor Against Jean-Pierre Bemba Gombo, para. 202 (June 15, 2009).

149. *Prosecutor v Bemba*, Case No. ICC-01/05–01/08, Trial Chamber III, Decision giving notice to the parties and participants that the legal characterisation of the facts may be subject to change in accordance with Regulation 55(2) of the Regulations of the Court, para. 5 (September 21, 2012); Dienke de Vos, "Why We Should Be Watching the ICC on 21 March," *IntLawGrrls*, February 29, 2016, https://ilg2.org/2016/02/29/why-we-should-be-watching-the-icc-on-21-march/#more-8751.

150. *Prosecutor v. Bemba*, Case No. ICC-01/05–01/08, Trial Chamber III, Judgment pursuant to Article 74 of the Statute, paras. 706–18 (March 21, 2016).

151. Alex Whiting, "Commanders Put on Notice," *Just Security*, June 29, 2016, www.justsecurity.org/31733/commanders-put-notice.

152. Kevin Jon Heller, "Legal Qualification of Facts under Regulation 55," in Carsten Stahn ed., *The Law and Practice of the International Criminal Court* (Oxford: Oxford University Press, 2015), 981, 982–83.

153. *Prosecutor v. Katanga*, Case No. ICC-01/04–01/07, Trial Chamber II, Decision on the implementation of Regulation 55 of the Regulations of the Court and severing the charges against the accused persons, para. 7 (November 21, 2012) (*Katanga* Decision on the implementation of Regulation 55).

154. Press Release, "ICC Trial Chamber II Acquits Mathieu Ngudjolo Chui" (December 18, 2012), www.icc-cpi.int/pages/item.aspx?name=PR865.

155. Heller, "Legal Qualification of Facts under Regulation 55," 1001–02.

156. *Katanga* Decision on the implementation of Regulation 55, paras. 7–8 and n. 21.

157. *Prosecutor v. Katanga*, Case No. ICC-01/04–01/07–3436-AnxI, Minority Opinion of Judge Christine Van den Wyngaert, para. 310.

158. Ibid., para. 311. Katanga withdrew his appeal because he was eligible for release within a year of the judgment under the sentence he received, thus preventing the Appeals Chamber's review of the verdict on the recharacterized charges.

159. Rigney, "'The Words Don't Fit You,'" 532–33; Heller, "Legal Qualification of Facts under Regulation 55," 1003; Dov Jacobs, "The ICC Katanga Judgment: A Commentary (Part 2): Regulation 55 and the Modes of Liability," *Spreading the Jam* (March 11, 2014), http://dovjacobs.com/2014/03/11/the-icc-katanga-judgment-a-commentary-part-2-regulation-55-and-the-modes-of-liability/.

160. Heller, "Legal Qualification of Facts under Regulation 55," 994–1003.

161. Carsten Stahn, "Modification of the Legal Characterization of Facts in the ICC System: A Portrayal of Regulation 55," *Criminal Law Forum* 16 (2005), 1, 25, and n. 79.

162. Rigney, "'The Words Don't Fit You,'" 518, 521–22.

163. Jenia Iontcheva Turner, "Defense Perspectives on Fairness and Efficiency at the International Criminal Court," in Kevin Jon Heller, Jens Ohlin, Sarah Nouwen, Fred Megret, and Darryl Robinson eds., *Oxford Handbook on International Criminal Law* (Oxford: Oxford University Press, 2017) (forthcoming), SMU Deadman School of Law Legal Studies Research Paper No. 349, at 1, 7, http://dx.doi.org/10.2139/ssrn.2940483.

164. Ibid., 7.

165. Ibid., 9, 12–18, 33–34.

166. Ibid., 18.

167. Ibid., 3, 21–22.

168. Gerard J. Mekjian and Mathew C. Varughese, "Hearing the Victim's Voice: Analysis of Victims' Advocate Participation in The Trial Proceeding of the International Criminal Court," *Pace International Law Review* 17 (2005), 1, 11.

169. Susana SáCouto, "Victim Participation at the International Criminal Court and the Extraordinary Chambers in the Courts of Cambodia: A Feminist Perspective," *Michigan Journal of Gender and the Law* 18 (2012), 297, 301.

170. Sergey Vasiliev, "Victim Participation Revisited—What the ICC Is Learning about Itself," in Stahn ed., *The Law and Practice of the International Criminal Court*, 1134–36.

171. Rome Statute, arts. 75, 79; Tom Dannenbaum, "The International Criminal Court, Article 79, and Transitional Justice: The Case for an Independent Trust Fund for Victims," *Wisconsin International Law Journal* 28 (2010), 234, 240–42.

172. International Criminal Court, *Twenty-Third Diplomatic Briefing: Figures from the Registry*, at 3 (May 29, 2013), www.icc-cpi.int/iccdocs/db/Registry-Figures-30-April-2013.pdf.

173. Mugambi Jouet, "Reconciling the Conflicting Rights of Victims and Defendants at the International Criminal Court," *St. Louis University Public Law Review* 26 (2007), 249, 255–56; Brianne N. McGonigle, "Bridging the Divides in International Criminal Proceedings: An Examination into the Victim Participation Endeavor of the International Criminal Court," *Florida Journal of International Law* 21 (2009), 93 106.

174. Jouet, "Reconciling the Conflicting Rights of Victims and Defendants," 254–55.

175. Basic Principles and Guidelines on the Right to Remedy and Reparation for Victims of Gross Violations of International Human Rights Law and Serious Violations of International Humanitarian Law, G.A. Res. 60/147, U.N. Doc. A/RES/60/147 (March 21, 2006); Declaration of Basic Principles of Justice for Victims of Crime and Abuse of Power, G.A. Res. 40/34, U.N. Doc A/RES/40/34 (November 29, 1985); Elisabeth Baumgartner, "Aspects of victim participation in the proceedings of the International Criminal Court," *International Review of the Red Cross* 90 (2008), 409, 410.

176. Pablo de Greiff, "Justice and Reparations," in Jon Miller and Rahul Kumar eds., *Reparations: Interdisciplinary Inquiries* (Oxford: Oxford University Press, 2007), 162.

177. Goran Sluiter, Hakan Friman, and Suzannah Linton et al. eds., *International Criminal Procedure: Principles and Rules* (Oxford: Oxford University Press, 2013), 1299–1300.

178. Rome Statute, art. 68(3).
179. Baumgartner, "Aspects of victim participation," 425–38.
180. Rome Statute, arts. 15(3), 19(3).
181. *Situation in the Democratic Republic of Congo*, Case No. ICC-01/04, Pre-Trial Chamber I, Decision on the Applications for Participation in the Proceedings of VPRS 1, VPRS 2, VPRS 3, VPRS 4, VPRS 5 and VPRS 6, para. 12 (January 17, 2006).
182. *Situation in the Democratic Republic of the Congo*, Case No. ICC-01/04-556, Appeals Chamber, Judgment on victim participation in the investigation stage of the proceedings in the appeal of the OPCD against the decision of Pre-Trial Chamber I of 7 December 2007 and in the appeals of the OPCD and the Prosecutor against the decision of Pre-Trial Chamber I of 24 December 2007, paras. 45, 55–57 (December 19, 2008); SáCouto, "Victim Participation at the International Criminal Court," 347.
183. Rome Statute, art. 19(3); ICC RPE, Rules 50, 59.
184. Sluiter et al. eds., *International Criminal Procedure: Principles and Rules*, 1317.
185. Ibid., 1319.
186. Baumgartner, "Aspects of victim participation," 428–29; Caroline L. Davidson, "No Shortcuts on Human Rights: Bail and the International Criminal Trial," *American University Law Review* 60 (2010), 1, 65, and n. 319.
187. *Prosecutor v. Lubanga Dyilo*, Case No. ICC-01/04-01/06-1432, Appeals Chamber, Judgment on appeals of The Prosecutor and The Defence against Trial Chamber I's Decision on Victims' Participation of January 18, 2008, para. 4 (July 11, 2008) (*Lubanga* Judgment on appeals of Decision on Victims' Participation); *Prosecutor v. Lubanga Dyilo*, Case No. ICC-01/04-01/06-1119, Trial Chamber I, Decision on victims' participation, paras. 101–18 (January 18, 2008); McDermott, *Fairness in International Criminal Trials*, 122.
188. Christine Van den Wyngaert, "Victims before International Criminal Courts: Some Views and Concerns of a Trial Judge," *Case Western Journal of International Law* 44 (2011), 475, 486.
189. *Lubanga* Judgment on appeals of Decision on Victims' Participation, para. 97.
190. Rome Statute, art. 68(3).
191. Damaška, "The International Criminal Court," 28.
192. McDermott, *Fairness in International Criminal Trials*, 122–23.
193. Jouet, "Reconciling the Conflicting Rights of Victims and Defendants," 262–63.
194. Damaška, "The International Criminal Court," 28–29.
195. McDermott, *Fairness in International Criminal Trials*, 122.
196. Ibid.
197. Hakan Friman, "Participation of Victims in the ICC Criminal Proceedings and the Early Jurisprudence of the Court," in Goran Sluiter and Sergey Vasiliev eds., *International Criminal Procedure: Towards a Coherent Body of Law* (London: Cameron May, 2009), 220–21.
198. Christine Chung, "Victims' Participation at the International Criminal Court: Are Concessions of the Court Clouding the Promise?" *Northwestern University Journal of International Human Rights* 6 (2008), 459, 501–03.
199. Van den Wyngaert, "Victims before International Criminal Courts," 481–83.
200. Jouet, "Reconciling the Conflicting Rights of Victims and Defendants," 261–62.
201. *Prosecutor v. Katanga*, Case No. ICC-01/04-01/07-474, Pre-Trial Chamber I, Decision on the Set of Procedural Rights Attached to Procedural Status of Victim at the Pre-Trial Stage of a Case, paras. 101–03, 110–12 (May 13, 2008).

202. John D. Ciorciari and Anne Heindel, "Victim Testimony in International and Hybrid Criminal Courts: Narrative Opportunities, Challenges, and Fair Trial Demands," *Virginia Journal of International Law* 56 (2017), 265, 320.

203. *Lubanga*, Judgment on appeals of Decision on Victims' Participation, paras. 86, 99–101, 104.

204. *Prosecutor v. Katanga and Chui*, Case No. ICC-01/04–01/07 OA 11, Appeals Chamber, Judgment on the Appeal of Mr. Katanga Against the Decision of Trial Chamber II of January 22, 2010 Entitled "Decision on the Modalities of Victim Participation at Trial," paras. 44–48, 110–14 (July 16, 2010).

205. Kweku Vanderpuye, "Traditions in Conflict: The Internationalization of Confrontation," *Cornell International Law Journal* 43 (2010), 513, 565–66; Baumgartner, "Aspects of victim participation," 425.

206. Sluiter et al. eds., *International Criminal Procedure: Principles and Rules*, 1339.

207. Emily Haslam and Rod Edmunds, "Common Legal Representation at the International Criminal Court: More Symbolic than Real?" *International Criminal Law Review* 12 (2012), 871, 872.

208. Jennifer Easterday, "Major Changes at the ICC: the Registry's ReVision," *Open Society Justice Initiative*, August 24, 2015, www.ijmonitor.org/2015/08/major-changes-at-the-icc -the-registrys-revision/.

209. Mariana Pena and Gaelle Carayon, "Is the ICC Making the Most of Victim Participation?" *International Journal of Transitional Justice* 7 (2013), 518, 531–35.

210. Sara Kendall and Sarah Nouwen, "Representational Practices at the International Criminal Court: The Gap between Juridified and Abstract Victimhood," *Law and Contemporary Problems* 76 (2014), 235, 261–62.

211. International Federation for Human Rights, "Five Myths about Victim Participation in ICC Proceedings" (2014), www.fidh.org/en/issues/international-justice/international -criminal-court-icc/16592-five-myths-about-victim-participation-in-icc-proceedings.

212. Pena and Carayon, "Is the ICC Making the Most of Victim Participation?" 523–27.

213. Sluiter et al. eds., *International Criminal Procedure: Principles and Rules*, 132.

214. Eric Engle, "The International Criminal Court, the United States, and the Domestic Armed Conflict in Syria," *Chicago-Kent Journal of International and Comparative Law* 14 (2013), 146, 163. For accounts of realist critiques, see generally Kenneth W. Abbott and Duncan Snidal, "Why States Act through Formal International Organizations," *Journal of Conflict Resolution* 42 (1998) 3; John J. Mearsheimer, "The False Promise of International Institutions," *International Security* 19 (Winter 1994–95), 5, 14–15, 37–39.

215. Chris Mahony, "The Justice Pivot: U.S. International Criminal Law Influence from Outside the Rome Statute," *Georgetown Journal of International Law* 46 (2015), 1071, 1083–84.

216. Sylvia A. Fernández de Gurmendi, "The Role of the International Prosecutor," in Roy S. Lee ed., *The Making of the Rome Statute* (The Hague, Netherlands: Kluwer Law International, 1999), 175–77.

217. Richard John Galvin, "The ICC Prosecutor, Collateral Damage, and NGOs: Evaluating the Risk of a Politicized Prosecution," *University of Miami International and Comparative Law Review* 13 (2005), 1, 3–4.

218. Alexander K. A. Greenawalt, "Justice without Politics? Prosecutorial Discretion and the International Criminal Court," *New York University Journal of International Law and Politics* 39 (2007), 583, 590–92; Allison Marston Danner, "Enhancing the Legitimacy and Accountability of Prosecutorial Discretion at the International Criminal Court," *American Journal of International Law* 97 (2003), 510, 536–37.

219. U.N. GAOR, Report of the Ad Hoc Committee on the Establishment of an International Criminal Court, para. 121, U.N. Doc. A/50/22 (September 6, 1995).

220. Rome Statute, arts. 13(c), 15.

221. Ibid., art. 15(b).

222. Danner, "Enhancing the Legitimacy and Accountability of Prosecutorial Discretion," 515.

223. Richard J. Goldstone and Gary Jonathan Bass, "Lessons from the International Criminal Tribunals," in Sarah B. Sewell and Carl Kaysen eds., *The United States and the International Criminal Court: National Security and International Law* (Maryland: Rowman and Littlefield Publishers, 2000), 51–52.

224. Matiangai V. S. Sirleaf, "Regionalism, Regime Complexes, and the Crisis in International Criminal Justice," *Columbia Journal of Transnational Law* 54 (2016), 699, 711–12.

225. Rome Statute, arts. 15, 17, 53.

226. Ibid., art. 53(1)(c). (Prosecutor may decline to initiate an investigation where there are "substantial reasons" to believe it would "not serve the interests of justice"); 53(2)(c) (Prosecutor may conclude that a prosecution "is not in the interests of justice".)

227. Ibid., art. 15(4). Two of the three members of the Pre-Trial Chamber may vote to approve the prosecution's request for an investigation.

228. Ibid., art. 53(3). See also Kevin Jon Heller, "The Pre-Trial Chamber's Dangerous Comoros Review Decision," *Opinio Juris*, July 17, 2015, http://opiniojuris.org/2015/07/17/the-pre-trial-chambers-problematic-comoros-review-decision/ (comparing the different standards of review applicable to the ICC Prosecutor's decision not to open a formal investigation). See also Sluiter et al. eds., *International Criminal Procedure: Principles and Rules*, 147 (noting that the degree to which a decision not to prosecute a case is reviewable remains a gray area).

229. Jenia Iontcheva Turner, "Nationalizing International Criminal Law," *Stanford Journal of International Law* 41 (2005), 1, 11; David Tolbert, "International Criminal Law: Past and Future," *University of Pennsylvania Journal of International Law* 30 (2009), 1281, 1283.

230. Margaret M. deGuzman, "Choosing to Prosecute: Expressive Selection at the International Criminal Court," *Michigan Journal of International Law* 33 (2012), 265, 267–70.

231. Robert Cryer, *Prosecuting International Crimes: Selectivity and the International Criminal Law Regime* (Cambridge: Cambridge University Press, 2005), 192.

232. Alex Whiting, "International Justice Year-in-Review: Looking Backwards, Looking Forwards," *Just Security*, January 19, 2016, www.justsecurity.org/28869/international-criminal-justice-2015-part-1.

233. Carmel Agius, "2015 Brandeis Institute of International Judges Report: International Courts, Local Actors," *University of Pacific Law Review* 47 (2016), 371, 398. The absence of cooperation prompted the ICC to suspend its investigations into the Darfur situation.

234. David Smith, "ICC Chief Prosecutor Shelves Darfur War Crimes Probe," *The Guardian*, December 14, 2014, www.theguardian.com/world/2014/dec/14/icc-dar fur-war-crimes-fatou-bensouda-sudan.

235. *Situation in Darfur, Sudan, in the Case of Prosecutor v. Al-Bashir*, Case No. ICC-02/05-01/09, ICC Pre-Trial Chamber II, Decision under article 87(7) of the Rome Statute on the noncompliance by South Africa with the request by the Court for the arrest and surrender of Omar Al-Bashir, paras. 123, 140 (July 6, 2017).

236. Ibid., paras. 137–39.

237. Angela Mudukuti, "Non-Compliance But No Referral—The ICC Muddies the Waters," *Justice in Conflict* (July 20, 2017), www.justiceinconflict.org/2017/07/20/non-compliance-but-no-referral-the-icc-muddies-the-waters/.

238. International Criminal Court, "Statement of the Prosecutor on the International Criminal Court, Fatou Bensouda, On the Withdrawal of Charges against Mr. Uhuru Muigai Kenyatta, International Criminal Court" (2014), www.icc-cpi.int/Pages/record .aspx?docNo=ICC-01/09–02/11–983; Wolfgang Kaleck, *Double Standards: International Criminal Law and the West* (Brussels: Torkel Opsahl Academic EPublisher, 2015), 95–96.

239. *Prosecutor v. Kenyatta*, Case No. ICC-I01/09–02/11, Trial Chamber V(B), Second decision on Prosecution's Application for a finding of non-compliance under Article 87(7) of the Statute, para. 38 (September 19, 2016).

240. Rome Statute, art. 87(7); Thomas Obel Hansen, "Referring Kenya to the ICC Assembly of States Parties, Part 2: Implications for Cooperation and Enforcement," *Justice in Conflict*, October 4, 2016, https://justiceinconflict.org/2016/10/04/referring-kenya-to-the -icc-assembly-of-states-parties-part-2-implications-for-cooperation-and-enforcement/.

241. Lilian V. Faulhaber, Recent Development, "American Servicemembers' Protection Act of 2002," *Harvard Journal on Legislation* 40 (2003), 537.

242. David Bosco, *Rough Justice: The International Criminal Court in a World of Power Politics* (Oxford: Oxford University Press, 2014), 180.

243. Mahony, "The Justice Pivot," 1104–06.

244. Marlise Simons, "U.S. Grows More Helpful to International Criminal Court, a Body It First Scorned," *New York Times*, April 2, 2013. Early signs suggest the Trump administration is retreating from this engagement, including through its threatened elimination of the US State Department's Office of Global Criminal Justice, which has coordinated the US response on international justice issues and served as the principal liaison to the ICC and other international and hybrid courts. Beth Van Schaack, "State Dept. Office of Global Criminal Justice on the Chopping Block: Time to Save It," *Just Security* (July 17, 2017), www.justsecurity.org/43213/u-s-office-global-criminal-justice-chopping-block/.

245. Mark Kersten, "Whatever Happens, the ICC's Investigation into US Torture in Afghanistan Is a Win for the Court," *Justice in Conflict*, November 17, 2016, https:// justiceinconflict.org/2016/11/17/whatever-happens-the-iccs-investigation-into-us-tor ture-in-afghanistan-is-a-win-for-the-court/.

246. Bosco, *Rough Justice*, 22; Mahony, "The Justice Pivot," 1094–96; William Schabas, "Prosecutorial Discretion v. Judicial Activism at the International Criminal Court," *Journal of International Criminal Justice* 6 (2008), 731, 742–43.

247. Máximo Langer, "The Diplomacy of Universal Jurisdiction: The Political Branches and the Transnational Prosecution of International Crimes," *American Journal of International Law* 105 (2011), 1, 2.

248. Rachel E. VanLandingham, "Criminally Disproportionate Warfare: Aggression as a Contextual War Crime," *Case Western Reserve Journal of International Law* 48 (2016), 215, 243.

249. Rome Statute, art. 8 *bis* (2).

250. Ibid., art. 8 *bis* (1).

251. Ibid., arts. 15 *bis* (2), (3), 15 *ter* (2), (3).

252. Ibid., art. 15 *ter* (2).

253. Julie Veroff, Note, "Reconciling the Crime of Aggression and Complementarity: Unaddressed Tensions and a Way Forward," *Yale Law Journal* 125 (2016), 730, 743. See also Donald M. Ferencz, "Bringing the Crime of Aggression within the Active

Jurisdiction of the ICC," *Case Western Reserve Journal of International Law* 42 (2009), 531, 542 (describing the value of activating ICC jurisdiction over the crime of aggression).

254. Kai Ambos, "The Crime of Aggression after Kampala," *German Yearbook of International Law* 53 (2010), 463, 475–77.

255. Johan D. van der Vyver, "Prosecuting the Crime of Aggression in the International Criminal Court," *University of Miami National Security and Armed Conflict Law Review* 1 (2011), 1, 2.

256. Rome Statute, art. 15 *bis* (6).

257. Ibid., art. 15 *bis* (6)–(8).

258. Ibid., art. 15 *bis* (9); van der Vyver, "Prosecuting the Crime of Aggression," 2.

259. Ambos, "The Crime of Aggression after Kampala," 475–77.

260. Rome Statute, art. 15 *bis*.

261. Mahony, "The Justice Pivot," 1110.

262. Harold Hongju Koh and Todd F. Buchwald, "The Crime of Aggression: The United States Perspective," *American Journal of International Law* 109 (2015), 258, 273. Some commentators maintain that the United States' failure to obtain this express language does not mean, however, that crimes of aggression cover humanitarian intervention. See Jennifer Trahan, "Defining the 'Grey Area' Where Humanitarian Intervention May Not be Fully Legal, but Is Not the Crime of Aggression," *Journal on the Use of Force and International Law* 2 (2015), 42, 65.

263. Rome Statute, art. 16.

264. Ibid., art. 15 *bis*(4). Some commentators argue that this opt-out provision conflicts with a provision in the Rome Statute that prevents States from ratifying the statute subject to reservations. van der Vyver, "Prosecuting the Crime of Aggression," 47.

265. Charles Chenor Jalloh, "Africa and the International Criminal Court: Collision Course or Cooperation?" *North Carolina Central Law Review* 34 (2012), 203, 209–11; William A. Schabas, "Selecting 'Situations' at the International Criminal Court," *John Marshall Law Review* 43 (2010), 535, 549.

266. Jalloh, "Africa and the International Criminal Court," 210 (quoting Ugandan scholar, Mahmood Mamdani).

267. Sirleaf, "Regionalism, Regime Complexes, and the Crisis in International Criminal Justice," 703–04, 717.

268. Sewell Chan and Marlise Simmons, "South Africa to Withdraw from International Criminal Court," *New York Times*, October 21, 2016; "Gambia Is Latest African Nation to Quit International Criminal Court," *The Guardian*, October 26, 2016.

269. Norimitsu Onishi, "South Africa Reverses Withdrawal from International Criminal Court," *New York Times*, March 8, 2017.

270. David Bosco, "Is the International Criminal Court Crumbling before Our Eyes?" *Foreign Affairs*, October 26, 2016; Simon Allison, "African Revolt Threatens International Criminal Court's Legitimacy," *The Guardian*, October 27, 2016.

271. Asad Kiyani, "Group-Based Differentiation and Local Repression: The Custom and Curse of Selectivity," *Journal of International Criminal Justice* 14 (2016), 939, 950–51.

272. Ibid.; Kaleck, *Double Standards*, 91–94; Mark Kersten, *Justice in Conflict: The International Criminal Court's Interventions on Ending Wars and Building Peace* (Oxford: Oxford University Press, 2016), 164–65, 173–77; Payam Akhavan, "The Lord's Resistance Army Case: Uganda's Submission of the First State Referral to the International Criminal Court," *American Journal of International Law* 99 (2005), 403, 411.

273. Kaleck, *Double Standards*, 92.
274. Schabas, "Prosecutorial Discretion v. Judicial Activism," 747–48.
275. Phuong Pham, Patrick Vinck, and Eric Stover, "The Lord's Resistance Army and Forced Conscription in Northern Uganda," *Human Rights Quarterly* 30 (2008), 404.
276. Schabas, "Prosecutorial Discretion v. Judicial Activism," 753.
277. International Criminal Court, Situations and Cases, www.icc-cpi.int/en_menus/icc/situations%20and%20cases/Pages/situations%20and%20cases.aspx (last visited, June 8, 2017).
278. Office of the Prosecutor, International Criminal Court, *Situation in the Republic of Kenya*, Case No. ICC-01/09 Request for authorization of an investigation pursuant to Article 15, paras. 45, 53, November 26, 2009, www.icc-cpi.int/iccdocs/doc/doc785972.pdf; Kenneth Roth, "Africa Attacks the International Criminal Court," *New York Review of Books*, February 6, 2014, www.hrw.org/news/2014/01/14/africa-attacks-international-criminal-court.
279. Commission of Inquiry into the Post-Election Violence, *Report of the Commission of Inquiry into the Post-Election Violence*, October 15, 2008, www.dialoguekenya.org/cre port.aspx.
280. Kiyani, "Group-Based Differentiation and Local Repression," 940–41.
281. William A. Schabas, "Regions, Regionalism, and International Criminal Law," *New Zealand Yearbook of International Law* 4 (2007), 3, 14.
282. Yvonne M. Dutton, "Bridging the Legitimacy Divide: The International Criminal Court's Domestic Perception Challenge," 9–10 (forthcoming) (Manuscript on File with Author); Mark Kersten, "The Africa-ICC Relationship — More and Less than Meets the Eye (Part I)," *Justice in Conflict*, July 17, 2015, https://justiceinconflict.org/2015/07/17/the-africa-icc-relationship-more-and-less-than-meets-the-eye-part-1/.
283. Yvonne M. Dutton, "Enforcing the Rome Statute: Evidence of (Non) Compliance from Kenya, *Indiana International and Comparative Law Review* 26 (2016), 7, 24–25.
284. Assembly of the African Union, *Decision on the Meeting of African States Parties to the Rome Statute of the International Criminal Court (ICC)*, paras. 2–13, Assembly/AU/Dec.245(XIII) Rev. 1 (July 3, 2009).
285. Patryk I. Labuda, "The African Union's Collective Withdrawal from the ICC: Does Bad Law Make for Good Politics?" *EJIL: Talk!*, February 15, 2017, www.ejiltalk.org/the-african-unions-collective-withdrawal-from-the-icc-does-bad-law-make-for-good-politics/.

4

Procedure and Fairness in a Decentralized System

Criminal procedure serves multiple purposes. The relative importance of these purposes may vary, however, depending on the context. In domestic legal systems, where a central goal is maintaining public order, procedure helps streamline decisions on substantive and evidentiary issues to facilitate the prosecution of a high volume of cases. In international criminal justice, which prioritizes the prosecution of fewer but more extreme crimes in countries often devastated by internal armed conflict and political breakdown, procedure's demonstrative role in reestablishing the rule of law is particularly significant. Yet, regardless of the context, the *sine qua non* of criminal procedure is to make possible a fair adjudication of facts and principled determination of the guilt or innocence of accused persons. If procedure fails in that elemental task, it undermines not only ICL's core aim of assigning individual criminal responsibility, but also its broader goals, such as promoting peace and stability in affected countries and regions. As one judge explained, the "train of international criminal law" would go nowhere without sturdy "rails of international criminal procedure."[1] Procedure may thus be regarded both as an instrument for applying legal norms to behavior and as an end in itself.

ICL seeks to solidify and express norms of accountability through judicial proceedings. In a world where far more international crimes go unpunished than are prosecuted, this didactic function assumes particular salience.[2] Procedure plays a critical role not only because it provides the vehicle for implementing norms of individual criminal responsibility, but also because it conveys respect for human rights by demonstrating fairness and adherence to legal rules in the prosecution of mass atrocities.[3]

From the seed planted at Nuremberg – that individuals accused of the gravest crimes must still be provided due process – international criminal tribunals have developed an increasingly elaborate set of procedural rules. Numerous scholars have addressed the role of procedure in international criminal law,[4] and many today view international criminal procedure as a field in its own right.[5] One goal of these efforts is to identify common standards and practices across international and hybrid tribunals, notwithstanding their respective differences. A recent expert study, for example, provides a comprehensive account of the general rules and principles of international criminal procedure, including which rules constitute its immutable core.[6]

Yet, despite significant improvements and greater systemization, procedural law is still described as the "Achilles heel of international criminal justice."[7] As the previous two chapters suggest, continuing concerns include: limits on a defendant's access to evidence and the ability to confront it; the length of trials, particularly in light of the presumption of innocence and limits on provisional release; an over-reliance on documentary evidence in place of oral testimony; and structural imbalances between the prosecution and defense.

In some respects, the challenges facing international criminal justice resemble those confronted by national criminal justice systems, which also face pressure to balance a defendant's fair trial rights against the need to hold individual perpetrators accountable. Yet, these challenges are different and in some ways more pronounced at the international level. Crime control through incapacitation is not a central feature of ICL, in contrast to domestic criminal law.[8] International courts do not have their own police force,[9] and international criminal procedure lacks domestic criminal procedure's focus on deterring law enforcement misconduct through the erection of rules designed to constrain police behavior.[10] Additionally, international criminal procedure operates amid a set of practical and normative challenges generally not faced on the domestic level, including widespread barriers to accessing evidence and witnesses, a mandate to include and protect victims, and the sheer gravity of the crimes themselves. In domestic criminal law, an extraordinary crime is the exception; in ICL, it is the norm, thus placing a constant downward pressure on procedural rights designed to protect defendants. Moreover, ICL's *sui generis* procedures, which combine elements from different traditions without necessarily considering how they fit together, can jeopardize the rights of the accused.[11] In ICL, the critical question is not whether a particular procedural rule derives from the civil or common law, but rather whether it comports with fair trial standards.[12]

Human rights law, to be sure, plays an important role in determining the content of the fair trial standards that international tribunals are obligated to respect.[13] The statutes for international tribunals all base their fair trial provisions on those contained in the International Covenant on Civil and Political Rights (ICCPR).[14] The Rome Statute, moreover, expressly provides that the ICC's interpretation of law must be "consistent with internationally recognized human rights."[15] International criminal tribunals have also drawn on the jurisprudence of international human rights tribunals in interpreting those provisions.[16] Human rights law thus encompasses a set of due process and fair trial guarantees that offer a baseline against which to measure international criminal proceedings.[17] But while international criminal tribunals apply international human rights law in their decisions, they are not strictly bound by it as a matter of treaty law.[18] Human rights law, moreover, is often expressed in generalized terms, and states have a considerable margin of appreciation (or discretion) in interpreting and applying it within their respective criminal jurisdictions.[19] Human rights law thus may provide insufficient guidance on the myriad of questions that arise in international criminal prosecutions.[20] In some instances, human rights law may appear insufficiently attuned to the particular challenges ICL faces on such issues as the provisional pretrial release of defendants, the protection of confidential information provided to the prosecution by third parties, and the need to ensure the safety of witnesses and victims.

In confronting these issues, judges, lawyers, NGOs, and other international criminal justice actors operate in a highly decentralized system that relies heavily on national courts for the enforcement of international norms. Although initially envisioned as a global court, the ICC remains limited in its reach and capacity. The ICC's emphasis on national prosecutions is partly a product of its design. Complementarity, which gives primacy to domestic jurisdictions to prosecute international crimes, is central to the Court. But the emphasis on national prosecutions is also a product of the practical realities that the ICC confronts, including jurisdictional limitations, budgetary and other resource constraints, and a lack of enforcement power. The stand-alone *ad hoc* tribunals for the former Yugoslavia and for Rwanda, which helped revitalize international criminal justice in the 1990s, faced some similar challenges, leading to increased emphasis on national prosecutions as part of their respective completion strategies. Despite the attention given to the ICTY and ICTR, the bulk of prosecutions arising from the conflicts in the former Yugoslavia and Rwanda have taken place in domestic courts.[21] In the former Yugoslavia, local Serbian, Croatian, and Bosnian courts have prosecuted more than 2600 individuals,[22] compared with 161 indictments before the ICTY.[23] In Rwanda, local courts have handled more than 120,000 accused individuals, while the ICTR completed sixty-four trials. Two million additional cases were processed in Rwanda's *gacaca* system, a traditional Rwandan community justice mechanism.[24]

ICL has no supreme court to harmonize existing jurisprudence, and individual tribunals can, and sometimes do, reach different conclusions on issues.[25] Indeed, different chambers of the same tribunal can reach divergent conclusions, as demonstrated by conflicting ICTY decisions on imposing counsel on uncooperative defendants or limiting a defendant's right to be present at trial due to disruptive behavior.[26] The rules themselves also may vary across international tribunals or national jurisdictions. Such a decentralized and nonhierarchical system of international criminal justice risks fragmentation. The diverse traditions underlying ICL magnify this risk.[27]

Such diversity, however, may also be viewed positively, as long as courts adhere to certain overarching principles, including the right of an accused person to a fair trial.[28] Decentralization can help foster the gradual development of generally accepted procedures, while simultaneously allowing for innovations that respond to the various challenges of prosecuting international crimes and to the different legal and cultural contexts in which those crimes occur.[29]

Decentralization also underscores the importance of procedure's didactic function. Courts adjudicating international crimes model the interpretation and application of procedure for a broad and diverse audience. This audience includes, first and foremost, the country (or region) in which the crimes took place. It also includes the larger global community of states, nongovernment organizations, and other actors within the international justice space. The multiplicity of fora, both domestic and international, applying ICL creates the potential for dialogue and cross-fertilization, as the procedures adopted by one court can inform those used by others.[30]

Scholars and practitioners have accordingly attempted to find ways to address pluralism's challenges and opportunities.[31] Allowing for acceptable margins of discretion can increase the possibilities for creative problem solving on matters of procedure. It can also encourage greater compliance with international norms at the national level and facilitate the diffusion of those norms across divergent contexts.[32] In the area of procedure, a primary challenge is to allow for experimentation while still maintaining rigorous fair trial standards, regardless of the enormity of the crime or the value of a conviction to the larger goal of accountability.

This chapter focuses on two ways of understanding ICL's relationship with fair trial rights in the decentralized landscape of international criminal justice. Here, the ICC functions less as a global court than as a catalyst since most prosecutions of international crimes continue to take place before national courts or hybrid tribunals, which combine international and domestic features. The chapter first examines the development of procedural protections through the ICC's complementarity regime and the referral of cases by the ICTY and ICTR to national jurisdictions. It then discusses the growing role played by hybrid tribunals and their potential contributions to fair trial standards employed in prosecuting international crimes.

***

The Rome Statute's complementarity regime demonstrates the important, but ultimately circumscribed, role the ICC can play in advancing international criminal justice. International criminal tribunals, from Nuremberg to the ICTY and ICTR, have traditionally asserted primacy over national courts. Primacy dictates that if a national court chooses to prosecute an individual that court must still defer to the international tribunal should the tribunal elect to prosecute that person.[33] In *Tadić*, the ICTY Appeals Chamber upheld the system of primacy against a challenge by the defendant who had been arrested in Germany on charges of torture and aiding and abetting genocide, which are crimes under German law, and transferred to the ICTY. *Tadić* sought to challenge his transfer. The Appeals Chamber rejected the challenge, explaining that the Security Council had acted "on the part of the community of nations" by establishing a judicial body to address matters that affected international peace and security, and that state sovereignty should not function as a shield against the rule of law.[34] In general, primacy is animated by the concern that the state (or states) where the international crimes occurred – such as those in the former Yugoslavia – will not effectively prosecute them, whether because national forces opposing accountability are too strong or existing judicial institutions are too weak (or both). A state, for example, might undertake proceedings intended to protect the accused or fail to pursue an investigation or prosecution aggressively.[35] Primacy has also been linked to the goal of establishing peace and stability in an affected country or region.[36] Primacy can serve the further goal of facilitating the development of a uniform body of ICL by giving an international criminal tribunal the power to issue authoritative rulings.[37]

The Rome Statute, by contrast, adopts a regime of complementarity. As set forth in Article 17, national courts possess primary jurisdiction, and the ICC exercises jurisdiction only when the state with jurisdiction over the crime is unable or unwilling to carry out the investigation or prosecution.[38] A state or individual defendant may challenge the admissibility of a case before the ICC based on the existence of a genuine domestic investigation or prosecution of the person concerned for substantially the same conduct that the ICC Prosecutor is pursuing.[39] The ICC, in effect, must defer to national courts when they are functioning properly.[40] Under complementarity, therefore, the ICC operates less as a world court proactively asserting jurisdiction over the worst atrocities than as a court of last resort, intervening where necessary to fill gaps in accountability.[41] Or, as the ICC Appeals Chamber has explained, "the complementarity principle ... strikes a balance between safeguarding the primacy of domestic proceedings vis-à-vis the International Criminal Court on the one hand, and the goal of the Rome Statute to 'put an end to impunity' on the other hand."[42]

The Rome Statute's prioritization of, and deference to, domestic prosecutions reflects concerns voiced by states during treaty negotiations that an international criminal court would interfere with national sovereignty.[43] Various countries, including the United States, resisted the creation of a tribunal that could second-guess national courts.[44] The Rome Statute's complementarity regime seeks to ease the political friction created by a permanent international criminal tribunal. It is also a product of the ICC's practical limitations. Even if the Rome Statute had given the ICC primacy over core international crimes, the Court would still lack the necessary resources to fulfill this mandate, as funding restrictions have limited the Court's docket since the outset.[45]

Complementarity, however, serves positive ends as well. National prosecutions are typically held closer to where crimes were committed, are conducted by individuals from the same country as the accused, and make it easier for witnesses and victims to participate in proceedings. National prosecutions also can help build local capacity, thus contributing to greater stability in an affected country or region.[46] In addition to bolstering legal institutions, domestic prosecutions of international crimes can vindicate the rule of law in places where it has collapsed.[47] Even when overseen by international mechanisms, domestic prosecutions may thus be better situated than purely international prosecutions to contribute to a process of reconciliation in states recovering from mass atrocities.[48] At a time when the ICC is suspected of politically motivated prosecutions, complementarity provides a way for the Court to enhance its legitimacy and promote its long-term viability.[49]

The focus on strengthening the capacity of national jurisdictions to undertake prosecutions for international crimes is commonly referred to as positive complementarity.[50] Positive complementarity recognizes that the Rome Statute does more than establish an international tribunal with jurisdiction over the most serious international crimes; it also creates a system of judicial enforcement at both the domestic and international level and reinforces the duty of states to prosecute those offenses.[51] In theory, as former ICC Prosecutor Luis Moreno-Ocampo explained, the Court will achieve its greatest success not by the existence of international trials, but by their absence, with national institutions assuming the main responsibility of prosecuting serious international crimes.[52] Positive complementarity thus stresses the ICC's role as a catalyst, an institution that can strengthen accountability not only by conducting trials, but also by inspiring others to do so. Views differ, however, on how actively the ICC should encourage or assist national prosecutions. Moreno-Ocampo himself subsequently emphasized the ICC's important role in prosecuting international crimes, notwithstanding the complementarity principle.[53]

Positive complementarity highlights the ICC's potential to enhance accountability within the decentralized framework of international criminal justice. Through complementarity, the ICC can strengthen aspects of national criminal justice systems that facilitate the prosecution of atrocities, including by pressuring countries to enact domestic legislation covering the crimes contained in the Rome Statute, establishing specialized national tribunals, and improving mechanisms necessary for the effective prosecution of international crimes, such as witness protection programs.[54] The ICC's emphasis on more localized prosecutions of international crimes could also help encourage the development of regional accountability mechanisms, such as the proposed African Court of Justice and Human Rights, which would add to the region's human rights court a separate chamber with jurisdiction over crimes under the Rome Statute as well as crimes of particular regional concern, such as trafficking in humans, terrorism, and piracy.[55]

Complementarity, however, also provides opportunities for strengthening due process safeguards and other features of national legal systems designed to protect defendants. One way to bolster fair trial safeguards is by increasing capacity and expertise, such as through training and education programs for lawyers and judges. Another is through the threat of ICC intervention.

The ICC's admissibility decisions concerning Libya illustrate the possibility for complementarity to reinforce the link between prosecuting exceptional crimes and protecting fair trial rights. Following the Security Council's referral of the situation in the Libyan Arab Jamahiriya to the ICC in 2011, the Pre-Trial Chamber issued warrants for the arrest of Colonel Muammar Gaddafi, Saif Al-Islam Gaddafi, his son and heir-apparent, and Abdullah Al-Senussi, Libya's former intelligence chief, for crimes against humanity committed during the 2011 uprising.[56] Proceedings against Colonel Muammar Gaddafi ended after he was killed, but continued against Saif Gaddafi and Al-Senussi. Libya brought admissibility challenges in both the *Gaddafi* and *Al-Senussi* cases, arguing that it was willing and able to try the defendants. In May 2013, the Pre-Trial Chamber rejected Libya's admissibility challenge in *Gaddafi* and reminded Libya of its obligation to surrender the suspect to the Court. Several months later, however, the Pre-Trial Chamber reached the opposite conclusion in *Al-Senussi*, finding the case inadmissible before the ICC because Libya was willing and able to investigate the crimes.

In 2015, a Libyan tribunal in Tripoli tried and convicted Saif Gaddafi, Al-Senussi, and thirty other members of the former dictatorship, sentencing Saif Gaddafi, Al-Senussi, and seven others to death, and twenty-three others to terms of life imprisonment.[57] Four defendants were acquitted and one was referred to a mental institution.[58] The tribunal tried Saif Gaddafi *in absentia* because he remained in the custody of a militia group in Zintan, a mountainous region southwest of the capital, Tripoli, and the group refused to release him. International monitors and human rights groups generally criticized the trial,[59] although a report by the International Bar Association, while describing the trial's flaws, noted that judges and lawyers attempted to safeguard the defendants' rights and ensure that the proceedings were handled with professionalism.[60] The militia holding Saif Gaddafi announced it had released him in June 2017 under an amnesty law passed by a parliament based in eastern Libya. The attorney general's office in Tripoli stated, however, that Saif Gaddafi is still wanted under the 2015 conviction and launched an investigation into his release. [61] Saif Gaddafi still also faces charges before the ICC.

The thrust of complementarity is to defer to national prosecutions where a state is genuinely willing and able to investigate and prosecute the alleged crimes. *Gaddafi* and *Al-Senussi* surface a different question: whether the ICC can, through complementarity, ensure not only that a state genuinely seeks to hold a suspect accountable, but also that it does so in a manner that respects the suspect's due process rights. Unlike in prior cases, where states had not yet begun proceedings, thus foreclosing an admissibility challenge under ICC jurisprudence,[62] in *Gaddafi* and *Al-Senussi*, Libya had initiated proceedings against the two suspects. In its admissibility challenges, Libya argued that its domestic proceedings sought to bring the suspects to justice in a manner that would promote accountability and the rule of law, while adhering to applicable international standards.[63] In rejecting Libya's admissibility challenge in *Gaddafi*, the Pre-Trial Chamber not only said Libya failed to establish that the domestic proceedings covered the same conduct at issue before the ICC, as Article 17 of the Rome Statute requires for such challenges,[64] but also noted Libya's inability to try the defendant in accordance with international fair trial standards. That latter deficiency, the Pre-Trial Chamber explained, impacted Libya's ability to carry out the proceedings in accordance with Libyan law, including with the international human rights guarantees that Libya is legally obligated to follow.[65] The Pre-Trial Chamber expressed concerns, for example, about Libya's ability to fulfill its duty to secure counsel for the defendant, its capacity to ensure that the defendant had proper time and facilities to prepare his defense, and its lack of control over the defendant himself.[66]

In *Al-Senussi*, the Pre-Trial Chamber also discussed the relevance of due process concerns in the admissibility determination. It noted that "certain violations of the procedural rights of the accused may be relevant to the assessment of the independence and impartiality of the national proceedings that the Chamber is required to make, having regard to the principles of due process recognized under international law," in determining a case's admissibility.[67] Such violations, the Pre-Trial Chamber said, could be inconsistent with a state's asserted intent to bring a suspect to justice, as required by Article 17(2)(c) of the Rome Statute.[68] But unlike in *Gaddafi*, in *Al-Senussi* the ICC upheld Libya's challenge and found the case inadmissible, citing the suspect's entitlement to legal representation under Libyan law, the absence of delay, the opportunity to confront adverse evidence, and the independence and impartiality of the domestic proceedings.[69] In distinguishing the prior admissibility ruling in *Gaddafi*, the Pre-Trial Chamber observed that Saif Gaddafi was not in the control of the Libyan national authorities and that efforts to secure legal representation for him had failed.[70] By contrast, the Pre-Trial Chamber said, Al-Senussi was in the custody of the central government in Tripoli and there was no basis to conclude that he would be unable to secure adequate legal representation for criminal proceedings in Libya.[71]

The Appeals Chamber subsequently affirmed the Pre-Trial Chamber's admissibility rulings in both cases.[72] In *Al-Senussi*, the Appeals Chamber acknowledged that due process deficiencies, such as lack of meaningful access to counsel, could potentially affect the complementary analysis.[73] It concluded, however, that such deficiencies did not provide a *per se* ground for a case's admissibility before the ICC, but rather were merely factors for the Court to consider in determining whether domestic proceedings were being conducted impartially and independently, and with the intent of bringing the accused person to justice.[74] The primary focus of the complementarity analysis, the Appeals Chamber said, should be on whether a state had established sham proceedings designed to insulate suspects from international criminal responsibility rather than on whether a state's proceedings adequately protected the fair trial rights of accused individuals.[75] The Appeals Chamber deemed the asserted due process deficiencies, including inadequate assurances of legal representation and of the ability to summon witnesses, too speculative.[76] In *Gaddafi*, the Appeals Chamber relied on an alternative ground in affirming the finding that the case was admissible before the ICC – namely, that the proceedings in Libya did not cover the same (or substantially the same) conduct as the ICC warrant – and did not address the issue of due process deficiencies in Libya.[77]

The two Libya cases highlight the debate over whether the complementarity analysis should consider factors that make it easier to convict a suspect as well as those that help insulate a suspect from criminal responsibility. Some commentators observe that States Parties to the Rome Statute failed to register concerns about national jurisdictions prosecuting alleged perpetrators in proceedings that lack due process guarantees and that the Article 17 inquiry was instead designed to focus on the risk of individuals escaping punishment.[78] Others maintain that the ICC weakens state sovereignty by scrutinizing a national jurisdiction's adherence to fair trial standards.[79] Most views, however, endorse an approach to complementarity in which the ICC accords at least some weight to due process considerations. As an informal Panel of Experts noted in 2003, while the ICC is not a "human rights court," human rights standards can still play a role in determining whether domestic proceedings are being carried out genuinely, as the Rome Statute requires.[80] While observers may differ over the weight to assign a country's adherence to fair trial standards, accountability should not be pursued at any cost.[81] Even the Appeals Chamber's decision in *Al-Senussi*, which prioritizes accountability in national courts, still leaves some space for fair trial considerations. As one commentator notes, *Al-Senussi* and *Gaddafi* reflect the ICC's reliance on a predictive due process analysis in which the Court gauges whether a state will be willing and able to abide by due process norms in its future investigation and prosecution of the suspect.[82] In *Al-Senussi*, for example, the Appeals Chamber observed that although in the past it had not been possible to appoint counsel for Al-Senussi in Libya, such appointment could occur in the future.[83] The Appeals Chamber also noted the Prosecutor's ability to seek review of the ICC's inadmissibility ruling were the appointment of counsel not to occur.[84]

Several scholars have nevertheless criticized the ICC for failing to do more to ensure due process in domestic proceedings. Jennifer Trahan, for example, maintains that the Appeals Chamber set too high a bar in *Al-Senussi* when it suggested that a state's procedures must "completely lack fairness" or be "so egregious" that they are no longer capable of providing "any form of justice" for due process concerns to be dispositive.[85] Trahan argues that the ICC's complementarity analysis should engage in more exacting scrutiny of national jurisdictions that retain the death penalty, particularly when coupled with due process deficiencies, as in *Gaddafi* and *Al-Senussi*.[86] Most States Parties to the ICC do not permit the death penalty as a permissible punishment in their domestic legislation, and other international and hybrid tribunals created through the UN allow only the imposition of prison terms.[87] Although the Rome Statute contemplates that the ICC may still deem cases inadmissible where a national jurisdiction retains the death penalty,[88] evolving human rights norms have strengthened arguments for finding cases admissible before the ICC where the national jurisdiction could impose the death penalty, especially where the state in question appears unprepared to enforce due process protections.[89]

The ICC may not be violating human rights law by finding inadmissible a case in which the national jurisdiction lacks adequate due process safeguards. But it is foregoing an opportunity to express and entrench the link between fair trial standards and international criminal justice. Further, convictions achieved without due process will remain vulnerable to future challenge and criticism, while reinforcing ICL's past association with vengeful justice. The ICC should instead create incentives for states to ensure rigorous fair trial standards by conditioning state control over prosecutions of nationals charged with crimes under the Rome Statute on adherence to those standards.[90]

There are several possible ways to help facilitate this outcome. States Parties could seek to amend the Rome Statute to require express consideration of a state's due process safeguards in the ICC's complementarity analysis, although the high bar for amendments to the Rome Statute makes adoption and ratification of such an amendment unlikely.[91] The ICC could also give greater priority to due process safeguards in national courts when interpreting Article 17. In addition, the UN, states, NGOs, and legal experts could provide increased assistance to domestic systems to prosecute international crimes in accordance with international fair trial guarantees.[92]

✳✳✳

The ICTY and ICTR's referral of cases to national courts provides another example of how international tribunals can help bolster fair trial standards through domestic prosecutions of international crimes. The ICTY and ICTR initially had primary jurisdiction over international crimes committed in the former Yugoslavia and Rwanda, respectively. In 2003, the UN Security Council adopted a Completion Strategy for both tribunals, which it elaborated over time. In addition to setting deadlines for the investigation and prosecution of cases and mandating a focus on high-ranking officials, the Security Council emphasized the need for the ICTY and ICTR to refer cases to national courts.[93] While financial considerations were the main impetus, a desire to increase local capacity also motivated the shift away from primacy. The ICTY, for example, was perceived as chilling the development of domestic judicial institutions in Bosnia-Herzegovina and the exercise of domestic jurisdiction over war crimes committed there.[94]

As part of their respective completion strategies, the ICTY and ICTR each amended their rules to authorize referrals to national courts. Under Rule 11 *bis*, each tribunal could refer a case to a state with jurisdiction over the offense that was willing and adequately prepared to prosecute.[95] The state, however, also had to demonstrate that, in addition to conducting an effective prosecution, it would provide the accused with a fair trial. The state, moreover, could not allow the death penalty. These requirements sought to ensure that cases would "not be referred to jurisdictions that do not observe the minimum guarantees of procedural fairness and international human rights."[96]

In 2010, the Security Council established the International Residual Mechanism for Criminal Tribunals (MICT) to perform a number of essential functions of the ICTY and ICTR after the tribunals complete their work and to maintain their respective legacies.[97] These responsibilities include: tracking fugitives; conducting investigations and trials for contempt of court and false testimony committed during proceedings before the ICTY, ICTR, or MICT; conducting appeals and review proceedings (such as where new facts are discovered that might affect the validity of a prior judgment); and protecting victims and witnesses.[98] Another responsibility of the MICT, which began operating in parallel with the ICTY and ICTR, is to monitor cases that those tribunals referred to national courts[99] and to determine whether certain additional cases are suitable for referral, including cases of individuals who are not among the most senior leaders most responsible for crimes.[100] The MICT Statute makes a state's adherence to fair trial guarantees – under both the treaties establishing the tribunals and applicable human rights instruments, including the ICCPR – a crucial factor both in assessing whether to refer cases to the national jurisdiction and in monitoring those cases that have been referred.[101] This assessment turns on several considerations, including: the national code of criminal procedure's compliance with international human rights standards; the presumption of innocence; the equality of arms between the prosecution and defense; the ability to conduct trials without undue delay; the protection of victims and witnesses; judicial independence; and the equal treatment of all individuals, regardless of nationality, religion, or political views.[102] The MICT is also tasked with responding to requests for assistance from national authorities that are prosecuting Rwandan or Yugoslav defendants found within their territory.[103]

Following the introduction of Rule 11 *bis*, Rwanda abolished the death penalty, created a new legal framework for referred cases, and provided various fair trial safeguards for transferred defendants.[104] The ICTR Trial Chambers initially denied the Prosecutor's requests for the referral of cases to Rwanda based on concerns about Rwanda's compliance with these fair trial safeguards,[105] citing, for example, the defense's difficulty obtaining documents and access to witnesses.[106] In first granting a request for referral in 2011, the ICTR focused on the changes made by Rwanda, including its elimination of life imprisonment as a potential penalty for transferred cases, establishment of additional protections to facilitate the testimony of witnesses, and provision of detention facilities that conform to international standards.[107] Subsequent grants of referrals by the ICTR to Rwanda followed.[108] The MICT similarly noted improvements in Rwanda's criminal justice system and enhanced fair trial protections in approving transfers from the ICTR to Rwanda.[109] Rwanda's abolition of the death penalty is particularly notable given the Rwandan government's previous insistence that sentencing genocide perpetrators to death was critical to post-conflict justice and reconciliation.[110] Referrals by the ICTY under

Rule 11 *bis* have also focused attention on due process issues in national courts in the former Yugoslavia.[111]

The referral of cases by the ICTY and ICTR to national jurisdictions suggests the potential for international tribunals to impact domestic prosecutions of international crimes.[112] It also demonstrates a desire to increase local ownership of the transitional justice process in a manner that strengthens adherence to fair trial protections in prosecuting exceptional crimes. It further addresses complaints about infringements of state sovereignty previously leveled against the ICTY and ICTR.[113]

Both the ICC's complementarity regime and the *ad hoc* tribunals' referral of cases to national courts highlight opportunities to build on the principle that responsibility for international crimes is best achieved within a framework that protects a defendant's rights. Referrals by the ICTY and ICTR, in particular, illustrate how international tribunals can strengthen due process guarantees beyond their own limited capacity to prosecute individual cases by requiring national courts to uphold those guarantees. They suggest, in short, how norms of procedural fairness might develop within a largely decentralized system of international criminal justice, where jurisdiction is spread across multiple tribunals and where national courts continue to play an essential role in preventing impunity.

***

Another important development in ICL has been the increased reliance on hybrid tribunals to address past and ongoing atrocities around the globe. Although there is no fixed definition, hybrid tribunals – also called mixed or internationalized tribunals – typically combine international and domestic elements, including in their composition of judges, lawyers, and other staff, substantive and procedural law, and financing. Hybrid tribunals thus seek to leverage the resources and expertise of both the international community and the state where the crimes occurred.[114] Hybrids are created through a combination of domestic legislation and international instruments. They have been established by different means, including: agreements negotiated between the United Nations and the host country, as in Sierra Leone and Cambodia; UN administrations exercising sovereignty in trust in post-conflict situations, as in East Timor and Kosovo; or a UN Security Council resolution based on the Security Council's peacekeeping power under Chapter VII of the UN Charter, as in Lebanon (where the Security Council unilaterally approved an agreement it had previously reached with Lebanon after the Lebanese government failed to take the necessary internal measures to bring the agreement into force).[115] Hybrid tribunals represent a form of accountability sharing between the individual states or regions where they operate and the international community.[116] Since hybrid tribunals are typically created at the invitation of or by an agreement with the host state, they are more consensual in nature than the ICTY and ICTR, which were effectively imposed on the countries in question.[117]

Hybrid tribunals initially developed in post-conflict settings where a fully international tribunal was deemed infeasible or where an international tribunal existed but was incapable of handling the total volume of cases.[118] Hybrid tribunals, broadly defined, include the Special Court for Sierra Leone (SCSL), the Extraordinary Chambers in the Courts of Cambodia (ECCC), the Special Panels for Serious Crimes in Dili, East Timor (SPSC), the Regulation 64 Panels in the Courts of Kosovo (Regulation 64 Panels), the War Crimes Chamber (WCC) of the State Court of Bosnia-Herzegovina, the Kosovo Specialist Chambers and Specialist Prosecutor's Office, the Extraordinary African Chambers in Senegal, the Special Tribunal for Lebanon (STL), and the Special Criminal Court (SCC) in the Central African Republic. The international community has contemplated hybrid mechanisms to address other past and current atrocities, including in Syria, Colombia, South Sudan, Sri Lanka, the Democratic Republic of Congo, and Chad.[119] As the ICC's limitations have become more apparent, hybrid tribunals have emerged as an increasingly prominent feature of the international criminal justice landscape.

Hybrid tribunals differ in how they blend domestic and international elements. Foreign judges typically sit alongside national judges, but those relationships may be structured in various ways. Also, in some cases special chambers and investigative units are embedded within an existing domestic system that benefits from international assistance and expertise through seconded personnel and the provision of technical support, as illustrated by the special WCC within the State Court of Bosnia-Herzegovina.[120] Hybrid tribunals generally apply international law, but in some cases they apply domestic law, as informed by international standards. The jurisdiction of hybrid tribunals also differs. The SCSL and ECCC, for example, have jurisdiction to prosecute only those individuals who bear the greatest responsibility for crimes committed within those tribunals' specified geographic and temporal parameters.[121] The SPSC in East Timor exercised jurisdiction over a wider group of defendants. The government of Kosovo, in agreement with the European Union, recently created the Kosovo Specialist Chambers and Specialist Prosecutor's Office, referred to jointly as the Kosovo Relocated Specialist Judicial Institution (KRSJI), specifically to prosecute offenses committed by one side, the Kosovo Liberation Army, an ethnic Kosovar Albanian paramilitary group that sought Kosovo's independence from Serbia.[122] Although hybrid tribunals are ordinarily situated in the country or region where the crimes occurred, they can be located in an external location, such as The Hague, where the STL and KRSJI are based, and where the SCSL, which was otherwise located in Freetown, conducted its trial of former Liberian leader Charles Taylor for security reasons. Taylor is presently serving his sentence in the United Kingdom as part of an international agreement for similar reasons.[123]

Hybrid tribunals offer several potential advantages over purely international or domestic courts. They involve national institutions and actors in administering justice for past atrocities, which can increase local ownership, enhance the tribunal's legitimacy within the affected country, and help restore public confidence in that country's legal institutions.[124] Situating the tribunal in the state or region where the atrocities occurred can help enable the participation of witnesses, victims, and affected communities. At the same time, the involvement of international judges, lawyers, and organizations can supply needed expertise, help build national capacity, and facilitate the penetration of international norms at the domestic level. While the degree of collaboration and coordination with national governments may vary, hybrid tribunals, where successful, can help shore up domestic judicial institutions and restore the rule of law.[125] Hybrids are also typically less expensive to operate than stand-alone international tribunals, such as the ICC and *ad hoc* tribunals like the ICTY and ICTR, and less dependent on international funding (although hybrids can face significant financial hurdles of their own, especially where they depend on voluntary contributions, as has happened in the past).[126]

Hybrid tribunals can, moreover, be tailored to a particular country's legal culture and to the specific political and social causes underlying the crimes and mass violence in that country. Hybrids also can complement the work of international tribunals, which may lack the capacity to handle the sheer volume of cases, as Regulation 64 Panels in Kosovo and the special WCC in Bosnia-Herzegovina have done for the ICTY,[127] and as the SCC seeks to do for the ICC by sharing responsibility for crimes committed in the Central African Republic.[128] Further, some hybrids can assert pendant jurisdiction over relevant crimes under domestic law. The ECCC, for example, has jurisdiction over several domestic crimes, such as homicide and religious persecution, that were based on the national criminal code in place at the time the Khmer Rouge took power but that were not enforced during and after the Khmer Rouge era.[129] These domestic offenses were included in part because of concerns that certain charges based on international law might not meet rigorous standards of legality under the *nullum crimen sin lege* principle since the offending conduct predated developments in ICL.[130] The capacity of hybrid tribunals to incorporate domestic law can also fill gaps in international criminal statutes. For example, the jurisdiction of the KRSJI, created to prosecute crimes by the Kosovo Liberation Army, includes organ-trafficking and other offenses that were committed after the conclusion of the war in Kosovo and that therefore fall outside the jurisdiction of the ICTY statute, which requires a nexus to the armed conflict in the former Yugoslavia.[131] Additionally, hybrid tribunals can prosecute a single defendant, as illustrated by the Extraordinary African Chambers in the Senegal court system, which tried and convicted the former dictator of Chad, Hissène Habré, whose government was responsible for widespread political killings, systematic torture, and arbitrary arrests.[132]

Hybrid tribunals, in short, offer a means of combining elements of domestic and international legal institutions and adapting those elements to fit a particular local context. Rather than a second-best alternative, they are increasingly viewed as an integral part of ICL and important courts in their own right.[133]

Hybrids nevertheless pose several concerns. Although hybrid tribunals typically have a majority of international judges and apply international criminal law,[134] their inclusion of national officials and their responsiveness to local demands makes them vulnerable to political control and interference. This vulnerability can manifest itself in two main ways. One is through political capture by domestic forces opposed to accountability and determined to shield officials from criminal responsibility. The risk of capture is greatest where a regime change was not truly effective and elites from the prior government remain in power.[135] While this type of interference can potentially be reduced by giving international judges and personnel more control, hybrid courts are ultimately a shared enterprise and have less ability than the two original *ad hoc* tribunals and the ICC to trump local actors. Mixed panels of domestic and international judges, moreover, can encounter difficulties that stem from a clash of legal cultures or judicial systems.[136] Budgetary and other resource constraints can exacerbate these challenges. In the past, hybrid tribunals have been criticized on these grounds. For example, the ECCC, created to seek justice for atrocities committed by the Khmer Rouge between 1975 and 1979, has been plagued by charges of corruption, including claims of payments to Cambodian officials by ECCC staff in return for positions on the court, the acceptance of bribes by an individual judge,[137] and political interference, including pressure by Cambodian Prime Minister Hun Sen, himself a former Khmer Rouge military commander, to limit the ECCC's reach.[138] The SPSC, established to try serious offenses committed during the last stages of Indonesia's military occupation of East Timor, has been criticized for prioritizing political considerations, shielding senior officials, and failing to deliver on its promise of justice to Timorese citizens.[139]

Another way that political interference can manifest itself is when a new regime engages in show trials bent on vengeance rather than justice. Such trials undermine, rather than advance, the rule of law at the domestic and international level.[140] Trials that deny due process and impartiality compromise the most important goals of hybrid institutions and tarnish their legacy.[141] Ensuring a majority of international judges can enhance a hybrid tribunal's commitment to fairness.[142] But even where domestic actors do not seek to tilt the balance so extremely, they may insist on concessions such as the availability of the death penalty or the use of *in absentia* trials that jeopardize the goal of imposing criminal responsibility in a manner consistent with fair trial standards and other human rights norms.[143]

Despite some successes, hybrids have proven vulnerable to fair trial deficiencies. The SPSC, for example, faced a number of obstacles, including inadequate funding, an uncertain division of responsibility between the East Timor government and the UN, and a lack of knowledge of international standards among East Timor judges.[144] The defense bore a disproportionate brunt of these shortcomings, undermining defendants' right to counsel and the equality of arms.[145] The defense, for example, had no budget even for such key tasks as sending investigators or counsel into the field to locate witnesses or bringing those witnesses to Dili, East Timor's capital, where the tribunal was located, to testify at trial. The SPSC, as one commentator has observed, inhabited "an entirely different judicial world" than the more professionalized ICTY and ICTR.[46] While the SPSC completed a significant number of trials between 2000 and 2005 before the UN ceased funding it – many lasting only a few days and nearly all resulting in convictions – its lack of attention to the rights of the accused weakened its legitimacy and ability to deliver justice in a fair and impartial manner.[47]

The ECCC is often cited as an example of how hybrid tribunals are susceptible to domestic political interference that can shield individuals from criminal responsibility, especially in countries with historically weak legal institutions and judicial systems.[48] Several of the ECCC's features that have proven problematic, such as its coequal national and international prosecutors, majority of domestic judges, and degree of local control over court administration, resulted from accommodations to Cambodian sovereignty during the prolonged negotiations between Cambodian and UN officials to establish the tribunal.[49] The ECCC has also fallen short in protecting the rights of defendants. A common critique has focused on the sweeping power and broad discretion given to investigating judges. The way in which the judges have exercised their exclusive authority and enormous discretion to conduct investigations has contributed to defense claims of bias, procedural irregularities, and an absence of transparency.[50]

Another critique has centered on the ECCC's unwieldy mix of procedural rules. The framework agreement for the ECCC requires the use of procedures in accordance with Cambodian law, with guidance from international procedural rules in the event of a gap or an ambiguity.[51] Cambodia, however, lacked an authoritative procedural code and the procedures it did have when the ECCC was created were ill-suited to trying mass crimes. The relationship between Cambodian and international law, however, was uncertain and difficult to reconcile. It was hard to determine, for example, when Cambodian law was inconsistent with international law,[52] eventually leading the ECCC in 2007 to promulgate Internal Rules on procedure and evidence to consolidate applicable domestic and international law.[53] The ECCC's lack of predictability has posed concerns about ensuring the defendants' due process rights and opened the tribunal to charges of "cherry-picking to achieve desired outcomes."[54] While the ECCC has had some successes, including its contribution to international criminal law jurisprudence on joint criminal enterprise liability, innovations in victim participation, and effective outreach to the local population, the ECCC's procedural deficiencies have compromised its legacy.[55]

The Iraq Special Tribunal (IST), a national tribunal established with international support after the fall of Baghdad to try crimes committed during Saddam Hussein's regime, has been widely criticized for its due process failures. The Bush administration believed that the IST would be a superior post-conflict mechanism to either a UN-backed *ad hoc* international tribunal or a hybrid tribunal like the Special Court for Sierra Leone that more equally balanced domestic and international elements. The Bush administration insisted that the IST would have greater support among Iraqis and give them greater ownership of the transitional justice process.[156] The tribunal's defenders saw it as a genuine partnership between Iraqi officials and the Coalition Provisional Authority, the transitional government of Iraq established after the US-led invasion.[157] The tribunal's design, however, enabled the United States to exercise behind-the-scenes influence.[158] Further, as human rights groups and other NGOs had cautioned, Iraq's judiciary lacked the capacity to handle the complicated trials that the crimes of Saddam Hussein's regime necessitated and the Iraqi criminal justice system lacked important legal safeguards.[159] The tribunal, which was later renamed the Iraqi High Criminal Court (or Iraqi High Tribunal), eventually prosecuted Saddam Hussein and other senior Ba'ath party officials. It also provoked substantial criticism, including for a lack of judicial independence, defects in substantive law, and procedural shortcomings, thus leaving a questionable legacy.[160]

Other hybrid tribunals have achieved greater success in delivering accountability in a manner that respects the rights of accused individuals. The SCSL, which was established in 2002 to address atrocities committed during Sierra Leone's civil war from 1991 to 2002, including the widespread use of child soldiers, illustrates several positive features of hybrid tribunals and their potential utility as a transitional justice mechanism.[161] The SCSL enjoyed several advantages over other hybrid tribunals, including a clear mandate (to try those most responsible for international law violations during the relevant time period), a UN-appointed administration that operated the court relatively free of domestic political interference, largely positive national will towards the court, more stable funding, and better infrastructure and management.[162] These advantages helped the SCSL provide a judicial process that not only more capably served victims and witnesses, but also better protected the rights of defendants in a manner visible to the local population.[163] Notably, the SCSL created a Defense Office as a formal organ of the tribunal, which it intended to serve as a "fourth pillar" to safeguard the rights of defendants and provide a counterweight to the prosecution.[164] While the office did not achieve its full potential due to limits on its autonomy,[165] it nonetheless represents an important innovation.[166] The absence of an independent defense organ at the ICC, by contrast, remains a persistent concern.[167] The SCSL also sought to meet international standards on such operational matters as simultaneous translations and the issuance of daily transcripts that, in addition to improving the court's efficiency, contributed to fairer trials.[168] Critics note that the SCSL fell short in its contributions to national legal development in Sierra Leone and failed to incorporate local perspectives in a way that would have maximized support among Sierra Leoneans, who often viewed the court as an outside institution with little effect on their daily lives.[169] Yet, despite these critiques, the SCSL, which closed in 2013 after completing its mandate, is generally viewed more favorably than other hybrid tribunals.[170]

Another hybrid tribunal, the Special Tribunal for Lebanon (STL), was established in 2009 to prosecute individuals in connection with the 2005 terrorist attack that killed Lebanon's former Prime Minister Rafik Hariri and 22 others and with related attacks. The STL, the first international court to focus specifically on terrorism, illustrates the diverse form hybrids can take. The STL was created by the UN Security Council under its Chapter VII powers (based on a treaty with Lebanon) and combines international and national judges.[171] The tribunal, however, also applies Lebanese substantive and procedural law, which it interprets in light of relevant international treaties and custom.[172] The STL is thus effectively an international court in origin and composition that applies a state's domestic criminal law.

The STL contains several innovations, serving as what one commentator calls "a judicial laboratory for the development of human rights standards triggered by international criminal proceedings."[173] The STL is the only international tribunal (other than the ICC) to include a human rights enabling clause that supplements the specific human rights standards listed in its internal legal instruments.[174] The STL Statute requires that judges be guided by international fair trial standards when adopting the tribunal's Rules of Procedure and Evidence.[175] The STL has exceeded the baseline procedural requirements of human rights law in several areas. It has adopted a strict exclusionary rule, which bars the admission of evidence obtained in violation of human rights law to avoid compromising the integrity of the proceedings or undermining the procedural protections afforded the accused.[176] Other international criminal tribunals, by contrast, employ more flexible, balancing-oriented approaches that consider such factors as the status of the human rights norm that was violated and the value and reliability of the evidence.[177] The STL has also increased a defendant's ability to pursue an interlocutory appeal, recognized the right of suspects to communicate freely with defense counsel and to access their criminal case file, and bolstered protections against anonymous witness testimony by requiring that convictions not be based exclusively or significantly on such testimony.[178] Additionally, the STL has established an independent Defense Office as an organ of the court to protect the rights of the accused. This office expands on the precedent created by the SCSL and has the potential to contribute significantly towards achieving equality of arms.[179]

However, the STL's most significant – and controversial – provision concerns *in absentia* trials. The STL is the first international tribunal to provide expressly for a trial in the defendant's absence since the IMT allowed Martin Bormann's trial *in absentia* at Nuremberg.[180] The STL can conduct trials *in absentia* if a defendant waives his right to be present, has not been handed over to the tribunal by state authorities within a reasonable time, or escapes and cannot be found after all reasonable steps have been taken to secure his appearance.[181] Adequate notice must be provided to the accused and the accused must be represented by counsel, either of his own selection or on appointment by the court.[182] If tried *in absentia*, the accused can request a new trial unless he had defense counsel of his choosing at the original trial.[183] A principal motive behind the STL's provision for *in absentia* trials was the concern that Lebanon or Hezbollah, the political and military organization that controls large portions of territory in Lebanon, would refuse to hand over suspects to the tribunal.[184] Nothing, moreover, in the relevant UN Security Council resolutions imposes an obligation on states to cooperate with the STL,[185] and Lebanese law, reflecting its civil law heritage, provides for *in absentia* proceedings.[186]

The STL's provision for *in absentia* trials could significantly impact fair trial guarantees.[187] Other modern international criminal tribunals have refused to adopt such provisions, primarily because they weaken the truth-seeking function of international criminal trials and raise fairness concerns.[188] The Rome Statute, for example, requires the presence of the accused during trial[189] and provides that the ICC Trial Chamber may remove a defendant from the courtroom only as an exceptional measure, where the defendant continues to disrupt the trial.[190] The Trial Chamber, moreover, must enable the defendant to observe the trial and instruct counsel from outside the courtroom.[191] But while international law strongly disfavors *in absentia* trials, it does not categorically prohibit them. Human rights law allows for *in absentia* trials in limited circumstances, where a defendant waives his right to be present and adequate legal safeguards are provided.[192] Moreover, even national jurisdictions that generally grant criminal defendants the right to be present at their trial permit some exceptions to this right, such as when an accused person flees the jurisdiction or receives valid notice of the charges and fails to respond to a summons.[193] And international criminal tribunals have allowed trials to proceed where a defendant refuses to attend further proceedings in order to prevent the defendant from impeding the administration of justice.[194] The ICTY, moreover, initially exercised its authority to consider evidence and witness testimony without the accused present to reconfirm an unexecuted indictment and issue an international arrest warrant, before halting the practice after the tribunal grew more successful at obtaining custody over suspects.[195]

The STL will need to grapple with various fair trial concerns. The STL Statute appears to allow for constructive notice of the indictment through the indictment's publication in the media or its communication to the accused's state of residence or nationality rather than mandating actual notice.[196] Also, even when a court, such as the STL, appoints counsel to represent the defendants, the presumed inability of counsel to communicate with his or her clients makes it difficult to mount a full defense.[197] The STL Statute should not be interpreted to allow for *in absentia* trials when a defendant wishes to attend his trial, but the state prevents him from doing so, and thus the defendant cannot attend for circumstances outside his control.[198] Another question is how the STL will be able to guarantee the right to retrial once the tribunal has been discontinued.[199] While the establishment of a residual mechanism to conduct such future proceedings could help address this issue, the uncertainty about future proceedings shows how hybrid tribunals, which are generally temporary in nature, face questions that domestic courts do not ordinarily confront. At the same time, the STL's provision for *in absentia* trials suggests a hybrid tribunal's capacity for experimentation in the face of persistent obstacles, such as the difficulty of apprehending suspects – an obstacle that may be more acute for the STL, but is one that other international and hybrid courts continually face.

The STL has thus far commenced an *in absentia* trial against four defendants accused of involvement in the bombing that killed former Prime Minister Hariri and is conducting an investigation into three related attacks.[200] The prosecution alleges that the defendants in the assassination of Hariri were closely associated with Hezbollah, which has denounced the STL and refused to cooperate with it.[201] Ultimately, the success of the STL's experimentation with *in absentia* trials will depend on how rigorously its safeguards are administered and how scrupulously such trials protect the rights of accused persons.

Hybrid tribunals also offer an attractive model for responding to emerging challenges for which an international tribunal may not be feasible or desirable. One recent proposal, for example, contemplates an extraterritorial Somali anti-piracy court that would be staffed by internationally trained Somali and diaspora judges and based in a secure location. The tribunal, which would be established through treaties between Somalia, the host state, and the apprehending states, would serve as a focal point for regional and international anti-piracy efforts and help bolster the rule of law in Somalia.[202] Another proposal is to create a tribunal to prosecute individuals responsible for the 2014 downing of Malaysian Air Flight 17. The envisaged tribunal, modeled loosely on the Lockerbie tribunal established after the 1988 bombing of Pan Am Flight 103 over Lockerbie, Scotland, would be located in a neutral forum and would be the product of negotiations between states with competing claims to jurisdiction. However, unlike the Lockerbie tribunal, which applied only Scots law, the proposed Malaysian Air Flight 17 tribunal would combine Malaysian and Ukrainian law. The hybrid tribunal could provide a means of sidestepping Russia's prior veto of a proposed UN Security Council resolution to create an international criminal tribunal.[203]

Given the constraints faced by the ICC and the political and financial obstacles to the creation of new major standalone tribunals modeled on the ICTY and ICTR, hybrids will likely play a prominent role in ICL's future. In part, increased reliance on hybrid tribunals is a consequence of the limitations of international tribunals. But hybrids also possess positive features. They can provide a transitional justice mechanism more closely tailored to the diverse political, social and cultural contexts in which international crimes occur. Such tailoring can help fortify a hybrid tribunal's legitimacy among the local population and facilitate its efforts in rebuilding national legal institutions. Significant criticism has been directed at the ICC and the two *ad hoc* international tribunals for failing to respond to local preferences and to the diverse constituencies in affected countries.[204] Hybrid tribunals can be designed to avoid, or at least mitigate, these problems. They also have the potential to catalyze local efforts to establish rule of law institutions and foster human rights norms within domestic legal systems,[205] even if they have often failed to do so in the past.[206] Creators of hybrid tribunals should accordingly do more to incorporate local actors in designing these tribunals and to facilitate the participation of broader segments of society in their operation.[207]

Hybrid tribunals nevertheless present risks as well as opportunities. The same responsiveness to local preferences and conditions that makes hybrids appealing can impede their establishment.[208] It also makes them susceptible to the injection of regressive elements of domestic law once operational.[209] Some tribunals, moreover, are effectively hybrid in name only, featuring little, if any, international involvement, and thus lack the international personnel and expertise that can help maintain fair trial standards.[210]

More locally grounded accountability mechanisms are similarly vulnerable not only to capture by local elites, but also to procedural unfairness. For example, Rwanda harnessed *gacaca*, an informal civil dispute resolution mechanism traditionally used to resolve claims involving such matters as property and marital relations, to address crimes committed before and during the Rwandan genocide.[211] Rwanda's *gacaca* courts show how an existing and respected local institution can be used as a transitional justice mechanism. But the courts also faced criticism because of the judges' lack of impartiality and competence, and because they often failed to protect the due process rights of defendants.[212]

Even as hybrids and other more locally grounded accountability mechanisms proliferate, international tribunals will remain an important model, not only for the development of substantive standards of liability, but also for the elaboration of procedures employed to prosecute international crimes. Despite their shortcomings, the procedures utilized by the ICTY, ICTR, and ICC provide an example for hybrid tribunals. In the increasingly pluralistic and decentralized landscape of international criminal justice, the interaction among tribunals will be critical to the development and maintenance of fair trial standards.[213] Human rights tribunals can play a role in this process as well. Human rights courts can, for example, reinforce fair trial rights in their review of war crimes prosecutions by individual states[214] or through their review of decisions by hybrid tribunals that fall within their jurisdiction, a function the European Court of Human Rights has performed through its review of decisions by the WCC of the State Court of Bosnia-Herzegovina.[215]

Alternative mechanisms to criminal trials will also remain a tool for addressing mass violence. Truth and reconciliation commissions, for example, may seek to uncover and document past human rights abuses and allow victims to confront perpetrators without imposing criminal sanctions to assist societies transitioning from civil war or from an authoritarian regime to a more democratic form of government.[216] Although the South African Truth and Reconciliation Commission is the best known example, numerous countries have employed some form of truth commission.[217] Such commissions, moreover, may be employed contemporaneously with international or hybrid tribunals. In East Timor and Sierra Leone, for example, truth commissions helped address broader factors that led to the atrocities in each country, conducted outreach to victims, and advocated for systemic reforms.[218] Truth commissions might also be used in conjunction with criminal prosecutions in ICC situation countries.[219]

The potential value of such alternative accountability mechanisms should not, however, obscure the critical point about prosecuting international crimes. Whenever a court seeks to address past atrocities through a criminal trial – whether alone or in conjunction with some form of truth commission – that trial's credibility and legitimacy will depend ultimately on the adequacy and fairness of its procedures.

NOTES

1. Göran Sluiter, Hakan Friman, and Suzannah Linton et al. eds., *International Criminal Procedure: Principles and Rules* (Oxford: Oxford University Press, 2013), 5 (quoting Judge O-Gon Kwon).
2. Mirjan Damaška, "What Is the Point of International Criminal Justice?" *Chicago-Kent Law Review* 83 (2008), 329, 345.
3. Gregory S. Gordon, "Toward an International Criminal Procedure: Due Process Aspirations and Limitations," *Columbia Journal of Transnational Law* 45 (2007), 635, 710.
4. Yvonne McDermott, *Fairness in International Criminal Trials* (Oxford: Oxford University Press, 2016), 2.
5. See generally Sluiter et al. eds., *International Criminal Procedure: Principles and Rules.*
6. Ibid., 8.
7. Albert Eser, "Procedural Structure and Features of International Criminal Justice: Lessons from the ICTY," in Bert Swart, Alexander Zahar, and Göran Sluiter eds., *The Legacy of the International Criminal Tribunal for the Former Yugoslavia* (Oxford: Oxford University Press, 2011).
8. McDermott, *Fairness in International Criminal Trials*, 9.
9. Mark Drumbl, "Collective Violence and Individual Punishment: The Criminality of Mass Atrocity," *Northwestern University Law Review* 99 (2005), 539, 590.
10. McDermott, *Fairness in International Criminal Trials*, 9.
11. Megan Fairlie, "The Marriage of Common and Continental Law at the ICTY and Its Progeny, Due Process Deficit," *International Criminal Law Review* 4 (2004), 243, 243–44.
12. Kai Ambos, "International Criminal Procedure: 'Adversarial', 'Inquisitorial' or 'Mixed'"? *International Criminal Law Review* 3 (2003), 1, 35.
13. Sonja B. Starr, "Rethinking 'Effective Remedies': Remedial Deterrence in International Courts," *New York University Law Review* 83 (2008), 693, 711.
14. McDermott, *Fairness in International Criminal Trials*, 17–18.
15. Rome Statute of the International Criminal Court, art. 21, July 17, 1998, 2187 U.N.T.S. 90 (Rome Statute).
16. McDermott, *Fairness in International Criminal Trials*, 19; Starr, "Rethinking 'Effective Remedies,'" 711; Kenneth S. Gallant, "International Criminal Courts and the Making of Public International Law: New Roles for International Organizations and Individuals," *John Marshall Law Review* 43 (2010), 603, 616.

17. Göran Sluiter, "The Law of International Criminal Procedure and Domestic War Crimes Trials," *International Criminal Law Review* 6 (2006), 605, 610.
18. Frédéric Mégret, "Beyond 'Fairness': Understanding the Determinants of International Criminal Procedure," *UCLA Journal of International Law and Foreign Affairs* 14 (2009), 37, 52.
19. Ibid., 53–54.
20. Ibid., 53.
21. Asad Kiyani, "Group-Based Differentiation and Local Repression: The Custom and Curse of Selectivity," *Journal of International Criminal Justice* 14 (2016), 939, 944–46.
22. Ibid., 945. Croatian courts have prosecuted the overwhelming majority of these cases. Ibid.
23. UN ICTY Website, "Key Figures of the Cases," www.icty.org/en/cases/key-figures-cases.
24. Kiyani, "Group-Based Differentiation and Local Repression," 945–46.
25. Elies van Sliedregt and Sergey Vasiliev, "Pluralism: A New Framework for International Criminal Justice," in Elies van Sliedregt and Sergey Vasiliev eds., *Pluralism in International Criminal Law* (Oxford: Oxford University Press, 2014), 12–17.
26. McDermott, *Fairness in International Criminal Trials*, 13.
27. Carsten Stahn and Larissa van den Herik, "'Fragmentation', Diversification, and '3D' Legal Pluralism: International Criminal Law as the Jack-in-the-Box?" in Larissa Van den Herik and Carsten Stahn eds., *The Diversification and Fragmentation of International Criminal Law* (Leiden: Brill-Nijhoff, 2012).
28. Antonio Coco, "Understanding International Criminal Law through an Analysis of the Defense of Mistake of Law," 23–25 (forthcoming) (Manuscript on File with Author); Flavia Lattanzi, "Introduction," in Van den Herik and Stahn eds., *The Diversification and Fragmentation of International Criminal Law*, 2–3.
29. Jens David Ohlin, "A Meta-Theory of International Criminal Procedure: Vindicating the Rule of Law," *UCLA Journal of International Law and Foreign Affairs* 14 (2009), 77, 112–13.
30. Sluiter et al. eds., *International Criminal Procedure: Principles and Rules*, 6.
31. See, for example, Alexander K. A. Greenawalt, "The Pluralism of International Criminal Law," *Indiana Law Journal* 86 (2011), 1063, 1068.
32. William W. Burke-White, "A Community of Courts: Towards a System of International Criminal Law Enforcement," *Michigan Journal of International Law* 24 (2002), 1, 77–85; Bruno Simma, "Fragmentation in a Positive Light," *Michigan Journal of International Law* 25 (2004), 845, 846.
33. José E. Alvarez, "Crimes of States/Crimes of Hate: Lessons from Rwanda," *Yale Journal of International Law* 24 (1999) 365, 385–86.
34. *Prosecutor v. Tadić*, Case No. IT-94-AR72, Appeals Chamber, Decision on the Defence Motion for Interlocutory Appeal on Jurisdiction, paras. 58, 62 (October 2, 1995).
35. Bartram S. Brown, "Primacy or Complementarity: Reconciling the Jurisdiction of National Courts and International Criminal Tribunals," *Yale Journal of International Law* 23 (1998), 383, 404.
36. Mohamed M. El Zeidy, "The Principle of Complementarity: A New Machinery to Implement International Criminal Law," *Michigan Journal of International Law* 23 (2002), 869, 882.
37. Brown, "Primacy or Complementarity," 408.
38. Rome Statute, art. 17(1).
39. Ibid., art. 19; *Prosecutor v. Muthaura, Kenyatta and Ali*, Case No. ICC-01/09–02/11 OA, Appeals Chamber, Judgment on appeal of the Republic of Kenya against the decision of

Pre-Trial Chamber II of 30 May 2011 entitled "Decision on the Application by the Government of Kenya Challenging the Admissibility of the Case Pursuant to Article 19(2)(b) of the Statute," para. 39 (August 30, 2011).

40. Carey Shenkman, Note, "Catalyzing National Judicial Capacities: The ICC's First Crimes against Humanity Outside Armed Conflict," *New York University Law Review* 87 (2012), 1210, 1234–35.

41. Megan A. Fairlie, "The United States and the International Criminal Court Post-Bush: A Beautiful Courtship but an Unlikely Marriage," *Berkeley Journal of International Law* 29 (2011), 528, 560–61.

42. *Prosecutor v. Katanga and Chui*, Case No. ICC-01/04-01/07 OA 8, Appeals Chamber, Judgment on the Appeal of Mr. Germain Katanga against the Oral Decision of Trial Chamber II of 12 June 2009 on the Admissibility of the Case, para. 85 (September 25, 2009) (*Katanga* Judgment on the Appeal of the Oral Decision on the Admissibility of the Case).

43. John T. Holmes, "The Principle of Complementarity," in Roy S. Lee ed., *The International Criminal Court: The Making of the Rome Statute* (The Hague: Kluwer Law International, 1999), 41, 41–42.

44. David J. Scheffer, "Staying the Course with the International Criminal Court," *Cornell International Law Journal* 47 (2002), 35, 87.

45. William W. Burke-White, "Proactive Complementarity: The International Criminal Court and National Courts in the Rome System of International Justice," *Harvard International Law Journal* 49 (2008), 53, 54.

46. Elizabeth B. Ludwin King, "Big Fish, Small Ponds: International Crimes in National Courts," *Indiana Law Journal* 90 (2015), 829, 848.

47. Ohlin, "A Meta-Theory of International Criminal Procedure," 107–08.

48. Rosanna Lipscomb, "Restructuring the ICC Framework to Advance Transitional Justice: A Search for a Permanent Solution in Sudan," *Columbia Law Review* 106 (2006), 182, 197–99.

49. Samuel C. Birnbaum, "Predictive Due Process and the International Criminal Court," *Vanderbilt Journal of Transnational Law* 48 (2015), 307, 309–10; Michael A. Newton, "The Complementarity Conundrum: Are We Watching Evolution or Evisceration?" *Santa Clara Journal of International Law* 8 (2010), 115, 119–23, 144.

50. Report of the Bureau on Stocktaking: Complementarity, 8th Session of the Assembly of States Parties (ASP), Mar. 22–25, 2010, Doc. ICC-ASP/8/51, para. 16 (March 18, 2010).

51. Burke-White, "Proactive Complementarity," 56.

52. Luis Moreno-Ocampo, Prosecutor of the ICC, "Statement Made at the Ceremony for the Solemn Undertaking of the Chief Prosecutor of the International Criminal Court," The Hague, Netherlands (June 16, 2003), www.icc-cpi.int/NR/rdonlyres/D7572226-264A -4B6B-85E3-2673648B4896/143585/030616_moreno_ocampo_english.pdf.

53. Luis Moreno-Ocampo, Prosecutor of the ICC, "Building a Future on Peace and Justice," Address in Nuremberg, Germany (June 24–25, 2007), www.icc-cpi.int/NR/rdonlyres/ 4E466EDB-2B38-4BAF-AF5F-005461711149/143825/LMO_nuremberg_20070625_ English.pdf.

54. Linda E. Carter, "The International Criminal Court in 2021," *Southwestern Journal of International Law* 18 (2011), 199, 208; Shenkman, "Catalyzing National Judicial Capacities," 1233.

55. Matiangai V. S. Sirleaf, "Regionalism, Regime Complexes, and the Crisis in International Criminal Justice," *Columbia Journal of Transnational Law* 54 (2016), 699, 701, 726–27.

56. *Situation in the Libyan Arab Jamahiriya*, Case No. ICC-01/11–14, Pre-Trial Chamber I, Warrant of Arrest for Saif Al-Islam Gaddafi (June 27, 2011); *Situation in the Libyan Arab Jamahiriya*, Case No. ICC-01/11–15, Pre-Trial Chamber I, Warrant of Arrest for Abdullah Al-Senussi (June 27, 2011).

57. Human Rights Watch, "Libya: Flawed Trial of Gaddafi Officials; Defendants Alleged Limited Access to Lawyers, Ill-Treatment," July 28, 2015, www.hrw.org/news/2015/07/28/libya-flawed-trial-gaddafi-officials.

58. Ibid.

59. Chris Stephen, "Gaddafi's son Saif al-Islam sentenced to death by court in Libya," *The Guardian* (July 28, 2015), www.theguardian.com/world/2015/jul/28/saif-al-islam-sentenced-death-by-court-in-libya-gaddafi-son.

60. Mark S. Ellis, International Bar Association, "Trial of the Libyan Regime: An Investigation into International Fair Trial Standards" (November 2015), www.ibanet.org/Article/NewDetail.aspx?ArticleUid=759f1431-4e10-450d-998e-21349fd8bf26.

61. Ayman Al-Warfalli, "Gaddafi's Son Saif Freed in Libya, Whereabouts Unclear: Lawyer," *Reuters* (June 11, 2017), www.reuters.com/article/us-libya-security-saif/gaddafis-son-saif-freed-in-libya-whereabouts-unclear-lawyer-idUSKBN192092.

62. *Katanga* Judgment on the Appeal of the Oral Decision on the Admissibility of the Case, paras. 75–79.

63. *Prosecutor v. Gaddafi and Al-Senussi*, Case No. ICC-01/11–01/11–130, Pre-Trial Chamber I, Application on Behalf of the Government of Libya pursuant to Article 19 of the ICC Statute, paras. 2, 10 (May 1, 2012).

64. *Prosecutor v. Gaddafi and Al-Senussi*, Case No. ICC-01/11–01/11–344-Red, Pre-Trial Chamber I, Decision on the admissibility of the case against Saif Al-Islam Gaddafi, para. 219 (May 31, 2013) (*Gaddafi* Decision on the admissibility of the case); Rome Statute, art. 17(3).

65. *Gaddafi* Decision on the admissibility of the case, 217.

66. Ibid., paras. 210–15.

67. *Prosecutor v. Saif Al-Islam Gaddafi and Abdullah Al-Senussi*, Case No. ICC-01/11–01/11–466-Red, Pre-Trial Chamber I, Decision on the admissibility of the case against Abdullah Al-Senussi, para. 235 (October 11, 2013) (*Al-Senussi* Decision on the admissibility of the case).

68. Ibid.

69. Ibid., paras. 218, 233, 258, 308; Angela Walker, Comment, "The ICC Versus Libya: How to End the Cycle of Impunity for Atrocity Crimes by Protecting Due Process," *UCLA Journal of International Law and Foreign Affairs* 18 (2014), 303, 312.

70. *Al-Senussi* Decision on the admissibility of the case, para. 308

71. Ibid.

72. *Prosecutor v. Gaddafi and Al-Senussi*, Case No. ICC-01/11–01/11, Appeals Chamber, Judgment on the appeal of Libya against the decision of Pre-Trial Chamber I of May 31, 2013 entitled "Decision on the admissibility of the case against Saif Al-Islam Gaddafi" (May 21, 2014) (*Gaddafi* Judgment on appeal of decision on the admissibility of the case); *Prosecutor v. Gaddafi and Al-Senussi*, Case No. ICC-01/11–01/11, Appeals Chamber, Judgment on the appeal of Mr. Abdullah Al-Senussi against the decision of Pre-Trial Chamber I of October 11, 2013 entitled "Decision on the admissibility of the case against Abdullah Al-Senussi," para. 299 (July 24, 2014) (*Al-Senussi* Judgment on appeal of decision on the admissibility of the case).

73. *Al-Senussi* Judgment on appeal of decision on the admissibility of the case, paras. 191, 220.

74. Ibid., para. 220.

75. Ibid., para. 221.

76. Ibid., paras. 200–201, 244(i).

77. *Gaddafi* Judgment on appeal of decision on the admissibility of the case, paras. 212–14.

78. See, for example, Kevin Jon Heller, "The Shadow Side of Complementarity: The Effect of Article 17 of the Rome Statute on National Due Process," *Criminal Law Forum* 17 (2006), 255, 257, 279; Marcus Benzing, "The Complementarity Regime of the International Criminal Court: International Criminal Justice between State Sovereignty and the Fight against Impunity," *Max Planck Yearbook of United Nations Law* 7 (2003), 591, 612.

79. M. Christopher Pitts, "Being Able to Prosecute Saif Al-Islam Gaddafi, Applying Article 17(3) of the Rome Statute to Libya," *Emory International Law Review* 27 (2013), 1291.

80. ICC Office of the Prosecutor, Informal Expert Paper, "The Principle of Complementarity in Practice," para. 23 (2003), www.icc-cpi.int/NR/rdonlyres/20BB4494-70F9-4698-8E30-907F631453ED/281984/complementarity.pdf.

81. Darryl Robinson, "The Impact of the Rome Statute on National Law," in Antonio Cassese, Paola Gaeta, and John R. W. D. Jones eds., *The Rome Statute of the International Criminal Court: A Commentary* (vol. 1) (Oxford: Oxford University Press, 2002), 1849, 1866; Albin Eser, "For Universal Jurisdiction: Against Fletcher's Antagonism," *Tulsa Law Review* 39 (2004), 955, 963. A version of a due process approach would, for example, consider due process violations in the complementarity analysis where those violations are particularly severe. See Jonathan O'Donohue and Sophie Rigney, "The ICC Must Consider Fair Trial Concerns in Determining Libya's Application to Prosecute Saif al-Islam Gaddafi Nationally," *EJIL: TALK!* (June 8, 2012), http://perma.cc/8G9Q-3N3D.

82. Birnbaum, "Predictive Due Process and the International Criminal Court," 312.

83. *Al-Senussi* Judgment on appeal of decision on the admissibility of the case, para. 201.

84. Ibid., para. 201; Rome Statute, art. 19(10).

85. *Al-Senussi* Judgment on appeal of decision on the admissibility of the case, paras. 190, 229. See Jennifer Trahan, "The International Criminal Court's Libya Case(s) — The Need for Consistency with International Human Rights as to Due Process and the Death Penalty," *International Criminal Law Review* 17 (2017), 803, 819, 826.

86. Trahan, "The International Criminal Court's Libya Case(s)," 835–37.

87. Ibid., 805–06.

88. Rome Statute, art. 80.

89. Trahan, "The International Criminal Court's Libya Case(s)," 843.

90. Mark S. Ellis, "The International Criminal Court and Its Implication for Domestic Law and National Capacity Building," *Florida Journal of International Law* 15 (2002), 215, 241.

91. Rome Statute, art. 121(3)–(4).

92. Elena Baylis, "Reassessing the Role of International Criminal Law: Rebuilding National Courts through Transnational Networks," *Boston College Law Review* 50 (2009), 1, 81–84.

93. S.C. Res. 1503, U.N. Doc. S/RES/1503 (August 28, 2003); Dafna Gozani, "Beginning to Learn How to End: Lessons on Completion Strategies, Residual Mechanisms, and Legacy Considerations from *Ad Hoc* International Criminal Tribunals to the International Criminal Court," *Loyola Los Angeles International and Comparative Law Review* 36 (2015), 331, 342–56.

94. William W. Burke-White, "The Domestic Influence of International Criminal Tribunals: The International Criminal Tribunals for the Former Yugoslavia and the Creation of the State Court of Bosnia and Herzegovina," *Columbia Journal of Transnational Law* 46 (2008), 279, 309–10.

95. ICTY Rules of Procedure and Evidence, Rule 11 *bis*; ICTR Rules of Procedure and Evidence, Rule 11 *bis*; Olympia Bekou, "Rule 11 *Bis*: An Examination of the Process of Referrals to National Courts in ICTY Jurisprudence," *Fordham International Law Journal* 33 (2010), 723, 723–24.

96. Address of Judge Theodor Meron, President of the International Criminal Tribunal for the former Yugoslavia, to the United Nations Security Council (The Hague, June 29, 2004), www.icty.org/en/press/address-judge-theodor-meron-president-international -criminal-tribunal-former-yugoslavia-unit-0.

97. Statute of the International Residual Mechanism for Criminal Tribunals, S.C. Res. 1966, Annex 1, U.N. Doc. S/RES/1966 (December 22, 2010) (MICT Statute).

98. United Nations Mechanism for International Criminal Tribunals, "Functions of the MICT," www.unmict.org/en/about/functions.

99. MICT Statute, art. 6.

100. Ibid., arts. 1(3), 6(1).

101. Ibid., art. 6.

102. Letter from the Secretary-General, to the President of the Security Council, paras. 48, 55, 72, U.N. Doc. S/2002/678 (June 19, 2002); Walker, "The ICC Versus Libya," 340.

103. MICT Statute, art. 28(3).

104. Amelia S. Canter, Note, "'For These Reasons, The Chamber: Denies the Prosecutor's Request for Referral': The False Hope of Rule 11 *Bis*," *Fordham International Law Journal* 32 (2009), 1614, 1616.

105. Sara Kendall and Sarah M. H. Nouwen, "Speaking of Legacy: Toward an Ethos of Modesty at the International Criminal Tribunal for Rwanda," *American Journal of International Law* 110 (2016), 212, 225.

106. *Prosecutor v. Kanyarukiga*, Case No. ICTR-2002–78-R11bis, ICTR Appeals Chamber, Decision on the Prosecution's Appeal against Decision on Referral under Rule 11*bis*, paras. 19, 21 (October 30, 2008).

107. Kendall and Nouwen, "Speaking of Legacy," 225.

108. Ibid.

109. *Prosecutor v. Munyarugarama*, Case No. ICTR-02–79-R11bis, ICTR, Decision on the Prosecutor's Request for Referral of the Case to the Republic of Rwanda, paras. 33–34, 52 (June 28, 2012).

110. Sigall Horovitz, "International Criminal Courts in Action: The ICTR's Effect on Death Penalty and Reconciliation in Rwanda," *George Washington International Law Review* 48 (2016), 505, 508.

111. Bekou, "Rule 11 *Bis*," 770.

112. Burke-White, "The Domestic Influence of International Criminal Tribunals," 309.

113. El Zeidy, "The Principle of Complementarity," 882–89.

114. David Cohen, "'Hybrid' Justice in East Timor, Sierra Leone, and Cambodia: 'Lessons Learned' and Prospects for the Future," *Stanford Journal of International Law* 43 (2007), 1, 2.

115. Beth Van Schaack and Ronald Slye, *International Criminal Law and Its Enforcement: Cases and Materials* 3rd ed. (Minnesota: Foundation Press, 2015), 98; John Cerone, "The Politics of International Justice—U.S. Policy and the Legitimacy of the Special Tribunal for Lebanon," *Denver Journal of International Law and Policy* 40 (2011–12), 44, 53–54.

116. Etelle R. Higonnet, "Restructuring Hybrid Courts: Local Empowerment and National Criminal Justice Reform," *Arizona Journal of International and Comparative Law* 23 (2006), 347, 352.

117. Van Schaack and Slye, *International Criminal Law*, 99.
118. Laura A. Dickinson, "The Promise of Hybrid Courts," *American Journal of International Law* 97 (2003), 295.
119. Beth Van Schaack, "The Building Blocks of Hybrid Justice," *Denver Journal of International Law and Policy* 44 (2016), 169, 170. Such proposals, however, can face significant domestic opposition.
120. Beth Van Schaack, "'More than a Domestic Mechanism': Options for Hybrid Justice in Sri Lanka," Stanford Public Law Working Paper No. 2705097 (Dec. 17, 2015), 3–4, http://papers.ssrn.com/sol3/papers.cfm?abstract_id=2705097.
121. Jennifer Trahan, "Reflections on the Difficulties of Enforcing International Justice," *University of Pennsylvania Journal of International Law* 30 (2009), 1187, 1198–99.
122. Mark Kersten, "The New Kosovo Tribunal—Turning Victors' Justice on Its Head?" *Justice in Conflict*, January 18, 2016, https://justiceinconflict.org/2016/01/18/the-new -kosovo-tribunal-turning-victors-justice-on-its-head/.
123. Shahram Dana, "The Sentencing Legacy of the Special Court for Sierra Leone," *Georgia Journal of International and Comparative Law* 42 (2014), 615, 659; "Charles Taylor, Background," *International Justice Monitor*, www.ijmonitor.org/charles-taylor -background/.
124. Van Schaack, "The Building Blocks of Hybrid Justice," 172–73.
125. Office of the United Nations High Commissioner for Human Rights (OHCHR), *Rule-of-Law Tools for Post-Conflict States: Maximizing the Legacy of Hybrid Courts* (2008), www.ohchr.org/Documents/Publications/HybridCourts.pdf.
126. Lindsey Raub, Note, "Positioning Hybrid Tribunals in International Criminal Justice," *New York University Journal of International Law and Politics* 41 (2009), 1013, 1024–25.
127. Higonnet, "Restructuring Hybrid Courts," 354.
128. Mark Kersten, "Why Central African Republic's Hybrid Tribunal Could be a Game-Changer," *Justice in Conflict*, May 14, 2015, https://justiceinconflict.org/2015/05/14/why -central-african-republics-hybrid-tribunal-could-be-a-game-changer/.
129. Van Schaack, "The Building Blocks of Hybrid Justice," 252–53.
130. Ibid.
131. Ibid., 255; Petrit Collaku, "Kosovo President Signs War Court Agreement with Holland," *Balkan Insight* (February 29, 2016), http://www.balkaninsight.com/en/arti cle/kosovo-president-gives-green-light-for-the-start-of-the-special-court-02-29-2016.
132. Jaime Yaya Barry and Dionne Searcey, "Hissène Habré, Ex-Ruler of Chad, Loses War Crimes Appeal," *New York Times*, April 27, 2017; Human Rights Watch, "Q & A: The Case of Hissène Habré before the Extraordinary African Chambers in Senegal," *Human Rights News*, May 3, 2016, www.hrw.org/news/2016/05/03/qa-case-hissene-habre-extraor dinary-african-chambers-senegal#2.
133. Dickinson, "The Promise of Hybrid Courts," 296; Mark Kersten, "On the Rebirth of Hybrid Tribunals," *Justice in Conflict*, January 22, 2016, https://justiceinconflict.org/ 2016/01/22/on-the-rebirth-of-hybrid-tribunals/.
134. Chiara Giorgetti, "Using International Law in Somalia's Post-Conflict Reconstruction," *Columbia Journal of Transnational Law* 53 (2014), 48, 90.
135. Elizabeth Nielsen, "Hybrid International Criminal Tribunals: Political Interference and Judicial Independence," *UCLA Journal of International Law and Foreign Affairs* 15 (2010), 289, 293; Julian Ku and Jide Nzelibe, "Do International Criminal Tribunals

Deter or Exacerbate Humanitarian Atrocities?" *Washington University Law Review* 84 (2006), 776, 827–31.

136. Randall Peerenboom, "Human Rights and Rule of Law: What's the Relationship?" *Georgetown Journal of International Law* 36 (2005), 809, 920.

137. Seeta Scully, "Judging the Successes and Failures of the Extraordinary Chambers of the Courts of Cambodia," *Asian-Pacific Law and Policy Journal* 13 (2011), 300, 334–38.

138. Ibid., 314–15.

139. Jane E. Stromseth, "Pursuing Accountability for Atrocities after Conflict: What Impact on Building the Rule of Law?" *Georgetown Journal of International Law* 38 (2007), 251, 287; Jaya Ramji-Nogales, "Designing Bespoke Transitional Justice: A Pluralist Process Approach," *Michigan Journal of International Law* 32 (2010), 1, 33.

140. Nielsen, "Hybrid International Criminal Tribunals," 293.

141. OHCHR, *Rule-of-Law Tools for Post-Conflict States*.

142. Van Schaack, "The Building of Hybrid Justice," 235.

143. Ibid., 173.

144. Cohen, "'Hybrid' Justice in East Timor," 6–11.

145. Kate Kerr, Note, "Fair Trials at International Criminal Tribunals: Examining the Parameters of the International Right to Counsel," *Georgetown Journal of International Law* 36 (2005), 1227, 1247–51.

146. Jennifer Trahan, "A Critical Guide to the Iraqi High Tribunal's Anfal Judgment: Genocide against the Kurds," *Michigan Journal of International Law* 30 (2009), 305, 315–18; Cohen, "'Hybrid' Justice in East Timor," 16.

147. Cohen, "'Hybrid' Justice in East Timor," 16–17.

148. Suzannah Linton, "Putting Cambodia's Extraordinary Chambers into Context," *Singapore Yearbook of International Law* 11 (2007), 195, 204–08, 223–26.

149. John D. Ciorciari and Anne Heindel, "Experiments in International Criminal Justice: Lessons from the Khmer Rouge Tribunal," *Michigan Journal of International Law* 35 (2014), 369, 372–73; Neha Jain, "Between the Scylla and Charybdis of Prosecution and Reconciliation: The Khmer Rouge Trials and the Promise of International Criminal Justice," *Duke Journal of Comparative and International Law* 20 (2010), 247, 249.

150. Ciorciari and Heindel, "Experiments in International Criminal Justice," 387–91.

151. Agreement between the United Nations and the Royal Government of Cambodia Concerning the Prosecution under Cambodian Law of Crimes Committed during the Period of Democratic Kampuchea, June 6, 2003, 2329 U.N.T.S. 117.

152. Göran Sluiter, "Due Process and Criminal Procedure in the Cambodian Extraordinary Chambers," *Journal of International Criminal Justice* 4 (2006), 314, 320, 326.

153. Internal Rules (Rev. 9), Extraordinary Chambers in the Courts of Cambodia Internal Rules (January 16, 2015).

154. Ciorciari and Heindel, "Experiments in International Criminal Justice," 391–93.

155. Ibid., 373; John D. Ciorciari and Anne Heindel, "Victim Testimony in International and Hybrid Criminal Courts: Narrative Opportunities, Challenges, and Fair Trial Demands," *Virginia Journal of International Law* 56 (2016), 265, 320–21.

156. M. Cherif Bassiouni, "Post-Conflict Justice in Iraq: An Appraisal of the Iraq Special Tribunal," *Cornell International Law Journal* 38 (2005), 327, 343–44. See also Ryan

Swift, "Occupational Jurisdiction: A Critical Analysis of the Iraqi Special Tribunal," *New York International Law Review* 19 (2006), 99, 104–05.

157. Michael A. Newton, "The Iraqi Special Tribunal: A Human Rights Perspective," *Cornell International Law Journal* 38 (2005), 863, 876–77.

158. Bassiouni, "Post-Conflict Justice in Iraq," 343.

159. Kevin Jon Heller, "A Poisoned Chalice: The Substantive and Procedural Defects of the Iraqi High Tribunal," *Case Western Reserve Journal of International Law* 39 (2007), 261, 261–62, 290.

160. Nehal Bhuta, "Between Liberal Legal Didactics and Political Manichaeism: The Politics and Law of the Iraqi Special Tribunal," *Melbourne Journal of International Law* 6 (2005), 245, 271; Leila Sadat, "Fixing the Legitimacy Deficit in the Saddam Hussein Trial," in Michael P. Scharf and Gregory S. McNeal eds., *Saddam on Trial: Understanding and Debating the Iraqi High Tribunal* (Durham: Carolina Academic Press, 2006), 166; Heller, "A Poisoned Chalice," 261–62.

161. Tom Perriello and Marieke Wierda, International Center for Transitional Justice, *The Special Court for Sierra Leone Under Scrutiny* 1–2 (March 2006), www1.umn.edu/humanrts/instree/SCSL/Case-studies-ICTJ.pdf.

162. Cohen, "'Hybrid' Justice in East Timor," 11–14, 19; Nielsen, "Hybrid International Criminal Tribunals," 319–20.

163. Antonio Cassese, *Report on the Special Court for Sierra Leone* (2006), 65, www.rscsl.org/Documents/Cassese%20Report.pdf.

164. Special Court for Sierra Leone, *Second Annual Report of the President of the Special Court for Sierra Leone: For the Period 1 January 2004–17 January 2005*, at 19, www.rscsl.org/Documents/AnRpt2.pdf.

165. Charles Chernor Jalloh, "Special Court for Sierra Leone: Achieving Justice?" *Michigan Journal of International Law* 32 (2011), 395, 437–40.

166. Richard J. Wilson, "'Emaciated' Defense or a Trend to Independence and Equality of Arms in Internationalized Criminalized Tribunals?" *Human Rights Brief* 15 (No. 2) (Winter 2008), 6.

167. Guénaël Mettraux et al., "Expert Initiative on Promoting Effectiveness at the International Criminal Court," paras. 145, 148 (December 2014), http://ilawyerblog.com/wp-content/uploads/2014/12/Final-Report-Swiss-Expert-Group-2-Dec-2014.pdf; Masha Fedorova, *The Principle of Equality of Arms in International Criminal Proceedings* (Cambridge: Intersentia, 2012), 451.

168. Cohen, "'Hybrid' Justice in East Timor," 22.

169. Mohamed Suma, International Center for Transitional Justice, *The Charles Taylor Trial and Legacy of the Special Court for Sierra Leone* 2 (September 2009), www.ictj.org/sites/default/files/ICTJ-SierraLeone-Special-Court-2009-English.pdf; Ramji-Nogales, "Designing Bespoke Transitional Justice" 36–38.

170. The Residual Special Court for Sierra Leone, created to carry out the SCSL's continuing functions, remains in place. See Special Court for Sierra Leone, Residual Court for Sierra Leone (established February 1, 2012), www.rscsl.org/.

171. S.C. Res. 1757, art. 1 (May 30, 2007) (STL Statute).

172. Nicolas A. J. Croquet, "The Special Tribunal for Lebanon's Innovative Human Rights Framework: Between Enhanced Legislative Codification and Increased Judicial Law-Making," *Georgetown Journal of International Law* 47 (2016), 351, 353–54.

173. Ibid., 433, 436.

174. Ibid, 357.

175. STL Statute, art. 28(2); Croquet, "The Special Tribunal for Lebanon's Innovative Human Rights Framework," 357.

176. Special Tribunal for Lebanon, Rules of Procedure and Evidence, Rule 162, STL/BD/2009/01/Rev.6.

177. Croquet, "The Special Tribunal for Lebanon's Innovative Human Rights Framework," 367–72.

178. Ibid., 432.

179. Charles Chernor Jalloh, "The Special Tribunal for Lebanon: A Defense Perspective," *Vanderbilt Journal of Transnational Law* 47 (2014), 765, 772–73.

180. Maggie Gardner, "Reconsidering Trials *In Absentia* at the Special Tribunal for Lebanon: An Application of Tribunal's Early Jurisprudence," *George Washington International Law Review* 43 (2011), 91.

181. STL Statute, art. 22(1).

182. Ibid., art. 22(2).

183. Ibid., art. 22(3).

184. Gardner, "Reconsidering Trials *In Absentia* at the Special Tribunal for Lebanon," 107–08.

185. Sarah Williams, *Hybrid and Internationalised Criminal Tribunals: Selected Jurisdictional Issues* (Oxford: Hart, 2012), 370.

186. Cerone, "The Politics of International Justice," 58.

187. Wayne Jordash and Tim Parker, "Trials *in Absentia* at the Special Tribunal for Lebanon: Incompatibility with International Human Rights Law," *Journal of International Criminal Justice* 8 (2010), 487, 489; Chris Jenks, "Notice Otherwise Given: Will in Absentia Trials at the Special Tribunal for Lebanon Violate Human Rights?" *Fordham International Law Journal* 33 (2009), 72, 84, 100.

188. Gardner, "Reconsidering Trials *In Absentia* at the Special Tribunal for Lebanon," 104–05.

189. Rome Statute, art. 63(1).

190. Ibid., art. 63(2).

191. Ibid.

192. Human Rights Committee, General Comment No. 32, para. 36, U.N. Doc CCPR/C/GC/32 (August 23, 2007); *Colozza v. Italy*, 89 Eur. Ct. H.R. (ser. A), 14 (1985); Cerone, "The Politics of International Justice," 58.

193. Beth Van Schaack, "Trials in Absentia under International, Domestic, and Lebanese Law," *Just Security*, January 18, 2014, www.justsecurity.org/5839/trials-absentia/.

194. Sluiter et al. eds., *International Criminal Procedure: Principles and Rules*, 768; *Nahimana v. Prosecutor*, Case No. ICTR 99–52-A, ICTR Appeals Chamber, Judgment, paras. 88, 94, 100, 109 (November 28, 2007); *Prosecutor v. Sesay*, Case No. SCSL-04–15-T, SCSL Trial Chamber, Ruling on the Issue of the Refusal of the Third Accused, Augustine Gbao, To Attend Hearing of the Special Court for Sierra Leone on July 7, 2004 and Succeeding Days, paras. 7–8 (July 12, 2004).

195. Van Schaack, "The Building Blocks of Hybrid Justice," 267.

196. McDermott, *Fairness in International Criminal Trials*, 71.

197. Charles Chenor Jalloh, "Does Living by the Sword Mean Dying by the Sword?" *Penn State Law Review* 117 (2013), 707, 742–43. This concern is magnified where *in absentia* proceedings are conducted by tribunals that have little regard for fair trial guarantees, such as the International Crimes Tribunal of Bangladesh, established to prosecute

crimes committed in 1971 by collaborators of the Pakistani Army in Bangladesh. See Geoffrey Robertson, *Report on the International Crimes Tribunal of Bangladesh* (Bosnia: International Forum for Democracy and Human Rights, 2015), 56–57, 84–85, 99.

198. William A. Schabas, "*In Absentia* Proceedings before International Criminal Courts," in Göran Sluiter and Sergey Vasiliev eds., *International Criminal Procedure: Towards a Coherent Body of Law* (London: Cameron May, 2009), 335, 379.

199. Parker and Jordash, "Trials *In Absentia* at the Special Tribunal for Lebanon," 498.

200. Gardner, "Reconsidering Trials *In Absentia* at the Special Tribunal for Lebanon," 107–08.

201. Special Tribunal for Lebanon, "The Cases," www.stl-tsl.org/en/the-cases.

202. Special Advisor to the Secretary-General on Legal Issues Related to Piracy Off the Coast of Somalia, Report of the Special Advisor to the Secretary-General on Legal Issues Related to Piracy Off the Coast of Somalia, Annex, U.N. Doc. S/2011/30, paras. 116–41. (January 25, 2011), https://cil.nus.edu.sg/wp/wp-content/uploads/2010/10/Lang_report_S -2011-301.pdf.

203. Van Schaack, "The Building Blocks of Hybrid Justice," 208–09.

204. Ramji-Nogales, "Designing Bespoke Transitional Justice," 26–27, 43.

205. Dickinson, "The Promise of Hybrid Courts," 296.

206. Ramji-Nogales, "Designing Bespoke Transitional Justice," 24, 30–31.

207. Ibid., 30–31.

208. See, for example, Patrick I. Labuda, "The Hybrid Court for South Sudan? Looking for a Way Forward (Part I)," *Justice in Conflict* (February 23, 2017), www.justiceinconflict.org/ 2017/02/23/the-hybrid-court-for-south-sudan-looking-for-a-way-forward-part-1/ (discussing the resistance of the government of South Sudan to the implementation of a hybrid tribunal for international crimes committed during the conflict in South Sudan).

209. Van Schaack, "The Building Blocks of Hybrid Justice," 249.

210. Ibid., 270–72 (describing the International Crimes Tribunal of Bangladesh).

211. Ramji-Nogales, "Designing Bespoke Transitional Justice," 54–55.

212. Ibid., 55–56.

213. Christoph J. M. Safferling, *Toward an International Criminal Procedure* (Oxford: Oxford University Press, 2001), 1–2.

214. Ireneusz C. Kamiński, "'Historical Situations' in the Jurisprudence of the European Court of Human Rights in Strasbourg," *Polish Yearbook of International Law* 30 (2010), 9, 41; *Kononov v. Latvia*, App. No. 36376/04, Eur. Ct. H.R., Judgment, paras. 143, 213, 227, 244 (May 17, 2010).

215. Van Schaack, "The Building Blocks of Hybrid Justice," 251; *Case of Maktouf and Damjanović v. Bosnia and Herzegovina*, App. Nos. 2312/08 and 34179/08, Eur. Ct. H. R., Judgment, paras. 65–75 (July 18, 2013).

216. Darryl Robinson, "Serving the Interests of Justice: Amnesties, Truth Commissions and the International Criminal Court," *European Journal of International Law* 14 (2003), 481, 504; Carrie J. Niebur Eisnaugle, Note, "An International 'Truth Commission': Utilizing Restorative Justice as an Alternative to Retribution," *Vanderbilt Journal of Transnational Law* 36 (2003), 209, 222–23. Some commissions, however, have authority to grant amnesty from criminal prosecution to individuals who participate in the truth-seeking process, a source of considerable controversy. Roy L. Brooks, "Post-Conflict Justice in the Aftermath of Modern Slavery," *George Washington International Law Review* 46 (2014), 243, 263.

217. United States Institute of Peace, "Truth Commission Digital Collection" (March 16, 2011), www.usip.org/publications/2011/03/truth-commission-digital-collection.

218. Stromseth, "Pursuing Accountability for Atrocities after Conflict," 320–22.

219. Alhagi Marong, "Unlocking the Mysteriousness of Complementarity: In Search of a *Forum Conveniens* for Trial of the Leaders of the Lord's Resistance Army," *Georgia Journal of International and Comparative Law* 40 (2011), 67, 84–85.

5

The Selectivity Challenge in International Criminal Law

The selection of situations and cases for prosecution remains one of the most intractable challenges facing the ICC and other international criminal tribunals.[1] Selectivity has historically had several, overlapping dimensions, including: victor's justice (the claim that the winning side of a conflict is not prosecuted); the insulation of officials of powerful nations and their allies from prosecution; shielding high-level officials while holding only less culpable, lower-level officials criminally responsible; and a disproportionate focus on particular countries and regions.

Since Nuremberg, ICL has had to contend with accusations of victor's justice. This critique was captured vividly in Justice Rahadbinod Pal's scathing dissent from the judgment of the Tokyo Tribunal, which he characterized as a political affair cloaked with a judicial appearance and as an exercise in formalized vengeance.[2]

Subsequent international tribunals have shown greater sensitivity to the importance of prosecuting international crimes regardless of the nationality of the perpetrator. The statutes for the ICTY and ICTR are neutral on their face as to the identity of the perpetrator, referring instead to crimes committed in a particular territory during a specified time period.[3] Moreover, the judges for these two *ad hoc* tribunals had no direct connection to the region that suffered the atrocities, in contrast to Nuremberg, where the tribunal was composed of judges from the winning side.[4] The ICTY brought war crimes cases against ethnic Serbs, Croats, and Muslims, including against Croatian generals.[5] In one important case, for example, the ICTY prosecuted Bosnian Muslim and Croat officials for their roles in crimes committed at a prison camp in Bosnia where Bosnian Serbs were grossly mistreated.[6] While the ICTY arguably focused disproportionately on crimes committed by Serb forces,[7] it brought "a semblance of balance to its indictments and prosecutions,"[8] and its greater focus on Serb crimes roughly approximated criminal responsibility on the ground, as Serb forces committed the vast majority of crimes.[9]

Proceedings at the ICTY raised a distinct set of concerns about the insulation of major powers from prosecution. Following NATO's bombing of Kosovo as part of Operation Allied Force, a group of law professors filed a war crimes complaint with the ICTY Prosecutor against American and Western European political and military leaders and pressed the Prosecutor to bring war crimes charges, including for the killing of civilians.[10] The ICTY Prosecutor appointed an independent committee to consider the allegations and subsequently informed the Security Council that she would not investigate further based on the committee's conclusions.[11] The report distinguished, for example, the use of cluster bombs by Serbian nationalist Milan Martić, whom the ICTY prosecuted for deliberately targeting the civilian population of Zagreb, from NATO's use of cluster bombs, which the report described as consistent with proportionality principles under International Humanitarian Law (IHL).[12] Critics nonetheless asserted that the investigation was biased towards NATO, selectively applied IHL's proportionality rules, and undermined the ICTY's claim to impartiality.[13] They also complained that the UN Security Council, led by the United States, excluded the crime of aggression from the ICTY statute, thus avoiding politically charged questions not only about the right of various states of the former Yugoslavia to declare their independence, but also about the legality of NATO strikes in Kosovo.[14] Defenses of the Prosecutor's decision emphasized that electing not to pursue NATO officials was consistent with a pre-existing prosecutorial policy of focusing on high-level officials responsible for the atrocities committed in the former Yugoslavia. In addition to the practical and political obstacles, a further investigation into Operation Allied Force did not appear likely to advance that stated prosecutorial goal.[15]

Selectivity issues were more pronounced at the ICTR, with its exclusive focus on prosecuting one side of the conflict (Hutu), despite evidence of grave violations committed by the other side (Tutsi).[16] Efforts by the ICTR's former Chief Prosecutor Carla Del Ponte to investigate Tutsi massacres of Hutus, which was vigorously opposed by the Tutsi-controlled government of Rwanda, helped prompt the United States and other members of the UN Security Council to seek her removal.[17] Such one-sided approaches to prosecuting mass atrocities triggered accusations of "victor's justice."[18] Cases such as that of Jean-Bosco Barayagwiza, a key figure in the violence that swept through Rwanda in 1994, also underscored how political pressures can influence prosecutorial decisions. In Barayagwiza's case, the government of Rwanda suspended cooperation with the ICTR after the Trial Chamber ordered the release of the accused Hutu génocidaire based on pretrial defects, prompting the Appeals Chamber to reverse the dismissal as too drastic a remedy.[19] The tribunal's exclusive focus on Hutu crimes as well as such instances of heavy-handed political interference prompted attacks on the ICTR's legitimacy.[20] The ICTR, however, rejected legal challenges by individual defendants claiming that their prosecution violated the principle of equality and upheld the Prosecutor's exercise of discretion in selecting defendants for investigation and prosecution absent evidence of invidious discrimination against a particular defendant.[21] The ICTY reached a similar result in deciding selectivity challenges brought before it by individual defendants.[22]

Selection decisions have also raised issues at hybrid tribunals.[23] One hybrid tribunal, the Special Court for Sierra Leone (SCSL), did prosecute individuals from all sides of the conflict.[24] But it has been criticized for prosecuting only cases of political expediency to the Sierra Leonean government.[25] Another hybrid tribunal – the recently established Kosovo Relocated Specialist Judicial Institution (KRSJI) – expressly contemplates prosecuting atrocities committed by members of the victorious party, the Kosovo Liberation Army (KLA), at the end of the war in Kosovo from 1998 to 2000, thus seeking to address the perceived failure of the prior tribunal for Kosovo, the Regulation 64 Panels, to address those crimes.[26] The degree to which the KRSJI will be able to prosecute members of the KLA, whom the local population widely views as heroes for carrying out a just war, remains to be seen.

As discussed previously, selectivity concerns are particularly acute at the ICC, which had raised hopes for a more depoliticized application of principles of individual criminal responsibility through the creation of an independent prosecutor, but which faces design limitations, including restrictions on its jurisdiction, and practical obstacles that make those hopes difficult to achieve. Critics frequently seize upon the Court's docket as evidence of various forms of selection bias, from protecting major powers and their allies from criminal responsibility to focusing disproportionately on crimes committed in certain regions (particularly, countries in Africa).[27] They also point to the ICC's past failures to investigate and prosecute all sides of a conflict, such as in Uganda, the Democratic Republic of Congo, and the Côte D'Ivoire.[28] The ICC's seeming powerlessness to address these concerns, especially given the continued UN Security Council influence over selection decisions, has colored perceptions of the Court's fairness and legitimacy.[29]

Selectivity concerns extend to potential new tribunals as well. They surround, for example, proposals for a future hybrid tribunal for Syria and Iraq that would focus only on crimes committed by the Assad regime or, alternatively, by ISIS, despite widespread international law violations committed by all sides of the conflict.[30] Any such focus would reinforce perceptions of a one-sided approach to international criminal justice and weaken the chances for lasting peace and security in the region.[31]

Paradoxically, ICL's selectivity problem has deepened even as it has benefitted from other advances that enhance the fairness of international criminal trials, such as greater attention to due process standards designed to protect individual defendants.[32] Continued asymmetries in the selection of situations and cases – even if largely the product of a tribunal's design and the practical obstacles it faces – will hinder the ICC and other international tribunals from satisfying broader conceptions of fairness rooted in the equal application of criminal responsibility under international law. The remainder of this chapter examines possible ways of addressing selectivity challenges in ICL, focusing mainly on the ICC. It then proposes

greater incorporation of distributive considerations in prosecutorial selection decisions, particularly through efforts designed to express the principle that no individual is above the law.

***

A trial's fairness is essential to its legitimacy in both international and domestic
settings.[33] International criminal courts gain moral authority from the fairness of
their proceedings, and the severity of the alleged crimes deepens the importance of
fairness to a trial's integrity.[34] Protections for the accused are thus particularly
significant in an area of law as "politicised, culturally freighted and passionately
punitive as war crimes."[35] International criminal trials, moreover, must be fair not
merely in some, but in all aspects.[36] Regardless of the forum, a trial's fairness is
commonly assessed in terms of its procedures – more specifically, whether those
procedures safeguard the rights of the accused and are applied equally to defendants.[37] The selection of situations, defendants, and crimes for prosecution, however, also represents an important measure of a tribunal's fairness and, by extension,
its legitimacy.

Unpacking the concept of legitimacy helps underscore the importance of selection decisions. Legitimacy may broadly be understood as acting with justification,[38]
although some political theorists have stressed that legitimacy additionally requires
the continuing consent of those subject to the exercise of political power and not
merely the justness *ex ante* of the state and its institutions.[39] For purposes of
discussion here, legitimacy may be divided along the following axis: legal, moral,
and sociological.[40] Legal legitimacy describes adherence to legal norms and procedures; moral legitimacy focuses on the justness of outcomes; and sociological
legitimacy measures the perception of relevant audiences.[41] Thus, while the first
two categories (legal and moral legitimacy) are based on intrinsic qualities, the third
category (sociological legitimacy) is based on perceptions by others.[42] If normative
legitimacy centers mainly on "the qualities of the ruler," sociological legitimacy
turns on "the attitudes of the ruled."[43]

While distinct conceptually, these categories are dynamic and can intersect in
various ways. Thomas Franck, for example, described legitimacy as "a property
of a rule or rule-making institution which itself exerts a pull towards compliance
on those addressed normatively because those addressed believe that the rule or
institution has come into being and operates in accordance with generally
accepted principles of right process."[44] Rights, Franck argued, are thus "defined,
acquired, and protected through the legitimate and legitimating processes of the
community."[45] As Franck's description suggests, a norm or norm-generating
institution that possesses legal and moral legitimacy is more likely to be perceived as such, as evidenced by increased compliance among relevant actors and
acceptance by relevant audiences. Similarly, Allen Buchanan and Robert
Keohane have observed that legitimacy for global governance institutions

implies the moral right of institutional agents to make rules and secure compliance with them and, correspondingly, provides a moral reason for people subject to those rules to follow them.[46]

The compliance pull that results from perceptions about an institution's adherence to principles of right process can increase that institution's fidelity to those principles through a type of feedback loop.[47] Abram Chayes accordingly described legitimacy as the product of a dynamic, negotiated process that rests ultimately on "the ability of a judicial pronouncement to sustain itself in the dialogue" with other political forces and "to generate assent over the long haul."[48] Because legitimate institutions typically have diffuse support among the public, the public will back those institutions' continued operation even when it disagrees with their decisions in particular cases.[49]

Legal and moral legitimacy do not, however, necessarily produce sociological legitimacy. The decision of a tribunal, for example, may be justified normatively because it emanates from "a fair and accepted procedure, is applied equally and without invidious discrimination, and does not offend minimum standards of fairness and equity."[50] The decision may also reach a morally just outcome. Yet, relevant audiences may still regard it as illegitimate, which in turn affects acceptance of the decision within a given society. In the context of a criminal trial, fairness thus necessarily implicates both the actual treatment of an accused individual and the perception of that treatment by the public.[51] In the context of international criminal justice, the audience is often broad and diverse, encompassing not only the individuals and societies directly affected by atrocities, but also a wider audience that includes other states, their citizens, and nongovernment organizations and other civil society actors.[52] Even if an international or hybrid tribunal has established trial procedures that are widely regarded as fair, the tribunal's choice of defendants for investigation and prosecution may still weaken its perceived legitimacy among at least some segments of this audience.

In the case of the ICC, the selection of situations for investigation and prosecution is most likely to impact the Court's standing within the broader international community. By contrast, the selection of cases within a given situation – and, particularly, the prosecution of only one side of a conflict in which atrocities were committed by all sides – has the greatest potential impact on directly affected communities. Such intraselectivity decisions can create "a problematic symbiosis between ICL and domestic arrangements of power that produce or depend upon systematic repression or violence" and can reinforce neocolonial patterns that marginalize certain domestic groups while privileging others.[53] Such decisions can also undermine the legitimacy of the ICC and other international courts within affected communities by conveying negative messages about a particular group's moral worth and claim to protection of the law.[54] Mark Kersten explains, for example, how the Ugandan government used an ICC prosecution to help weaken and delegitimize the rebel Lord's Resistance Army (LRA) in northern Uganda, while ensuring that the ICC Prosecutor did not investigate any members of the Ugandan government or military forces, including by withholding any possible cooperation. The resulting asymmetry, in which all ICC arrest warrants were issued for senior LRA commanders, undermined the post-conflict process in Uganda by helping frame the conflict simplistically as a battle between good and evil.[55] While the ICC can potentially mitigate such perceptions through its characterization of selection decisions, it cannot overcome them as long as its focus consistently remains on one side of a conflict.

The Rome Statute requires that the ICC Prosecutor treat like cases alike and apply a consistent set of criteria to each case.[56] But an *ex ante* commitment to treat like cases alike, which is a necessary component of fairness, may nevertheless be insufficient to achieve normative and sociological legitimacy even when coupled with the use of standards and procedures designed to realize that goal. The Rome Statute's threshold gravity requirement, for example, provides a potential means of grounding selection decision in generally applicable criteria.[57] If those decisions are made in a nonarbitrary manner through a fair process – and the chosen situations and cases objectively satisfy the minimum gravity threshold – the decisions can claim normative legitimacy.[58] But the minimum gravity threshold does not dictate which of the many potential international crimes the ICC should pursue given the Court's limited resources and other practical constraints.[59] The ICC Prosecutor's choice to pursue certain cases from among many potential ones thus exposes her to potential criticism. If the Prosecutor consistently selects the least serious cases without good reason, it could undermine the Court's normative legitimacy.[60] But even if the Prosecutor does not engage in such a skewed pattern of decision-making, and even if she provides cogent explanations about which situations and cases are selected and why, it will not necessarily ensure the Court's perceived legitimacy, particularly when those decisions collectively result in a predominant focus on particular regions or sides of a conflict. Studies of procedural and distributive justice in national criminal justice systems provide additional insights into the challenges confronting the ICC and other international criminal tribunals as they pursue the goals of fairness and accountability in the context of selection decisions.

***

Selection decisions are typically regarded as more important to the fairness and legitimacy of international tribunals than to domestic courts.[61] In national criminal justice systems, prosecutors are not only expected to pursue the most serious cases, but also possess the resources and means to do so in most circumstances.[62] Additionally, given the volume of cases prosecuted by domestic courts, the decision not to prosecute in particular instances is less likely to trigger broader questions about a system's overall legitimacy.[63] In many countries, moreover, prosecutors are accountable to the citizenry through the democratic process. Their selection choices can thus claim legitimacy because they reflect, at least to some degree, the views of the elected government and populace.[64] International courts, by contrast, handle far fewer cases, and prosecutors typically must make difficult choices about which, among a large number of international crimes, they have the resources and support to tackle. Selection decisions thus assume a greater symbolic importance. International courts, like other international institutions, also lack the grounding in domestic politics and the connection to ordinary citizens that national courts possess.[65] Moreover, given the relative weakness of coercive mechanisms, international tribunals, like other international institutions, depend heavily on securing compliance through their acceptance as legitimate, thus giving legitimacy an added practical dimension in this context.[66]

The contrast between the impact of selection decisions on domestic and international courts may, however, be less stark than is generally assumed. Selection decisions also matter in national criminal justice systems, sometimes in high-profile cases, but particularly in the aggregate. Patterns of prosecutorial decision-making, especially those that disproportionately target particular racial or ethnic groups, can erode a system's legitimacy among those groups, regardless how fair the legal procedures are in individual cases.[67] Also, the capacity of national justice systems to prosecute serious crimes varies significantly. While courts in advanced western democracies typically prosecute the most serious crimes committed within their respective jurisdictions, they too have faced challenges in ensuring equal application of the law, whether in confronting white-collar crime[68] or avoiding racial disparities in prosecution and sentencing.[69] States that have weak law enforcement capacity or that lack a strong rule-of-law tradition confront particular challenges. Such states not only fail to prosecute much serious crime, such as narcotic trafficking and public corruption, but also often conduct prosecutions in a manner that protects powerful interests and individuals.[70] In these circumstances, selection decisions can undermine the legitimacy of a criminal justice system and public institutions more generally.[71]

It should not be surprising, therefore, that studies of domestic law enforcement and criminal courts can help inform assessments of international criminal tribunals, both in their procedural and distributive dimensions.[72] In particular, studies of national criminal justice systems suggest how distributive considerations – which encompass the cases chosen for investigation and prosecution – can impact the perceived fairness and legitimacy of international criminal tribunals. They also underscore the risks of focusing solely on legal procedures designed to provide fair trials to individual defendants and excluding consideration of broader patterns of case selection in the administration of criminal justice.

Pioneering work by Tom Tyler and others emphasizes the role of procedural justice in local policing and courts. Tyler has shown how perceptions of legitimacy crystalize around judgments about the manner in which police and courts treat individuals. By shaping perceptions of law enforcement and judges, these interpersonal experiences help determine compliance with the law.[73] For Tyler, fair treatment, rather than fair outcomes, is the most critical factor in creating a perception of legitimacy and fostering compliance with public authority.[74] Procedural justice scholarship thus builds on the Weberian insight that power, when viewed as legitimate, is transformed into authority and triggers a duty to obey.[75] It has significant implications for the administration of criminal justice at the local level, where enforcement impacts large segments of the population and contributes to judgments about the legitimacy of law enforcement agents, prosecutors, and courts.[76] These institutions cannot continually violate norms of fair process and remain effective,[77] particularly in contexts where legal compliance depends more on moral compunction than on a fear of getting caught and punished for lawbreaking.[78]

Social identification plays an important role in theories of procedural justice. Fair treatment helps generate positive identification with legal structures and institutions by demonstrating that power-holders are acting in fair, justified, and measured ways.[79] It also signals to members of different social groups salient messages concerning their respective inclusion, status, and value within a given society.[80] The social identification resulting from fair treatment can motivate adherence to rules and laws governing behavior[81] and strengthen alignment with state actors and institutions.[82] Conversely, unfair treatment can weaken social identification and contribute to a sense of marginalization.[83] Such treatment can not only convey an abuse of power, but also alienate individuals from the group that the power holders represent.[84] This dynamic frequently plays out along racial and ethnic lines, reinforcing perceptions of outsider status among particular subgroups.[85]

Distributive factors also impact the fairness and legitimacy of national criminal justice systems. Whereas procedural justice concentrates on the treatment of individuals at the micro level, distributive justice focuses on broader patterns within a society.

The distribution of criminal law has a dual nature. First, it embodies an exercise of coercive power by legal institutions and actors – a form of corrective justice designed to punish wrongdoing.[86] This power includes choices regarding arrest, charging, prosecution, and sentencing. While these choices are directed primarily at individuals, they can produce racial disparities or other imbalances across groups when considered in the aggregate.[87] Second, criminal law represents a public good or resource that is distributed among communities and individuals in society.[88] It provides security and safety to members of society as well as satisfying public demands to hold responsible those individuals who violate shared norms.[89] The uneven distribution of criminal law resources across communities not only reflects power asymmetries, but also can contribute to different perceptions of the fairness of the state's exercise of criminal law authority. The media further shapes those perceptions within a society.[90]

Some scholars have elevated the importance of the fair treatment of individuals over distributive considerations. William Stuntz, for example, maintained that attitudes about law enforcement turn principally on the manner in which law enforcement treats individuals, and not on how law enforcement selects suspects or treats different groups collectively.[91] Some domestic courts, moreover, have reinforced the focus on procedural fairness for individual defendants by erecting barriers to claims targeting bias in charging and sentencing decisions.[92] But the distribution of criminal law authority – whether as a form of coercion or as a public resource – can affect its legitimacy, even where its exercise is procedurally fair on a micro-level. Institutionalized practices in criminal justice, including how courts and police treat different groups, and background knowledge of those practices, inform public perceptions.[93] Excessive focus on the fair treatment of individuals – at the expense of this broader social context – ignores a key factor contributing to the perceived fairness and legitimacy of criminal justice actors and institutions.

Some criminal justice scholars have drawn on concepts of social alienation to look beyond the procedural justice framework.[94] Monica Bell, for example, has addressed the lack of social inclusion across different groups under a theory of legal estrangement.[95] Legal estrangement theory places the community, rather than the personal interactions of individuals, at the center of how justice is experienced.[96] It also considers historical patterns and the role of collective memory in constructing social identity.[97] This focus on collective experience, including the experience of how public authority and resources are distributed across different communities, helps inform how those communities perceive criminal justice institutions.[98]

Theories of procedural and distributive justice map onto the international legal landscape in several ways. Legitimacy in the international sphere continues to depend partly on generally accepted principles of right process.[99] But it also can depend on the substantive distribution of benefits and goods across borders, and not simply within a given society.[100] Such benefits may include the equitable distribution of resources in the prosecution of international crimes and the equal application of international criminal law authority. Moreover, the difficulty of securing compliance through coercive measures in international affairs places greater emphasis on the compliance pull generated by the acceptance of ICL rules and decisions as fair and legitimate.[101] This acceptance is also critical to the internalization of international legal norms at the national and local level.[102]

The treatment of individuals, to be sure, continues to matter, and procedural safeguards remain a *sine qua non* of international criminal justice. But distributive considerations matter as well. International tribunals prosecute a relatively small number of cases, and the gap between the number of international crimes and the limited resources available to pursue them remains wide. Further, international criminal prosecutions often seek to reach a global audience as well as individuals, stakeholders, and communities in affected countries. The comparatively low number of international criminal prosecutions gives them greater symbolic weight than most domestic prosecutions. The selection of situations and cases for investigation and prosecution thus conveys significant information about an international criminal tribunal's priorities to multiple audiences at the local, national, and international level.

Further, international criminal prosecutions rely on legal norms that transcend borders and justify overriding national sovereignty. The procedural mechanisms by which criminal responsibility is imposed on individual defendants can promote acceptance of those norms and facilitate identification with international criminal justice institutions through an associative process. But even prosecutions that are procedurally fair in individual cases can still diminish identification with ICC's universal norms and increase marginalization when, in the aggregate, those prosecutions use skewed towards certain regions or against weaker countries or, within a given situation, are directed exclusively at one side of the conflict.

Prosecutions, moreover, are commonly viewed through the prism of past experiences and collective memory. International criminal prosecutions that appear to favor the victorious and insulate the powerful can reinforce a pre-existing sense of alienation and mistrust developed from past experience. Such perceptions can not only affect the willingness of governments to cooperate with international tribunals on practical challenges such as evidence collection and access to witnesses, but can also hinder acceptance of the legal norms that international criminal prosecutions aspire to advance and embed within societies.

Applying lessons of social psychology to survey data about how affected populations perceive international criminal courts, Stuart Ford has shown the important effect selection decisions can have on perceptions of legitimacy.[103] He argues that groups within an affected country or region are likely to view a tribunal as legitimate in direct relation to the degree to which that tribunal's charging decisions support a group's dominant internal narrative of the conflict.[104] This might suggest that any attempt by a tribunal to assign criminal responsibility will necessarily cause a net loss in perceived legitimacy among the affected population as a whole.[105] Yet, Ford also recognizes that this negative impact can be mitigated where courts help realign dominant internal narratives with what actually happened on the ground as part of a larger transitional justice process aimed at redressing past violence and abuses.[106] Prosecutorial charging decisions that seek to apportion blame among all responsible parties can contribute to this realignment, while bolstering a tribunal's perceived legitimacy and strengthening its normative legitimacy by attributing criminal responsibility to all sides, where such responsibility is warranted.

The importance of distributive considerations is magnified for courts established to enforce norms of international justice. The legitimacy of human rights courts, for example, is significantly influenced by perceptions of the most vulnerable groups since those groups form key constituencies that such courts are meant to serve. Decisions by human rights courts that elevate pragmatism over principle in response to external pressures can undermine their credibility and influence.[107] International criminal tribunals are similarly premised on universal norms of justice and generate expectations that those norms will be applied in a neutral manner, independent of power disparities among states. Greater emphasis on addressing distorting influences on selection decisions both across and within situations – especially where it requires resisting geopolitical pressures – can help counter perceptions that international prosecutions are necessarily directed against particular regions or invariably serve dominant power interests at the expense of weaker states or communities.

Thus far, ICL has achieved greater success in the area of procedural rather than distributive justice. The ICC provides the most notable example of this divide, with its elaborate procedural safeguards afforded an accused person, on the one hand, and its disproportionate focus on countries in Africa at the expense of international crimes committed elsewhere, on the other. Several factors help explain this focus, including: the number of prosecutions resulting from self-referrals by African states; the magnitude of the atrocities committed in several African countries; the ICC's design, which includes significant jurisdictional limitations and avenues for the exercise of Security Council influence; a myriad of practical obstacles from apprehending suspects to gathering evidence; and a fear of stoking major power opposition through controversial prosecutions and thereby weakening the Court at a relatively early stage in its development. Yet, the selectivity challenges the ICC faces are in several respects a more extreme version of those confronted by all international and hybrid criminal tribunals. The remainder of this chapter considers some ways of addressing these challenges to achieve more fully the goals of fairness and accountability in international criminal justice.

***

Various proposals seek to tackle selectivity issues in ICL. While these proposals focus mainly on the ICC, they contain principles broadly applicable to other international criminal tribunals. Some approaches advocate the adoption of formal legal standards that can be applied equally across a diverse set of situations and cases. Others emphasize the need to reconcile the aspiration of equal application of the law with the practical challenges international courts face and with ICL's other objectives, such as promoting peace and stability in societies devastated by war and civil strife.

Some commentators, joined by NGOs, maintain that no individual should escape accountability for grave crimes.[108] This position is grounded in the human rights norm of equality before the law.[109] It opposes impunity for international crimes and rejects the provision of amnesty to individuals who commit them. While this approach draws on retributivist rationales, it also contains an instrumentalist dimension that predicates the establishment of future peace and stability on ensuring legal accountability for past atrocities. Aggressively pursuing the equal application of individual criminal responsibility could help international criminal tribunals resist pressures to avoid controversial or politically sensitive prosecutions. At the same time, this categorical anti-impunity approach faces steep obstacles given the jurisdictional and practical constraints under which international tribunals, and the ICC in particular, operate. It thus faces significant limits as a path to enhancing fairness and legitimacy, and could have an adverse effect by raising expectations beyond current levels of feasibility.

Another approach concentrates less on outcomes and more on the process used to reach decisions. It relies on the notion, rooted in procedural justice theory, that legitimacy will result from the fairness of the process used to select situations and cases for investigation and prosecution. Allison Marston Danner, for example, has argued that prosecutorial decisions will be viewed as more legitimate if they result from a principled and transparent decision-making process.[110] Adopting publicly promulgated guidelines and methods for selecting situations and cases, she suggests, can help increase fairness and shield prosecutors from accusations of politicized prosecutions.[111] The ICC Prosecutor has drawn on this approach, seeking to channel prosecutorial discretion by articulating overarching standards of independence, impartiality, and objectivity, for the selection of both situations and cases.[112] Such standards can help enhance legitimacy by contributing to a perception, if not a reality, of bounded discretion and greater transparency.

Process-based approaches that rely on the articulation of generalized standards nonetheless have limitations. These standards do not dictate how the ICC should determine which situations or cases to pursue from among the various ones that cross the gravity threshold. The Rome Statute's gravity requirement is intended to help the ICC fulfill its goal of prosecuting "the most serious crimes of concern to the international community as a whole."[113] But the Rome Statute's lack of specificity about the meaning of gravity reflects a broader debate among the various parties that negotiated the treaty over which situations and cases the Court should prioritize and about when prosecution is appropriate.[114] Disagreement over interpretation of the gravity requirement arose in the ICC's first prosecution. In *Lubanga*, the Pre-Trial Chamber said that the bar should be set at widespread or systematic crimes and senior-level defendants who bear the greatest responsibility for those crimes,[115] but the Appeals Chamber rejected such a high bar.[116] In a separate opinion, one judge explained that the gravity requirement should exclude only insignificant crimes.[117] The Appeals Chamber, however, did not clarify how the ICC should choose from among situations and cases that cross the minimum gravity threshold.

The malleability of the factors articulated by the ICC Prosecutor to assess gravity – the scale, nature, manner of commission, and impact of the crimes – can lead the Prosecutor to privilege some factors over others given the limited resources at her disposal.[118] The term "interests of justice," which the ICC Prosecutor must consider in deciding whether to decline to undertake an investigation or bring charges for crimes that meet the gravity threshold,[119] is also ambiguous. It does not resolve, for example, whether, and to what extent, the existence of other, noncriminal transitional justice mechanisms, such as truth and reconciliation commissions, might justify a decision not to investigate or prosecute grave international crimes.[120]

Process-based approaches thus face hurdles not only because of the indeterminacy of the underlying criteria, but also because of the dilemmas commonly encountered in the transitional justice setting, where other priorities, such as maintaining peace and stability, can sometimes weigh against prosecution.[121] The need to determine when a state is engaging in a good-faith effort to investigate or prosecute international crimes under the Rome Statute's complementarity framework injects an additional layer of uncertainty into the selection process.[122] At the same time, relying on the uniform application of *ex ante* standards can create an unrealistic expectation that ICC violations will be treated equally if those standards are followed.

The ICC Prosecutor has rejected the need to address perceptions of unfairness in selection decisions. The Prosecutor is certainly correct that she should not, for example, seek to create "the appearance of parity within a situation between rival parties by selecting cases that would not otherwise meet the criteria" established by her office.[123] But refusing to allow perceptions of the need for greater parity to influence decisions where cases do not otherwise meet applicable selection criteria is not the same as allowing those perceptions to play some role when choosing from among cases that do meet those criteria. A more candid assessment of the importance of perceptions of parity could help the Court address the legitimacy deficit surrounding selection decisions, particularly given the significant resource constraints that effectively require the Prosecutor to forgo pursuing cases that satisfy the Rome Statute's threshold jurisdictional and admissibility requirements.

Other commentators place less emphasis on the neutral application of legal standards and seek other paths to enhancing the legitimacy of selection decisions. Some have argued, for example, that international criminal tribunals should abandon the aspiration of treating all international crimes the same, at least until tribunals gain more enforcement power. Stephanos Bibas and William Burke-White argue, for example, that tribunals should instead focus on the most egregious offenses, as measured by such factors as the number of victims and degree of harm and suffering inflicted.[124] Yet, even assuming one could objectively identify a "worst" set of crimes from among a broader spectrum of international criminal law violations, this focus could still produce asymmetric results in the selection of situations and cases. Concentrating on the "worst" crimes, for example, would not necessarily address the various complaints regarding selection decisions, from more recent criticisms of the ICC's focus on Africa to longstanding concerns about victor's justice and the insulation of officials from the most powerful nations from international criminal responsibility. To the contrary, a continued focus on mass atrocities would likely maintain the ICC's current trajectory of selection decisions since such atrocities are typically committed by weak or failed states, many of which are in Africa.[125] It would also limit the ICC's important role in developing nascent norms in areas where principles of international criminal responsibility are less firmly established.

Others question not only the possibility, but also the desirability of an apolitical international criminal tribunal. As Alexander Greenawalt has argued, the choice of whether, when, and whom to prosecute in societies undergoing transition after mass violence and social upheaval has significant ramifications.[126] Even if prosecutors could further the goals of independence and impartiality by applying objective legal criteria across the board, such policies would not necessarily advance ICL's broader ends, including the promotion of peace and stability. The ICC Prosecutor, Greenawalt maintains, should thus generally defer to decisions by legitimate political actors at the national level as they seek to navigate the thicket of competing policy demands and trade-offs facing societies in transition.[127] ICC intervention, he explains, should instead focus on cases of ongoing and unambiguous ICL violations by high-level officials. Greenawalt offers a more nuanced view of the Rome Statute's complementarity regime, with the ICC Prosecutor generally adopting a less interventionist stance in societies undergoing transition. His approach could lead to selection decisions more sensitive to local context and to the ICC's broader aims beyond imposing individual criminal responsibility for international crimes. But it is unlikely to alter negative perceptions resulting from distributive imbalances in the situations and cases before the Court.

Other approaches emphasize the symbolic importance of prosecutions in addressing selectivity challenges in international criminal law. While they vary in other respects, these approaches recognize the expressive value of prosecuting international crimes. Diane Orentlicher, for example, has described the utility of exemplary prosecutions. Even if most individuals suspected of international crimes cannot be prosecuted, she argues, targeted prosecutions of select individuals can help bolster the duty to prosecute under ICL and strengthen the norm of accountability.[128]

A generalized notion of exemplary prosecutions alone, however, will not resolve underlying debates about how a tribunal's scarce resources should be allocated or how the ICC Prosecutor should choose from among various situations and cases that meet the minimum level of severity. Margaret deGuzman has argued, therefore, that the ICC Prosecutor should instead focus her limited resources on articulating and expressing legal norms through illustrative prosecutions.[129] Such prosecutions would target particular offenses, such as attacks on peacekeepers, the use of child soldiers, or the destruction of cultural sites, to harness criminal law's potential to develop and entrench specific norms and values.[130] The ICC Prosecutor's recent decision to focus case selection more on historically under-prosecuted crimes, such as destruction of the environment, illegal exploitation of natural resources, and illegal dispossession of land, recognizes the utility of illustrative prosecutions.[131] This expressive approach thus prioritizes representative cases to strengthen both the impact and legitimacy of prosecutorial choices.

Reorienting the focus around the expression of norms through the prosecution of representative cases is particularly suited to international tribunals, such as ICC, where the number of crimes potentially subject to prosecution greatly outstrips capacity and where dependence on state cooperation remains a persistent challenge. It also offers an opportunity to build support among diverse constituencies, particularly if those norms are identified through a collaborative and inclusive process that incorporates local actors. Yet, this focus does not directly address the endemic perception of selectivity bias or its causes. Prioritizing the expression of particular international criminal law norms could still result in the disproportionate prosecution of cases from a particular region, a focus on one side of a conflict in which crimes are committed by all sides, and the continued insulation of powerful states and their allies from prosecution when they commit international crimes.

To address these concerns, an expressive approach to selection decisions should also incorporate a dimension of distributive fairness, a path the ICC has thus far resisted.[132] In particular, the ICC and other international criminal tribunals should seek to express the principle that no individual is above the law – both across and within situations – through their decisions to investigate and, where the evidence supports it, to prosecute. Even modest steps in this direction could contribute to an alternative narrative about the work of the ICC and other international tribunals and help counter the perception that international criminal justice merely tracks the preferences of the strong and their supporters.[133]

There are several possible paths for incorporating distributive considerations into the selection of situations and cases. At the ICC, the Office of the Prosecutor could make communicating the principle that no one is above the law an express goal to expand the Court's geographic focus and instantiate a commitment to pursuing international crimes committed by major powers to the extent they fall within the Court's jurisdiction. The Prosecutor could also prioritize her investigation of state actors to overcome past patterns of sheltering state forces and better ensure the prosecution of all sides of a conflict where warranted by the evidence. This prioritization would be consistent with the Rome Statute's gravity requirement since state involvement represents "the archetype of international crime and the paradigm of impunity."[134] It would also be consistent with the ICC's aim of securing "lasting respect for and the enforcement of international justice"[135] since the achievement of those ends depends on the Court's maintaining support among its various constituencies.

The ICC Prosecutor could additionally factor distributive considerations within the "interests of justice" analysis under the Rome Statute. Specifically, the Rome Statute provides that the Prosecutor may decline to initiate an investigation or pursue a prosecution where she concludes it would not serve "the interests of justice."[136] This provision is designed to give the Prosecutor discretion not to proceed in exceptional circumstances that warrant departure from the Rome Statute's broad anti-impunity norm.[137] The goal of communicating the principle of equal application of law, long considered a cornerstone of the rule of law,[138] could provide a reason for the ICC Prosecutor not to exercise this discretion and instead proceed with an investigation or prosecution of a crime that satisfies the statutory requirements of gravity and complementarity and that falls within the Court's jurisdiction. Also, the Pre-Trial Chamber could consider the importance of expressing this principle in its review of a decision by the ICC Prosecutor not to open a formal investigation or to pursue a prosecution based on the interests of justice.[139] Statutes for future international (or hybrid) tribunals could be drafted in a manner that not only exposes all sides of a particular conflict to potential prosecution for the commission of international crimes, but also makes the evenhanded application of individual criminal responsibility an explicit goal.

Additionally, ICC prosecutors and investigators could seek to identify opportunities to lessen their reliance on state cooperation for conducting investigations. The increased ability of individuals to document international crimes and upload them to the Internet by means of smart phones with cameras and connectivity, for example, could help decrease the dependence of ICC investigators on state authorities for gathering evidence of international crimes.[140] While the ICC will still need to rely heavily on states to arrest suspects and bring them to The Hague, and while the Court will have to ensure the authenticity and security of video evidence, such technological advances could provide the ICC with greater independence from state authorities in gathering evidence and selecting cases.

Limited resources, structural constraints, and practical obstacles will continue to impede efforts to achieve the equal application of law. Equal application of law, moreover, cannot be reduced to a quota or other easily measurable form of quantification. But the ICC and other international criminal tribunals could nevertheless mitigate criticisms surrounding the fairness of their selection decisions and bolster their legitimacy by drawing on the power of expressive prosecutions to entrench the norm that no person is above the law, much as the ICC has sought to express other norms through the prosecution of certain crimes, such as the use of child soldiers and the destruction of cultural property.

Placing greater emphasis on expressing the principle of equal application of law could, to be sure, potentially cause a tribunal to take action that has the unintended effect of undermining its credibility. A primary reason the ICC has sought to accommodate major power concerns thus far is that the Court fears alienating countries on which it depends for support in crucial areas such as collecting evidence, arresting suspects, and securing witness cooperation.[141] Prosecutions that have major power support, such as those based on Security Council referrals, tend to stand on firmer ground.[142] Further, unsuccessful efforts to pursue high-level officials from noncooperative states could backfire, causing the ICC to look weak and ineffective. The ICC's inability to secure the arrest of indicted Sudanese president Omar al-Bashir and its failed prosecution of senior Kenyan officials, including current president Uhuru Kenyatta, illustrate this risk, although negative perceptions stemming from the Court's disproportionate focus on Africa help explain the intensity of the backlash against the ICC in both situations.

These concerns are valid. They could, however, be moderated if prosecutions designed to express the principle of equal application of law focused on morally unambiguous crimes. In seeking to widen its geographic focus and, in particular, to confront international crimes committed by more powerful countries, the ICC Prosecutor could concentrate on instances where the legal norms are articulated in absolute terms, such as the intentional killing of civilians or torture.[143] The alleged torture and abuse of detainees by UK forces in Iraq and by US forces in Afghanistan fall within this category. Nonprosecution in such cases not only erodes these norms, but also sends the broader message that more powerful countries are above the law – a message that taints the ICC's goal of ending impunity for grave crimes. A prosecutor, by contrast, should proceed more cautiously where the norm is less sharply defined or more challenging to apply in practice because it is articulated as a general standard whose application depends on a balance of factors, such as the use of force that unintentionally causes disproportionate civilian harm and death (as opposed to the intentional killing of civilians, which is necessarily a war crime).[144]

The ICC Prosecutor initially declined to open an investigation into UK forces' alleged mistreatment of detainees in Iraq based on an assessment of relative gravity, which focused on the comparatively low number of victims there when measured against the number of victims in mass atrocities committed elsewhere.[145] The Prosecutor has since reopened a preliminary examination into possible crimes committed by UK forces in Iraq and has been conducting a preliminary examination in Afghanistan, including into possible crimes by US forces.[146] A report on ICC investigative activities issued just prior to the release of the executive summary of the US Senate Intelligence Committee's report on CIA torture in December 2014 indicated that American officials were potential targets.[147] The ICC Prosecutor subsequently announced that there was a reasonable basis to conclude that US soldiers and CIA agents had committed war crimes in Afghanistan, including torture, suggesting the likelihood that she would open a full investigation.[148] Neither the UK nor the US has demonstrated a genuine willingness to prosecute the alleged international crimes.[149]

Despite the relatively low number of victims compared to mass atrocities, prosecuting torture and forced disappearance committed by powerful states may be justified under a relative gravity assessment given the threat to bedrock international law norms and the alarm such egregious conduct causes in the international community, particularly where, as with the US secret detention and torture program, it emanates from the highest levels of the government.[150] Both situations present an opportunity for the ICC to show that it will pursue allegations of state-sponsored torture even when committed by the most powerful countries. Further action by the ICC Prosecutor could enhance the Court's overall reputation and legitimacy even if such action met with strong opposition and ultimately proved unsuccessful.[151]

The ICC's authorization for the Prosecutor to open a *proprio motu* investigation into possible international crimes committed in the Republic of Georgia during 2008 represents another potentially significant development.[152] The ICC Prosecutor is investigating the ethnic cleansing of Georgians from the breakaway region of South Ossetia as well as direct attacks on peacekeepers.[153] The investigation into crimes committed during the conflict in and around South Ossetia, which involved Georgia, Russia, and pro-Russian separatists, marks the Court's first investigation into a situation outside the African continent.[154] It also represents the first time that ICC prosecutors will be conducting an official investigation into the alleged crimes of a major world power.[155]

Negative perceptions about the ICC's fairness and legitimacy will persist if the Court fails to address the distributive dimensions of its selection decisions. The ICC necessarily remains confined by limits on its jurisdiction under the Rome Statute. The ICC Prosecutor also cannot realistically ignore the larger political context in which the Court operates. But the ICC can help counteract these perceptions by seeking to express the norm that no person is above the law through its investigations and prosecutions. Pursuing this goal not only would reinforce the principle of equal application of law, but also could prove more pragmatic than it might first seem by building broader support for the Court and strengthening the Court's reputation for fairness.

NOTES

1. See, for example, William A. Schabas, "Prosecutorial Discretion v. Judicial Activism at the International Criminal Court," *Journal of International Criminal Justice* 6 (2008), 731, 740, 749; Elena Baylis, "Outsourcing Investigations," *UCLA Journal of International Law and Foreign Affairs* 14 (2009), 121, 135. For a discussion of the impact of selection decisions on other tribunals, see, for example, Mark A. Drumbl, "Collective Violence and Individual Punishment: The Criminality of Mass Atrocity," *Northwestern University Law Review* 99 (2005) 539, 593.

2. *United States V. Araki*, Dissenting Opinion of Justice Radhabinod Pal, in *The Tokyo Major War Crimes Trial: The Records of the International Military Trinunal for the Far East* (vol. 105) (R. John Pritchard ed., 1981), 37.

3. Statute of the International Criminal Tribunal for the former Yugoslavia, art. 1, May 25, 1993, 32 I.L.M. 1192 (ICTY Statute), Statute of the International Criminal Tribunal for Rwanda, art. 1, November 8, 1994, 33 I.L.M. 1598 (ICTR Statute).

4. Virginia Morris and Michael P. Scharf, *An Insider's Guide to the International Criminal Tribunal for the Former Yugoslavia (A Documentary History and Analysis)* (Irvington-on-Hudson: Transnational Publishers, Inc., 1994), 332.

5. Victor Peskin, "Beyond Victor's Justice? The Challenge of Prosecuting the Winners at the International Criminal Tribunals for the Former Yugoslavia and Rwanda," *Journal of Human Rights* 4 (2005), 213, 227–28.

6. *Prosecutor v. Delalić*, Case No. IT-96–21-T, ICTY Trial Chamber, Judgment, para. 393, (November 16, 1998).

7. Vijay M. Padmanabhan, "Norm Internationalization through Trials for Violations of International Law: Four Conditions for Success and Their Application to Trials of Detainees at Guantanamo Bay," *University of Pennsylvania Journal of International Law* 31 (2009), 427, 444.

8. Victor Peskin, "Beyond Victor's Justice?" 228.

9. Stuart Ford, "Fairness and Politics at the ICTY: Evidence from the Indictments," *North Carolina Journal of International Law and Commercial Regulation* 39 (2013), 45, 93–94.

10. Andreas Laursen, "NATO, the War over Kosovo, and the ICTY Investigation," *American University International Law Review* 17 (2002), 765, 770–71.

11. ICTY, Committee Established to Review the NATO Bombing Campaign against the Federal Republic of Yugoslavia, Final Report to the Prosecutor, para. 3 (June 8, 2000), *reprinted in* 39 I.LM. 1257 (2000) (Final Report to the Prosecutor); Laursen, "NATO, the War over Kosovo, and the ICTY Investigation," 770–71.

12. Final Report to the Prosecutor, para. 27.

13. Michael Mandel, "Politics and Human Rights in International Criminal Law: Our Case against NATO and the Lessons to Be Learned from It," *Fordham International Law Journal* 25 (2001), 95, 95–97; Paolo Benvenuti, "The ICTY Prosecutor and the Review of the NATO Bombing Campaign against the Federal Republic of Yugoslavia," *European Journal of International Law* 12 (2001), 503, 506–09; Virgil Wiebe, "Footprints of Death: Cluster Bombs as Indiscriminate Weapons under International Humanitarian Law," *Michigan Journal of International Law* 22 (2000), 85, 125–37.

14. Chris Mahony, "The Justice Pivot: U.S. International Criminal Law Influence from Outside the Rome Statute," *Georgetown Journal of International Law* 46 (2015), 1071, 1079.

15. Allison Marston Danner, "Enhancing the Legitimacy and Accountability of Prosecutorial Discretion at the International Criminal Court," *American Journal of International Law* 97 (2003), 510, 540.

16. Carla De Ycaza, "Victor's Justice in War Crimes Tribunals: A Study of the International Criminal Tribunal in Rwanda," *New York International Law Review* 23 (2010), 53, 54–55.

17. Peskin, "Beyond Victor's Justice?" 444–45; Mahony, "The Justice Pivot," 1117–19.

18. Gerry J. Simpson, "Didactic and Dissident Histories in War Crimes Trials," *Albany Law Review* 60 (1997), 801, 805–06; William A. Schabas, "Victor's Justice: Selecting 'Situations' at the International Criminal Court," *John Marshall Law Review* 43 (2010), 535, 551–52.

19. *Barayagwiza v. Prosecutor*, Case No. ICTR-97-19-AR72, ICTR Appeals Chamber, Decision on Prosecutor's Request for Review or Reconsideration, paras. 71, 74–75 (March 31, 2000). See also Danner, "Enhancing the Legitimacy and Accountability of Prosecutorial Discretion," 510, 530–31.

20. Jenia Iontcheva Turner, "Defense Perspectives on Law and Politics in International Criminal Trials," *Virginia Journal of International Law* 48 (2008), 529, 593.

21. *Prosecutor v. Karemera*, Case No. ICTR-98-44-T, ICTR Trial Chamber III, Decision on Joseph Nzirorera's Motion for Selective Prosecution Documents, paras. 13–19 (September 30, 2009).

22. *Prosecutor v. Delalić*, Case No. IT-96-21-A, ICTY Appeals Chamber, Judgment, paras. 612–15 (February 20, 2001).

23. Beth Van Schaack, "The Building Blocks of Hybrid Justice," *Denver Journal of International Law and Policy* 44 (2016), 101, 188–89.

24. Leslie Haskell and Lars Waldorf, "The Impunity Gap of the International Criminal Tribunal for Rwanda: Causes and Consequences," *Hastings International and Comparative Law Review* 34 (2011), 49, 51.

25. Mahony, "The Justice Pivot," 1119. The SCSL has also been criticized from the other direction, with members of the public objecting to the decision to indict members of the

Civil Defense Forces, who were viewed as war heroes because they fought to preserve the constitutional order. Van Schaack, "The Building Blocks of Hybrid Justice," 189.

26. Mark Kersten, "The New Kosovo Tribunal—Turning Victors' Justice on its Head," *Justice in Conflict*, January 18, 2016, https://justiceinconflict.org/2016/01/18/the-new -kosovo-tribunal-turning-victors-justice-on-its-head/. See also Jaya Ramji-Nogales, "Designing Bespoke Transitional Justice: A Pluralist Process Approach," *Michigan Journal of International Law* 32 (2010), 1, 34–36.

27. Matiangai V. S. Sirleaf, "Regionalism, Regime Complexes, and the Crisis in International Criminal Justice," *Columbia Journal of Transnational Law* 54 (2016), 699, 712–13.

28. Ibid., 715.

29. Rosa Aloisi, "A Tale of Two Institutions: The United Nations Security Council and the International Criminal Court," in Dawn L. Rothe, James D. Meernik, and Thordis Ingadóttir eds., *The Realities of International Criminal Justice* (Leiden: Martinus Nijhoff, 2013), 147, 149.

30. Editorial, "The Crimes of Terrorists," *New York Times* (April 2, 2015); Jennifer Trahan, "Accountability for Crimes in Syria: Lessons Learned from the Field of International Justice," Syria Justice and Accountability Centre (June 2015), 1–2, http://syriaaccountability .org/wp-content/uploads/Syria-Lessons-from-tribunals.pdf.

31. Mark Kersten, "The ICC and ISIS: Be Careful What You Wish For," *Justice in Conflict*, June 11, 2015, https://justiceinconflict.org/2015/06/11/the-icc-and-isis-be-careful-what-you -wish-for/.

32. Yvonne McDermott, *Fairness in International Criminal Trials* (Oxford: University of Oxford Press), 1.

33. David Luban, "Fairness to Rightness: Jurisdiction, Legality, and the Legitimacy of International Criminal Law," in Samantha Besson and John Tasioulas eds., *The Philosophy of International Law* (Oxford: Oxford University Press, 2010), 575; Aaron Fichtelberg, "Democratic Legitimacy and the International Criminal Court: A Liberal Defense," *Journal of International Criminal Justice* 41 (2006), 765, 775; Sophie Rigney, Case Note, "'The Words Don't Fit You': Recharacterization of the Charges, Trial Fairness, and *Katanga*," *Melbourne Journal of International Law* 15 (2014), 515, 523.

34. Rigney, "'The Words Don't Fit You,'" 522.

35. Gerry J. Simpson, "War Crimes: A Critical Introduction," in Timothy L. H. McCormack and Gerry J. Simpson eds., *The Law of War Crimes: National and International Approaches* (Leiden: Martinus Nijhoff, 1997), 1, 15.

36. *Prosecutor v. Katanga*, Case No. ICC-01/04–01/07–3436-AnxI, Trial Chamber II, Minority Opinion of Judge Christine Van den Wyngaert, para. 311 (March 7, 2014).

37. Ian Hurd, *After Anarchy: Legitimacy and Power in the United Nations Security Council* (Princeton: Princeton University Press, 2007), 174.

38. Daniel Bodansky, "The Legitimacy of International Governance: A Coming Challenge for International Environmental Law?" *American Journal of International Law* 93 (1999), 596, 601.

39. A. John Simmons, *Justification and Legitimacy: Essays on Rights and Obligations* (Cambridge: Cambridge University Press, 2001), 126–30.

40. Richard H. Fallon, Jr. "Legitimacy and the Constitution," *Harvard Law Review* 118 (2005), 1787, 1789.

41. Ibid., 1794–99.

42. Danner, "Enhancing the Legitimacy and Accountability of Prosecutorial Discretion," 536.

43. Bodansky, "The Legitimacy of International Governance," 327.
44. Thomas M. Franck, *The Power of Legitimacy Among Nations* (Oxford: Oxford University Press, 1990), 24.
45. Thomas M. Franck, *Fairness in International Law and Institutions* (Oxford: Oxford University Press, 1998), 27.
46. Allen Buchanan and Robert O. Keohane, "The Legitimacy of Global Governance Institutions," *Ethics and International Affairs* 20 (2006), 405, 411.
47. Margaret M. deGuzman, "Gravity and the Legitimacy of the International Criminal Court," *Fordham International Law Journal* 32 (2009), 1400, 1437.
48. Abram Chayes, "The Role of the Judge in Public Law Litigation," *Harvard Law Review* 89 (1976), 1281, 1316.
49. James L. Gibson and Gregory A. Caldeira, "The Legitimacy of Transnational Legal Institutions: Compliance, Support, and the European Court of Justice," *American Journal of Political Science* 39 (1995), 459, 460.
50. Abram Chayes and Antonia Handler Chayes, *The New Sovereignty: Compliance with International Regulatory Agreements* (Cambridge: Harvard University Press, 1995), 127.
51. Carsten Stahn, "Between 'Faith' and 'Facts': By What Standards Should We Assess International Criminal Justice?" *Leiden Journal of International Law* 25 (2012) 251, 268–69.
52. Robert D. Sloane, "The Expressive Capacity of International Punishment: The Limits of the National Law Analogy and the Potential of International Criminal Law," *Stanford Journal of International Law* 43 (2007), 39, 41.
53. Asad Kiyani, "Group-Based Differentiation and Local Repression: The Custom and Curse of Selectivity," *Journal of International Criminal Justice* 14 (2016), 939, 949.
54. Ibid., 952.
55. Mark Kersten, *Justice in Conflict: The Effects of the International Criminal Court's Interventions on Ending Wars and Building Peace* (Oxford: Oxford University Press, 2016), 174–78.
56. Danner, "Enhancing the Legitimacy and Accountability of Prosecutorial Discretion," 537.
57. Rome Statute, art. 17(1)(2).
58. deGuzman, "Gravity and the Legitimacy of the International Criminal Court," 1440–41.
59. Ibid.
60. Ibid.
61. Margaret M. deGuzman, "Choosing to Prosecute: Expressive Selection at the International Criminal Court," *Michigan Journal of International Law* 33 (2012), 265, 268; Alexander K. A. Greenawalt, "Justice without Politics? Prosecutorial Discretion and the International Criminal Court," *New York University Journal of International Law and Politics* 39 (2007), 583, 656–57.
62. deGuzman, "Choosing to Prosecute," 269.
63. Ibid.
64. Greenawalt, "Justice without Politics?" 656–57.
65. Alison Duxbury, *The Participation of States in International Organisations: The Role of Human Rights and Democracy* (Cambridge: Cambridge University Press, 2011), 30.
66. Nigel Purvis, "Critical Legal Studies in Public International Law," *Harvard International Law Journal* 32 (1991), 81, 111.
67. Ben Bradford, Katrin Hohl, Jonathan Jackson, and Sarah MacQueen, "Obeying the Rules of the Road: Procedural Justice, Social Identity, and Normative Compliance," *Journal of Contemporary Criminal Justice* 31(2) (2015), 3.

68. Wolfgang Kaleck, *Double Standards: International Criminal Law and the West* (Brussels: Torkel Opsahl Academic EPublisher, 2015), 114–15.

69. Lawrence D. Bobo and Victor Thompson, "Unfair by Design: The War on Drugs, Race, and the Legitimacy of the Criminal Justice System," *Social Research* 73(2) (2006), 445; Stephen B. Bright, "Discrimination, Death and Denial: The Tolerance of Racial Discrimination in the Infliction of the Death Penalty," *Santa Clara Law Review* 35 (1995), 433, 439, 462–65.

70. Ivelaw L. Griffith, "Drugs and Democracy in the Caribbean," *University of Miami Law Review* 53 (1999), 869, 874; Angel Ricardo Orquendo, "Corruption and Legitimation Crises in Latin America," *Connecticut Journal of International Law* 14 (1999), 475, 490.

71. Steven E. Hendrix, "New Approaches to Addressing Corruption in the Context of U.S. Foreign Assistance with Examples from Latin America and the Caribbean," *Southwestern Journal of Law and Trade in the Americas* 12 (2005), 1, 5; Thomas M. DiBiagio, "Judicial Corruption the Right to a Fair Trial, and the Application of Plain Error Review," *American Journal of Criminal Law* 25 (1998), 595, 622 (discussing Mexico).

72. Stuart Ford, "A Social Psychology Model of the Perceived Legitimacy of International Criminal Courts: Implications for the Success of Transitional Justice Mechanisms," *Vanderbilt Journal of Transnational Law* 45 (2012), 405, 409–10, 454–55 (applying theories of sociological psychology to international criminal tribunals); Bernadette Atuahene, "The Importance of Conversation in Transitional Justice: A Study of Land Restitution in South Africa," *Law and Social Inquiry* 39 (2014), 902, 904 (applying procedural justice theories to transitional justice in South Africa).

73. Tom R. Tyler, *Why People Obey the Law* (New Haven: Yale University Press, 2006), 3–7.

74. Tom R. Tyler and Yuen J. Huo, *Trust in the Law: Encouraging Public Cooperation with the Police and Courts* (New York: Russell Sage Foundation, 2002), xiii–iv, 50.

75. Aziz Huq, Jonathan Jackson, and Rick Trinkner, "Acts that Legitimate: Widening the Array of Predicate Policing Practices," Public Law and Legal Theory Working Paper No. 603 (2016), 7, http://chicagounbound.uchicago.edu/cgi/viewcontent.cgi?article=2053&context=public_law_and_legal_theory.

76. Tyler and Huo, *Trust in the Law*, 90–93.

77. Morris Zelditch, Jr., "Theories of Legitimacy," in John T. Jost and Brenda Major eds., *The Psychology of Legitimacy: Emerging Perspectives in Ideology, Justice, and Intergroup Relations* (New York: Cambridge University Press, 2001), 33–53.

78. Bradford et al., "Obeying the Rules of the Road," 3.

79. Ben Bradford, Kristina Murphy, and Jonathan Jackson, "Officers as Mirrors: Policing, Procedural Justice and the (Re)Production of Social Identity," *The British Journal of Criminology* 54 (2014), 527, 528.

80. Bradford et al., "Obeying the Rules of the Road," 5–6.

81. Bradford et al., "Officers as Mirrors," 528.

82. Ben Bradford, Jenna Milani, and Jonathan Jackson, "Identity, Legitimacy and 'Making Sense' of Police Violence," Oxford Legal Studies Research Paper No. 41 (2016), 4–6, 11, https://papers.ssrn.com/sol3/papers.cfm?abstract_id=2793818.

83. Bradford et al., "Officers as Mirrors," 528.

84. Ibid.

85. Ibid., 533; Tyler and Huo, *Trust in the Law*, 139–43.

86. Ernest J. Weinrib, "Legal Formalism: On the Immanent Rationality of Law," *Yale Law Journal* 97 (1988), 949, 982, and n. 73.

87. See, for example, Crystal S. Yang, "Free at Last? Judicial Discretion and Racial Disparities in Federal Sentencing," *Journal of Legal Studies* 44 (2015), 75, 75–78 (discussing racial disparities in federal sentencing in the United States).

88. Aya Gruber, "A Distributive Theory of Criminal Law," *William and Mary Law Review* 52 (2010), 1, 11; Loïc Wacquant, "A Janus-Faced Institution of Ethnoracial Closure: A Sociological Specification of the Ghetto," in Ray Hutchison and Bruce D. Haynes eds., *The Ghetto: Contemporary Global Issues and Controversies* (Colorado: Westview Press, 2011), 1, 2.

89. Alon Harel, "Efficiency and Fairness in Criminal Law: The Case for a Criminal Law Principle of Comparative Fault," *California Law Review* 82 (1994), 1181, 1182–83.

90. Huq et al., "Acts that Legitimate," 4.

91. William J. Stuntz, "Local Policing After the Terror," *Yale Law Journal* 111 (2002), 2137, 2173–74.

92. See, for example, *United States v. Armstrong*, 517 U.S. 456, 465–68 (1996); Marc Price Wolf, Note, "Proving Race Discrimination in Criminal Cases Using Statistical Evidence," *Hastings Race and Poverty Law Journal* 4 (2007), 395, 414–21.

93. Charles R. Epp, Steven Maynard-Moody, and Donald P. Haider-Markel, *Pulled Over: How Police Stops Define Race and Citizenship* (Chicago: University of Chicago Press, 2014), 116–19.

94. See, for example, Monica C. Bell, "Police Reform and the Dismantling of Legal Estrangement," *Yale Law Journal* 126 (2017), 2054; Robert J. Sampson, *Great American City: Chicago and the Enduring Neighborhood Effect* (Chicago: University of Chicago Press, 2012), 365–67.

95. Bell, "Police Reform," 2067–68.

96. Ibid., 2087–88.

97. Ibid., 2106–07.

98. Ibid., 2108–09.

99. Franck, *The Power of Legitimacy Among Nations*, 24.

100. Charles R. Beitz, "International Liberalism and Distributive Justice: A Survey of Recent Thought," *World Politics* 51(2) (1999), 269. See also Gabriella Blum, "On a Differential Law of War," *Harvard International Law Journal* 52 (2011), 163, 181.

101. Franck, *Fairness in International Law and Institutions*, 6–7.

102. Yvonne M. Dutton, "Bridging the Legitimacy Divide: The International Criminal Court's Domestic Perception Challenge," *Columbia Journal of Transnational Law* 56 (forthcoming), https://papers.ssrn.com/sol3/papers.cfm?abstract_id=3016621, at 41–43.

103. Ford, "A Social Psychology Model," 409–11, 418–56.

104. Ibid., 409–10.

105. Ibid., 410.

106. Ibid., 411

107. Molly K. Land, "Justice as Legitimacy in the European Court of Human Rights," in Harlan Grant Cohen, Andreas Føllesdal, Nienke Grossman, and Geir Ulfstein eds. *Legitimacy and International Courts* (Cambridge: Cambridge University Press, forthcoming 2018), https://papers.ssrn.com/sol3/papers.cfm?abstract_id=2608578, at 12–14, 17, 22.

108. Greenawalt, "Justice without Politics?" 593.

109. Madeline Morris, "Few Reservations about Reservations," *Chicago Journal of International Law* 1 (2000), 341, 344.

110. Danner, "Enhancing the Legitimacy and Accountability of Prosecutorial Discretion," 536–37.

111. Ibid., 537.
112. Office of the Prosecutor [OTP], International Criminal Court, Policy Paper on Preliminary Examinations, para. 25 (November, 2013) (OTP, Policy Paper on Preliminary Examinations), www.icc-cpi.int/iccdocs/otp/OTP-Policy_Paper_ Preliminary_Examinations_2013-ENG.pdf; Office of the Prosecutor [OTP], Policy Paper on Case Selection and Prioritisation, para. 16 (September 15, 2016) (OTP Policy Paper on Case Selection and Prioritisation), www.icc-cpi.int/itemsDocuments/ 20160915_OTP-Policy_Case-Selection_Eng.pdf.
113. Rome Statute, preamble.
114. deGuzman, "Choosing to Prosecute," 283–84.
115. *Prosecutor v. Lubanga Dyilo*, Case No. ICC-01/04–01/06, Pre-Trial Chamber I, Decision concerning Pre-Trial Chamber I's Decision of February 10, 2006 and the Incorporation of Documents into the Record of the Case Against Mr. Thomas Lubanga Dyilo, Annex I, paras. 46, 50 (February 24, 2006).
116. *Situation in the Democratic Republic of the Congo*, Case No. ICC-01/04–169, Appeals Chamber, Judgment on the Prosecutor's appeal against the decision of Pre-Trial Chamber I entitled "Decision on Prosecutor's Application for Warrants of Arrest, Article 58," paras. 73–79 (July 13, 2006).
117. Ibid., Separate and partly dissenting opinion of Judge Georghios M. Pikis, paras. 39–41.
118. deGuzman, "Choosing to Prosecute," 295–96.
119. Rome Statute, art. 53(1)(c), (2)(c).
120. Darryl Robinson, "Serving the Interests of Justice: Amnesties, Truth Commissions and the International Criminal Court," *European Journal of International Law* 14 (2003), 481, 498–502.
121. Greenawalt, "Justice without Politics?" 653–54.
122. Rome Statute, art. 17.
123. OTP, Policy Paper on Case Selection and Prioritisation, para. 20.
124. Stephanos Bibas and William W. Burke-White, "Idealism Meets Domestic-Criminal-Procedure Realism," *Duke Law Journal* 59 (2010), 637, 681.
125. Kevin Jon Heller, "Situational Gravity under the Rome Statute," in Carsten Stahn and Larissa van den Herik eds., *Future Perspectives on International Criminal Justice* (The Hague: T. M. C. Asser Press, 2010), 227, 240.
126. Greenawalt," Justice without Politics?" 633; Allison Marston Danner and Jenny S. Martinez, "Guilty Associations: Joint Criminal Enterprise, Command Responsibility, and the Development of International Criminal Law," *California Law Review* 93 (2005), 75, 93–94.
127. Greenawalt, "Justice without Politics?" 660, 671–72.
128. Daniel F. Orentlicher, "Settling Accounts: The Duty to Prosecute Human Rights Violations of a Prior Regime," *Yale Law Journal* 100 (1991), 2537, 2598–99. See also Ruti G. Teitel, *Transitional Justice* (Oxford: Oxford University Press, 2000), 46–51 (describing the use of limited prosecutions and limited punishments in the transitional justice context).
129. deGuzman, "Choosing to Prosecute," 312.
130. Ibid., 314.
131. OTP, Policy Paper on Case Selection and Prioritisation, para. 41.
132. OTP, Policy Paper on Preliminary Examinations, paras. 28–29.
133. Mirjan Damaška, "What Is the Point of International Criminal Justice?" *Chicago-Kent Law Review* 83 (2008), 329, 361.
134. Kiyani, "Group-Based Differentiation and Local Repression," 956.

135. Rome Statute, preamble; deGuzman, "Gravity and the Legitimacy of the International Criminal Court," 1464.

136. Rome Statute, art. 53(1)(c), 53(2)(c).

137. Robinson, "Serving the Interests of Justice," 483–84.

138. Mark Ellis, "Toward a Common Ground Definition of the Rule of Law Incorporating Substantive Principles of Justice," *University of Pittsburgh Law Review* 72 (2010), 191, 193 (citing A.V. Dicey, *An Introduction to the Study of the Law of the Constitution* [1885]); Brian Z. Tamanaha, *On the Rule of Law: History, Politics, Theory* (Cambridge: Cambridge University Press, 2004), 63–64.

139. Rome Statute, art. 53(3)(a).

140. Alex Whiting, "The ICC's New Libya Case: Extraterritorial Evidence for an Extraterritorial Court," *Just Security* (August 23, 2017), www.justsecurity.org/44383/iccs-libya-case-extraterritorial-evidence-extraterritorial-court/ (discussing the ICC's heavy reliance on video evidence in issuing an arrest warrant for Mahmoud Mustafa Busayf Al-Werfalli, a militia leader in Libya, for war crimes and noting the use of video evidence for investigations of crimes committed in Syria).

141. David Bosco, *Rough Justice: The International Criminal Court in a World of Power Politics* (Oxford: Oxford University Press, 2014), 20.

142. Alexander K.A. Greenawalt, "Complementarity in Crisis: Uganda, Alternative Justice, and the International Criminal Court," *Virginia Journal of International Law* 50 (2009), 107, 154–56.

143. See generally Blum, "On a Differential Law of War," 186.

144. Luban, "Fairness to Rightness," 23. See also Blum, "On a Differential Law of War," 186–87. Another commentator maintains that the ICC Prosecutor should articulate a policy stating that she will not normally investigate allegations of collateral damage. Richard John Galvin, "The ICC Prosecutor, Collateral Damage, and NGOs: Evaluating the Risk of a Politicized Prosecution," *University of Miami International and Comparative Law Review* 13 (2005), 1, 90–91.

145. Letter from Luis Moreno-Ocampo, Chief Prosecutor of the ICC, 8–9 (February 9, 2006), www.icc-cpi.int/NR/rdonlyres/04D143C8-19FB-466C-AB77-4CDB2FDEBEF7/143682/OTP_letter_to_senders_re_Iraq_9_February_2006.pdf.

146. "ICC to investigate claims of abuse by UK forces in Iraq," *BBC News*, May 13, 2014, www.bbc.com/news/uk-27397695.

147. Office of the Prosecutor, International Criminal Court, "Report on Preliminary Examination Activities 2014," para. 94, December 2, 2014, www.icc-cpi.int/iccdocs/otp/OTP-Pre-Exam-2014.pdf.

148. Office of the Prosecutor, "Report on Preliminary Examination Activities 2016" paras. 211–13, November 16, 2016, www.icc-cpi.int/iccdocs/otp/161114-otp-rep-PE_ENG.pdf; Somini Sengupta and Marlise Simons, "U.S. Forces May Have Committed War Crimes in Afghanistan, Prosecutor Says," *New York Times*, November 14, 2016.

149. Aoife Duffy, "Searching for Accountability: British-Controlled Detention in Southeast Iraq, 2003–2008," *International Journal of Transitional Justice* 10 (2016), 410, 429–30 (describing the unwillingness of the United Kingdom to prosecute abuses of detainees by UK forces in Iraq and to penetrate the culture of impunity surrounding security force actions there); Sudha Setty, "Obama's National Security Exceptionalism," *Chicago-Kent Law Review* 91 (2015), 91, 97 (noting the failure of the United States to prosecute serious allegations of US torture).

150. Heller, "Situational Gravity under the Rome Statute," 244.

151. Mark Kersten, "Whatever Happens, the ICC's Investigation into US Torture in Afghanistan Is a Win for the Court," *Justice in Conflict*, November 17, 2016, https://justiceinconflict.org/2016/11/17/whatever-happens-the-iccs-investigation-into-us-torture-in-afghanistan-is-a-win-for-the-court/.

152. Nika Jeiranashvili, "Georgia—A Unique Test Case for the ICC," *International Justice Monitor*, March 8, 2017, www.ijmonitor.org/2017/03/georgia-a-unique-case-for-the-icc/.

153. "ICC authorises Russia-Georgia war crimes investigation," *BBC News*, January 17, 2016, www.bbc.com/news/world-europe-35422437.

154. Mark Kersten, "Why is the International Criminal Court stepping out of Africa and into Georgia," *Washington Post*, February 6, 2016, www.washingtonpost.com/news/monkey-cage/wp/2016/02/05/why-is-the-international-criminal-court-stepping-out-of-africa-and-into-georgia/?utm_term=.4b38a04d8c7a.

155. Ibid.

6

Accountability and Fairness: A Window into the Recurring Debate over Treating Terrorism as a Crime under International Law

The proliferation of global terrorism has increased pressure to bring terrorism within the orbit of international criminal justice. The possible paths range from making terrorism a crime under international law triable by the ICC to establishing a hybrid tribunal to address war crimes and crimes against humanity committed by terrorist groups generally or within specific geographical areas.

Terrorism's status under international law and, in particular, whether terrorism constitutes a crime under international law, is the subject of longstanding debate. Most experts still regard terrorism as a transnational, rather than an international, crime. Sectoral treaties, bilateral agreements, soft norms, and informal arrangements among states and their respective law enforcement and intelligence agencies remain the primary legal tools for addressing terrorism.[1] States rejected the proposal to include terrorism as a separate offense under the Rome Statute and efforts to establish a definition of terrorism through an international treaty remain stalled, suggesting lingering divisions over the meaning of the term itself.[2] For some, terrorism remains "a term without any legal significance."[3]

Counterterrorism law and policy has nevertheless become increasingly globalized. In addition to the growth of sectoral treaties and the proliferation of soft norms condemning terrorism, the UN Security Council has adopted resolutions requiring Member States to criminalize various forms of terrorist-related activity. In 2011, the Special Tribunal for Lebanon (STL), the hybrid tribunal created to prosecute those responsible for the assassination of Lebanon's former Prime Minister Rafik Hariri, ruled that there is a customary international law offense of transnational terrorism.[4] Some scholars and jurists argue that the gravity and widespread condemnation of terrorism warrant making it an international crime subject to prosecution by the ICC or a permanent hybrid tribunal.

The impulse to internationalize terrorism prosecutions illustrates the appeal of addressing mass violence through ICL. But it also suggests the challenges of holding perpetrators of severe crimes responsible under ICL while still upholding principles of due process and legality. The debate over subjecting terrorism to international criminal prosecution provides a window into the enduring tension between account-ability and fairness in ICL.

***

The terrorist attacks of September 11, 2001, triggered a massive increase in counter-terrorism legislation, regulation, and enforcement around the world. Subsequent events, from high-profile terrorist attacks in Europe to the spread of the Islamic State in Iraq and Syria (ISIS), have accelerated the creation of new legal tools for combatting terrorism. But international law concerning terrorism still "remains a work in progress – a halfway house between the ordinary application of general rules and a fully formed specialised regime."[5]

Terrorism has not traditionally been considered a separate subject of international law even though terrorism itself can cross international borders. Terrorism instead has served largely as a label to characterize certain prohibited methods and targets of violence.[6] It has been addressed through generally applicable norms of international law, including principles of nonintervention, the nonuse of force, state responsibil-ity, the law of armed conflict, international human rights law, and international criminal law.[7]

Until recently, states relied on sectoral treaties to address particular methods of violence, such as those targeting aircraft hijacking and hostage-taking, and to fill gaps in the existing legal framework.[8] Those treaties not only lack a definition of terror-ism, but also apply only to acts over which either no state or more than one state has jurisdiction.[9] Rather than providing for universal jurisdiction, by which any state could prosecute the offense based on its severity, they generally require states to criminalize certain conduct, establish extraterritorial jurisdiction over it, and coop-erate either by prosecuting or extraditing offenders.[10] States further rely on bilateral agreements to address transnational terrorist violence. But attempts to adopt a more comprehensive legal framework for terrorism have thus far failed to bear fruit, as illustrated by the stalled negotiations over the draft UN Comprehensive Convention on Terrorism, initially submitted by India in 1996,[11] and the deliberate exclusion of terrorism as a separate offense under the Rome Statute.[12] Proposals to add terrorism to the list of core international crimes subject to prosecution by the ICC, such as the proposal advanced by the Netherlands, have yet to gain traction.[13]

The principal obstacle to a more comprehensive legal framework for addressing terrorism remains the lack of a universally accepted definition of the term. The first antiterrorism conventions, adopted under the auspices of the International Civil Aviation Organization, excluded the term "terrorism" because no agreement on its content could be reached.[14] The growth of transnational terrorism has produced a flurry of international activity over the past several decades. This activity traces back to the 1979 kidnapping of American embassy personnel in Tehran and attacks carried out during the early-mid 1980s by various Islamic groups, frequently with state support.[15] But competing definitions persist. For example, a 1994 UN General

Assembly Declaration on Measures to Eliminate International Terrorism defines terrorism as "[c]riminal acts intended or calculated to provoke a state of terror in the general public, a group of persons or particular persons for political purposes."[16] It states that such acts "are in any circumstance unjustifiable, whatever the considerations of a political, philosophical, ideological, racial, ethnic, religious or any other nature that may be invoked to justify them."[17] The 1999 Convention for the Suppression of the Financing of Terrorism (Convention on Terrorism Financing) defines terrorism as "[a]ny . . . act intended to cause death or serious bodily injury to a civilian, or to any other person not taking an active part in the hostilities in a situation of armed conflict, when the purpose of such act, by its nature or context, is to intimidate a population, or to compel a government or an international organization to do or to abstain from doing any act."[18] One solution has been to avoid positing a single overarching definition of terrorism and instead to incorporate by reference definitions contained in existing conventions and protocols. The UN Security Council, for example, has described terrorism as conduct committed to cause death or serious bodily harm, with the intention of provoking a state of terror, where such conduct constitutes an offense under existing international antiterrorism conventions and protocols.[19]

The difficulty of defining terrorism under international law has traditionally arisen in the application of a crime of terrorism to two situations: first, to national liberation movements resisting foreign occupation and seeking self-determination; and second, to violence committed by state officials against their own citizens.[20] Continued conflict in the Middle East[21] and the divergent treatment by states under international humanitarian law (IHL) of violence committed by non-state actors[22] contribute to the definitional impasse.

Other factors also complicate elevating terrorism to the status of an international crime, including: a belief that the three existing core crimes (genocide, war crimes, and crimes against humanity) still represent the crimes of greatest concern to the international community; a fear of further overburdening the ICC by adding a crime of terrorism to its jurisdiction; a lack of necessity given aggressive domestic enforcement mechanisms and extensive international cooperation; and the risk of weakening the legitimacy of the ICC and other international tribunals because of terrorism's historically politicized nature.[23] Several recent developments have nevertheless strengthened the case for recognizing an international crime of terrorism, even as the term itself continues to elude precise definition.

***

Proposals to internationalize the legal treatment of terrorism date to at least 1937, when the League of Nations first proposed an international terrorism court.[24] Despite the failure to include a crime of terrorism within the Rome Statute and the stalling of negotiations over the draft UN Comprehensive Convention on Terrorism, other developments point to increased consensus on an overarching definition of terrorism. The UN General Assembly has roundly condemned terrorism, "wherever and by whomever committed,"[25] and urged development and codification of the law on terrorism.[26] It also eliminated an exception for armed liberation struggles from its antiterrorism resolutions.[27] In 1992, the UN Security Council declared terrorism a threat to international peace and security.[28] The Convention on Terrorism Financing, signed in 1990 and ratified by more than 175 states, provides a legal definition of terrorism in the context of prohibiting various types of terrorism financing.[29] The definition refers to acts prohibited by previous counterterrorism conventions, as well as "any other act" of terrorism, defined in turn as any "act intended to cause death or serious bodily injury to a civilian, or to any other person not taking an active part in the hostilities in a situation of armed conflict, when the purpose of such act, by its nature or context, is to intimidate a population, or to compel a government or an international organization to do or to abstain from doing any act."[30] Together with UN Security Council Resolution 1373, which commands all Member States to criminalize and prevent terrorism financing under their respective domestic laws,[31] the Convention has helped create what some view as a customary international norm prohibiting terrorism financing.[32]

International and hybrid tribunals have prosecuted acts of terrorism even though terrorism is not included as a separate offense in their respective statutes.[33] The ICTY statute, for example, does not reference terrorism, but ICTY prosecutors nonetheless successfully charged acts of terrorism as war crimes. In *Prosecutor v. Galic*, for example, the ICTY Trial Chamber determined that the defendant could be prosecuted for "[a]cts or threats of violence the primary purpose of which is to spread terror among the civilian population" based on Article 51(2) of Additional Protocol I to the 1949 Geneva Conventions.[34] In endorsing the Trial Chamber's analysis, the Appeals Chamber concluded that deliberately inflicting terror on the civilian population was a war crime under customary international law.[35] In his dissent, Judge Schomburg maintained that if the crime of terrorism were part of customary international law, it would have been included in the ICTY statute.[36] The Special Court for Sierra Leone (SCSL) also charged as war crimes offenses that included important elements of terrorism, such as acts of violence intended to spread terror among the civilian population.[37] Terrorism-related prosecutions by the SCSL, like those by the ICTY, did not, however, require the further special intent to intimidate persons in authority to submit to the perpetrators' political, ideological, or religious demands.[38] The ICTR statute references terrorism in defining the tribunal's subject matter jurisdiction,[39] but no documented terrorism prosecutions were brought before the tribunal.[40]

The STL, the first international criminal tribunal to prosecute terrorism, utilizes a domestic law definition of the term, based on Lebanon's criminal code.[41] In 2011, however, the Appeals Chamber ruled that terrorism had become a crime under customary international law.[42] The Appeals Chamber determined that the customary international law definition of terrorism has three central elements: (i) the perpetration of a criminal act (such as murder, kidnapping, or hostage-taking), or threatening such an act; (ii) the intent to spread fear among the population (which would typically entail the creation of public danger) or directly or indirectly coerce a national or international authority to take some action, or to refrain from taking it; and (iii) when the act involves a transnational element.[43] While Appeals Chamber's analysis has been sharply criticized for weak empirical grounding in state practice and flawed reasoning,[44] it reflects increased support for recognizing terrorism as a crime under international law.[45] Terrorism, as one scholar notes, still remains a serious transnational, treaty-based crime, but it has grown closer to becoming a true international crime.[46]

One of the most significant developments in the area of global counterterrorism has been the expansion of quasi-legislative activity by the UN Security Council.[47] Prior to the 9/11 attacks, the Security Council adopted Resolutions 1267 (in 1999) and 1333 (in 2000), which imposed duties on states to stop making any financial resources available to the Taliban or to al Qaeda, except for limited humanitarian reasons, and to freeze all assets or other financial resources intended to benefit either group.[48] Resolution 1373, adopted after the 9/11 attacks, built on these anti-terrorism financing measures by requiring Member States to criminalize prospectively and to prevent terrorist financing under their domestic law.[49] In 2004, the Security Council adopted Resolution 1566, which calls upon Member States to become parties to all relevant international conventions and protocols, to resolve all obstacles to drafting an international convention on terrorism, and to deny safe haven to any person who supports or facilitates a terrorist act or harbors a terrorism suspect.[50] In 2014, the Security Council adopted Resolution 2178, obligating Member States to take the following steps: prevent and suppress travel by individuals to another country to take part in terrorist acts or training; "prevent the movement of terrorists or terrorist groups" through their territory "by effective border controls and controls on issuance of identity papers and travel documents"; and prosecute and rehabilitate returning foreign terrorist fighters.[51] Resolution 2178 also urges Member States to "intensify and accelerate the exchange of operational information regarding actions or movements of terrorists or terrorist networks, including foreign terrorist fighters."[52] In addition to requiring states to adopt criminal legislation, Resolution 2178 provides for administrative and civil measures to achieve the goals of restricting travel, training, and support for terrorism, and preventing radicalization.[53] Although motivated principally by the rising flow of foreign fighters to join ISIS, Resolution 2178 is not limited to any specific group and represents a significant expansion of transnational counterterrorism enforcement through quasi-legislative activity by the Security Council.[54] Resolution 2178 thus "move[s] even farther down a path that diverges from the treaty-based global counterterrorism regime that predominated before 9/11."[55]

In light of these developments, some scholars argue that there is now sufficient consensus around key elements to constitute a universally accepted definition of terrorism that could supply the basis for jurisdiction before an international criminal tribunal.[56] Those core elements include: (i) the threat or use of violence; (ii) that is deliberately directed against the civilian population; (iii) with the intent to create fear or terror in that population. Additional elements vary, but they might include the desire to achieve a political goal, including by compelling a government or organization to perform (or refrain from performing) a particular action.[57] Specific proposals range from amending the Rome Statute to allow for prosecution of a crime of terrorism before the ICC[58] to creating a permanent hybrid court with jurisdiction over such crime.[59] Even if an international crime of terrorism has yet to cross from *lex ferenda* (what the law should be) to *lex lata* (established law), these developments suggest an overall trend in that direction.[60]

Several factors drive proposals to internationalize terrorism prosecutions. One is a desire to close jurisdictional gaps, which can occur, for example, where the state in which a terrorist attack occurs is unable or unwilling to prosecute the perpetrators.[61] This rationale is an impetus for proposals to include a crime of terrorism in the Rome Statute.[62] It also spurred the creation of the STL, which was established because of concerns that Lebanon's judicial system could not maintain its independence and stability during a high-profile investigation into the assassination of Lebanon's former prime minister.[63] In most instances, however, the underlying obstacles – from gathering evidence to arresting the suspects – will remain even if a case is prosecuted before an international or a hybrid tribunal.[64] The STL, for example, lacks custody over the defendants charged in the assassination of former Prime Minister Hariri and is thus trying them *in absentia*.[65] Additionally, the expansion of transnational counterterrorism mechanisms has decreased the gap-filling appeal of international tribunals by facilitating domestic prosecutions and fostering greater bilateral and regional coordination among states.[66]

Another justification for creating an international crime of terrorism is the opportunity it would provide to resolve lingering uncertainty over the definition of terrorism itself. Defining terrorism in an international criminal statute could help minimize fragmentation and reduce the risk of overbroad state application under domestic law.[67] But there is a significant possibility that including a crime of terrorism within the statute of the ICC or of another international tribunal would fail to resolve long-standing divisions over the definition of terrorism and might instead perpetuate ambiguity and overbroad application of terrorism-related offenses.

The strongest arguments for making terrorism an international crime are expressive, flowing from the gravity of terrorism itself. Terrorism shares important attributes with existing core international crimes in its potential to inflict massive harm on civilians, threaten political stability, and destroy the social fabric. Treating terrorism as a domestic or transnational crime may provide the most effective means of addressing the problem, as measured by criminal law's retributive, deterrent, and preventive purposes. National prosecutions, aided by transnational cooperation, will thus likely remain the predominant focus of counterterrorism enforcement for the foreseeable future. But national prosecutions do not necessarily convey the same message that international prosecutions of terrorism would.[68] International crimes are offenses not merely against particular individuals or states, but also against the broader conception of humanity and its shared values and interests.[69] Jürgen Habermas, for example, thus distinguishes terrorism from other forms of violence based on its desire to undermine the existing political system and public institutions.[70] In this regard, terrorism has more in common with war crimes and crimes against humanity than with the most egregious forms of private violence.[71] Proposals to add terrorism to the ICC's jurisdiction may accordingly be understood as an effort to connect two strands of international criminal law: crimes against the international order (such as genocide and crimes against humanity) and crimes under national law that have significant cross-border dimensions and effects but that do not transgress the same shared sense of humanity and values (such as drug trafficking).[72]

Terrorism, to be sure, can sometimes be prosecuted as an international crime under other jurisdictional heads, as ICTY and SCSL prosecutions of acts of terrorism as war crimes demonstrate. But such alternative bases of jurisdiction contain lacunae. War crimes require a nexus to armed conflict,[73] whereas terrorism often occurs during peacetime. Crimes against humanity, while sharing terrorism's focus on significant harm to civilians, require that the acts be part of a widespread or systematic attack perpetrated pursuant to a state or organizational policy[74] and exclude isolated and uncoordinated attacks.[75] Crimes against humanity thus fail to cover at least some acts of terrorism. Genocide demands a specific intent "to destroy, in whole or in part, a national, ethnical, racial or religious group, as such,"[76] which necessarily excludes a great deal of terrorist activity.

Treating terrorism as an international crime would do more than address these gaps, which could, in any event, potentially be filled by a state's domestic counterterrorism laws. It would help capture the gravity of terrorism and signal the opprobrium it warrants, whether the acts are instances of hyperterrorism, such as the 9/11 attacks, or targeted political violence, such as the assassination of key government figures. This expressive goal, rather than strictly functional considerations, best explains the appeal of labeling terrorism an international crime and prosecuting it before an international or a hybrid court.

***

Elevating terrorism to the status of an international crime would help convey its gravity and would reflect the increased global concern about this highly pernicious and destructive form of violence. But proposals to make terrorism an international crime also illustrate the enduring tensions within ICL between pursuing accountability for crimes of universal concern and upholding principles of fairness and legality. It is thus worth considering whether the aims of ICL can be achieved without sacrificing those principles or, less idealistically, whether any trade-offs are warranted given the severity of the crime, the risk of impunity, and the aspiration of establishing peace and security by bringing perpetrators to justice through a criminal trial. These considerations ultimately suggest caution in assessing proposals to make terrorism an international crime subject to prosecution by an international court or a hybrid tribunal.

One issue concerns the meaning of terrorism and, relatedly, the scope of individual responsibility for any crime of terrorism. There is still no universally accepted definition of terrorism and definitions vary in multiple respects even though there may be greater coherence than in the past. For example, the Convention on Terrorism Financing stresses the requirement of intimidating a population or threatening a government regardless of the purpose;[77] the STL's interpretation straddles several definitions;[78] and other definitions rely heavily on those contained in existing sectoral treaties.[79] Continued indeterminacy over the meaning of terrorism and overbroad articulations of the term jeopardize the principle of legality, which requires that crimes be set forth in precise and unambiguous language that narrowly defines the punishable offense[80] and which prohibits the retroactive imposition of criminal punishment on conduct that was not clearly defined when committed.[81] This principle seeks not only to ensure that individuals are able to receive notice of the proscribed conduct so that they can rationally adjust their behavior, but also to protect the public against arbitrary or oppressive government action based on ambiguities or gaps in the law.[82]

Individual states, moreover, continue to utilize different definitions of terrorism.[83] Indeed, terrorism may be defined differently even within a single country. The United States, for example, uses multiple definitions of terrorism across federal legislation and the executive branch,[84] including for international and domestic terrorism.[85] Many states continue to employ definitions of terrorism that lack the necessary precision and clarity to satisfy the principle of legality.[86]

Public authorities have historically abused the concept of terrorism to suppress particular groups or persecute political opponents.[87] Imprecise and overbroad definitions of terrorism can have a significant impact on individuals who are targeted and prosecuted under special antiterrorism powers, eroding human rights protections even within liberal western democracies.[88]

Increased international regulation through Security Council mandates heightens the risk of overbroad or abusive domestic prosecutions under a terrorism label. UN Security Council Resolution 1373, which requires states to criminalize terrorism financing,[89] and Resolution 1624, which commands states to prohibit by law incitement to commit terrorist acts,[90] have spurred a proliferation of domestic antiterrorism legislation that raises concerns about human rights protections not only among serial human rights violators, but among western states as well.[91] This increased top-down Security Council activity has prompted pushback, particularly from European courts, on the ground that global counterterrorism sanctions violate fundamental rights.[92] While Security Council resolutions may specify the need for states to observe human rights obligations when implementing counterterrorism measures,[93] the internationalization of counterterrorism enforcement continues to prioritize security.[94] Security might be similarly prioritized over fair trial standards and other human rights guarantees if a crime of terrorism were brought within the jurisdiction of an international tribunal.

Another important, if less obvious, concern about the potential scope of an international crime of terrorism is how it might be used in conjunction with existing modes of criminal responsibility. Despite the relative consensus on the definition of the core international crimes themselves, controversy over modes of liability persists, as the debate over the meaning and scope of co-perpetration and joint criminal enterprise illustrates.[95] The origins of this debate go back to the attempts to pursue conspiracy charges and organizational liability before the International Military Tribunal (IMT) at Nuremberg.[96] As described in Chapter 1, the London Charter controversially provided for conspiracy liability, but the IMT interpreted this provision restrictively and rejected its application to crimes against humanity and war crimes.[97] It also narrowed the grounds on which organizational liability could be obtained in the Subsequent Proceedings convened by the US military in the American Zone under Control Council Law No. 10,[98] as judges imposed requirements regarding the organization's purpose, the criminal intent of its members, and the prosecution's burden of proof.[99] The exclusion of conspiracy from the Rome Statute and the statutes of the ICTY and ICTR did not eliminate debate over related modes of criminal responsibility. Scholars and jurists, for example, have criticized the ICTY's expansive use of JCE for eroding the principle of individual criminal responsibility.[100]

The United States' continued effort since 9/11 to prosecute terrorism as a war crime in military commissions suggests how adopting an international crime of terrorism could undermine this principle. After the US Supreme Court invalidated the military commissions unilaterally created by President George W. Bush on separation of powers grounds,[101] Congress enacted legislation making a range of terrorism-related offenses prosecutable as war crimes,[102] including inchoate offenses such as material support for terrorism and conspiracy.[103] The exercise of military jurisdiction over material support for terrorism and conspiracy is controversial in part because international law does not recognize either as a war crime and because it allows individuals with minor roles in or mere provision of support to a terrorist organization to be branded as war criminals.[104] The US prosecution of those offenses in military commissions relies on theories of organizational liability that were advanced – and ultimately rejected – at Nuremberg to hold individuals criminally responsible for war crimes based on their membership in or nexus to a particular group, rather than any criminal act they personally committed. In defending this jurisdiction, a federal appeals court judge asserted that the United States should lead the international community by treating domestic offenses, such as providing financial assistance or pledging oneself to a terrorist group, as war crimes even if those offenses do not constitute crimes under international law.[105] This approach suggests how an international crime of terrorism, when coupled with doctrines of collective liability such as joint criminal enterprise, could potentially be used to prosecute more generalized forms of support to terrorist organizations. Prosecuting marginal figures in an international or a hybrid court for the crime of terrorism under such doctrines could undermine the notion of gravity and weaken the principle of individual culpability, both of which are important to ICL.[106]

The Security Council also has relied on broad conceptions of criminal responsibility in addressing terrorism, requiring Member States to criminalize financing and other forms of support for terrorist organizations or activity, short of direct involvement in a terrorist attack or plot. These directives may be defended as necessary measures to combat terrorist violence. But they risk criminalizing legitimate forms of conduct – a persistent critique by human rights bodies of current state practice in this area.[107] Resolution 2178's targeting of foreign fighters underscores this concern. In October 2015, the Council of Europe adopted an Additional Protocol to its 2005 Convention on the Prevention of Terrorism[108] to help European countries implement Resolution 2178 by specifying conduct to be criminalized under the respective laws of Member States.[109] The Additional Protocol, for example, directs Member States to criminalize travel and training abroad with the intent to commit or contribute to a terrorist offense as well as providing funding for such travel or training.[110] Since Resolution 2178 does not define terrorism, the Additional Protocol incorporates the definition contained in the 2005 Convention on the Prevention of Terrorism,[111] which defines terrorism by reference to existing international conventions and protocols.[112] Notably, the resolution also does not define foreign fighter, referring only to fighters belonging to certain terrorist groups without presenting this list as definitive.[113]

This approach poses several concerns. Resolution 2178 requires states to criminalize conduct, such as foreign travel, that individuals may engage in for legitimate reasons. The resolution thus creates a risk of overbroad application by authoritarian states seeking to exploit the terrorism label to suppress internal opposition and dissent.[114] More generally, it facilitates state law enforcement activity, as well as surveillance and administrative law measures, without providing targeted individuals the protections of precise legal categories.[115]

Resolution 2178 additionally seeks to apply the concept of terrorism and terrorist training to armed conflict, even though most of the conventions and protocols that the Convention on the Prevention of Terrorism relies on to define terrorism do not cover armed conflict.[116] Moreover, two of the international conventions potentially applicable to the armed conflict in Iraq and Syria – the International Convention against the Taking of Hostages (Hostages Convention)[117] and the International

Convention for the Suppression of Terrorist Bombings (Terrorist Bombings Convention)[118] – contain provisions that would exclude relevant conduct committed in armed conflict. Specifically, the Hostages Convention does not apply to acts of hostage-taking in the context of armed conflict[119] and the Terrorist Bombings Convention excludes "[t]he activities of armed forces during an armed conflict, as those terms are understood under international humanitarian law."[120] The Additional Protocol thus suffers from significant limitations in addressing the main problem it seeks to counter: individuals departing from European countries to join the fight in other countries, such as Iraq or Syria, currently experiencing armed conflict.[121] States nonetheless may attempt to rely on the Additional Protocol to legitimize expansive definitions of terrorism in domestic legislation enacted pursuant to the UN Security Council mandate.

Thus, beyond the recurring concerns about criminalizing legitimate activities by sweeping them under a terrorism label, Resolution 2178 highlights the difficulty of applying an international crime of terrorism to non-state actors engaged in armed conflict. Resolution 2178's failure to resolve what legal regime applies to terrorist groups reinforces the differences that exist among national approaches on this question.[122] While expanding the measures that states can take to address terrorism may give them added flexibility in dealing with new threats, it also can lead to fragmentation and abuse.[123] In short, the paradigmatic, post-World War II struggles for self-determination that previously precluded consensus on a definition of terrorism may be on the wane.[124] But controversy over the definition of terrorism persists and new challenges to establishing an international crime of terrorism have emerged.

***

In addition to the concerns arising from the definition of terrorism, terrorism prosecutions necessarily raise due process concerns. Even in liberal western democracies with ordinarily strong commitments to human rights, the invocation of terrorism tends to shift the balance significantly in favor of the state's interest in prosecution and punishment at the expense of the defendant's right to due process.[125] Terrorism prosecutions, moreover, commonly raise thorny evidentiary issues, involve the use of classified or other sensitive information, and depend on the cooperation of state security and intelligence agencies. The frequent use of secret evidence in terrorism prosecutions jeopardizes procedural safeguards.[126] There are reasons to question burdening international criminal tribunals with these additional challenges to delivering justice in a fair and consistent manner, especially where the aggressive approach national jurisdictions take in investigating and prosecuting terrorism generally eliminates the need for an international prosecution to fill an enforcement gap and prevent impunity.

International criminal tribunals rely heavily on external actors (particularly states) to gather evidence, apprehend suspects, and deliver them to the court.[127] But international tribunals have frequently encountered problems obtaining the necessary state cooperation.[128] Terrorism prosecutions would likely exacerbate these problems because states are often reluctant to share information related to national security, especially where the matter concerns an ongoing investigation or operation. States may additionally resist referring suspected terrorists to an international tribunal in order to maintain control over terrorism prosecutions for political or security reasons.[129]

Further, unlike ICL's core crimes, which tend to be addressed in the episodic manner in which they occur, terrorism is the focus of ongoing, widespread, and intensive law enforcement, intelligence, and military operations. Those operations tend to create pressure to relax the human rights protections that international criminal tribunals aspire to protect. Counterterrorism measures have historically weakened legal safeguards relating to arrest, detention, treatment, and trial in order to provide a supposedly more effective framework for combatting terrorism.[130] The procedural legitimacy that criminal justice derives from guaranteeing defendants due process of law tends to come under strain in the counter terrorism context.[131] Rather than leading by example through rigorous adherence to fair trial standards, international criminal tribunals could succumb to significant pressure to diminish those safeguards in adjudicating prosecutions for crimes of terrorism and become mired in a web of new procedural and evidentiary challenges.

Moreover, even if an international or a hybrid court scrupulously protects the rights of accused individuals in terrorism prosecutions, the manner in which jurisdiction over an international crime of terrorism is exercised could exacerbate ICL's selectivity problem. Global counterterrorism efforts rely heavily on countries with strong law enforcement capacity, powerful militaries, and extensive intelligence capabilities. Those countries that maintain dominance through conventional military superiority would likely exert their influence to prevent their respective government officials and armed forces from facing prosecution for abuses committed in combatting terrorism or for the crime of terrorism itself.[132] Meanwhile, elevating terrorism to an international crime would further concentrate prosecutorial attention and resources on weak or failed states that seek to counter the military superiority of more powerful states through the use of terrorist methods of warfare.[133] While such prosecutions might be justified on an individual basis, the collective shielding of dominant states and their allies, on the one hand, and the targeting of weaker states or nongovernment forces for the crime of terrorism, on the other, would deepen existing fairness concerns about ICL.

Past actions by the United States underscore these concerns. The United States has refused to ratify the Rome Statute, effectively precluding ICC jurisdiction over US personnel except potentially where a crime occurs on the territory of a Member State.[134] In an effort to foreclose that possibility, the United States negotiated a web of bilateral agreements designed to prevent the ICC from exercising jurisdiction over US personnel. These agreements – known as Article 98 agreements – rely on a provision of the Rome Statute that prevents the ICC from requesting that a State Party surrender an individual if that State has entered into an agreement or treaty with another nation that gives state or diplomatic immunity to said individual.[135] In 2002, the US Congress enacted the American Servicemembers' Protection Act (ASPA), which authorizes the United States to withhold military assistance from States Parties to the ICC that fail to enter into agreements with the United States barring those States Parties from surrendering US nationals to the Court.[136] While the Dodd Amendment to the ASPA permits the United States to assist international efforts to bring to justice high-level foreign officials accused of genocide, war crimes, or crimes against humanity, this exception remains narrow.[137]

At the same time that it has sought to preclude the exercise of ICC jurisdiction over US officials, the United States has committed widespread human rights violations in its Global War on Terrorism. Yet, despite the overwhelming evidence of the United States' systematic commission of torture and other war crimes after 9/11,[138] the US government has thus far largely insulated US officials from criminal responsibility, including those most responsible for designing and implementing America's secret detention, rendition, and interrogation program. No US official has been investigated or prosecuted by the ICC for international crimes committed on the territory of ICC Member States, which would be subject to the Court's jurisdiction under the Rome Statute even though the US government has consistently demonstrated that it is unwilling to prosecute responsible officials in US courts. Additionally, the United States has advocated for broad applications of complicity liability doctrines, such as aiding and abetting, to target terrorist organizations it opposes,[139] while pressing for narrow interpretations of the same doctrines to allow it to wage war by proxy, even where the groups it supports through weapons, training, and other assistance are committing international crimes.[140] The United States has argued, for example, that mere knowledge that an act would assist in the perpetration of a crime is sufficient for aiding and abetting liability in terrorism prosecutions before US military commissions at Guantánamo. But the United States has pressed for a more restrictive and nuanced standard that incorporates a purpose requirement when it supplies assistance to foreign governments that commit IHL violations, such as during Saudi-led military operations in Yemen aimed at terrorist groups there.[141]

Expanding the ICC's jurisdiction to include the crime of terrorism could thus intensify the selective application of international criminal law. The United States and other powerful countries would likely use international terrorism prosecutions – and the powerful stigma they carry – to advance their security interests while maintaining their own impunity for any crimes committed in the process, whether through the unlawful use of armed drone strikes, the abusive interrogation of prisoners, or other illegal actions. The alternative of prosecuting terrorism through a new *ad hoc* international or hybrid court would not eliminate these concerns, particularly if the jurisdiction of such a court were defined in a way that eliminated the possibility of prosecuting crimes committed by states in connection with their counterterrorism operations against non-state actors. If an international or a hybrid tribunal is to be given jurisdiction over a crime of terrorism, the exercise of that jurisdiction should not only rigorously respect due process safeguards for each defendant, but also strive to ensure that no individual is above the law.

***

Elevating terrorism to the status of an international crime subject to ICC jurisdiction would help convey the massive harm terrorism inflicts on innocent individuals and the magnitude of the threat it can pose to peace and stability. But the challenge of defining terrorism remains, as does the risk of overbroad use of the terrorism label. In time, sufficient consensus on the meaning of terrorism may develop to help mitigate some of these concerns and warrant terrorism's treatment as an international crime rather than a national crime with transnational dimensions. But even so, other challenges will persist, including the heavy reliance on national security and other sensitive information that can undermine fair trial safeguards. Establishing an international crime of terrorism, moreover, risks perpetuating selection decisions that embed major power influence and target non-state actors while shielding government forces even when they commit similar crimes. Future efforts to bring terrorism within the orbit of ICL should therefore remain attuned to the importance of pursuing accountability in a manner that fosters and maintains principles of fairness.

NOTES

1. Neil Boister, "Transnational Criminal Law?" *European Journal of International Law* 14 (2003), 953, 955.
2. Hans-Peter Gasser, "Acts of Terror, 'terrorism' and international humanitarian Law," *International Review of the Red Cross* 847 (2002) 547, 553.
3. Rosalyn Higgins, "The General International Law of Terrorism," in Rosalyn Higgins and Maurice Flory eds., *Terrorism and International Law* (London: Routledge, 1997), 28.
4. UN Special Tribunal for Lebanon, Case No. STL-11–01/I, STL Appeals Chamber, Interlocutory Decision on the Applicable Law: Terrorism, Conspiracy, Homicide, Perpetration, Cumulative Charging, paras. 83, 85–86, 102 (February 16, 2011) (STL Interlocutory Decision on the Applicable Law).
5. Ben Saul, "Terrorism and International Criminal Law: Questions of (In)Coherence and (Il)Legitimacy," in Gideon Boas, William A. Schabas, and Michael P. Scharf et al. eds., *International Criminal Justice: Legitimacy and Coherence* (United Kingdom: Elgar Publishing, 2012), 196.
6. Higgins, "The General International Law of Terrorism," 28.
7. Saul, "Terrorism and International Criminal Law," 193.
8. Erin Creegan, "A Permanent Hybrid Court for Terrorism," *American University International Law Review* 26 (2011), 237, 272 n.134.
9. Naomi Norberg, "Terrorism and International Criminal Justice: Dim Prospects for a Future Together," *Santa Clara Journal of International Law* 8 (2010), 11, 23.

10. Ben Saul, "Civilising the Exception: Universally Defining Terrorism," *Ius Gentium* 14 (2012), 79, 86–87.

11. Draft Comprehensive Convention on International Terrorism: Working Document Submitted by India, U.N. Doc. A/C.6/55/1 (August 28, 2000) (Draft Comprehensive Convention), www.satp.org/satporgtp/countries/india/document/papers/India_IntConv .htm.

12. Johan D. van der Vyver, "Prosecuting Terrorism in International Tribunals," *Emory International Law Review* 24 (2010), 527, 534–40; Christian Much, "The International Criminal Court (ICC) and Terrorism as an International Crime," *Michigan State International Law Review* 14 (2006), 121, 125–26.

13. Robert Kolb, "The Exercise of Criminal Jurisdiction over International Terrorists," in Andrea Bianchi ed., *Enforcing International Law Norms against Terrorism* (Oxford: Hart, 2004), 279–80.

14. Norberg, "Terrorism and International Criminal Justice," 22–23.

15. Ibid., 23–24.

16. GA. Res. 49/60, Annex, para. 3, U.N. Doc. A/RES/49/60 (December 9, 1994) (Declaration on Measures to Eliminate International Terrorism).

17. Ibid.

18. Convention for the Suppression of the Financing of Terrorism, art. 2(1)(b), G.A. Res. 54/109, U.N. Doc. A/RES/54/109 (December 9, 1999) (Convention on Terrorism Financing).

19. S.C. Res. 1566, Concerning Threats to International Peace and Security Caused by Terrorism, para. 3, U.N. Doc. S/RES/1566 (October 8, 2004).

20. Much, "The International Criminal Court (ICC) and Terrorism," 130.

21. Ibid.

22. Saul, "Terrorism and International Criminal Law."

23. Aviv Cohen, "Prosecuting Terrorists at the International Criminal Court: Revaluating an Unused Legal Tool to Combat Terrorism," *Michigan State International Law Review* 20 (2012), 219, 224–28.

24. Convention for the Prevention and Punishment of Terrorism, art. 1(2), League of Nations Doc. C.547M.384 1937 V (1937). The proposed convention defined terrorism as "criminal acts directed against a State and intended or calculated to create a state of terror in the minds of particular persons or a group of persons or the general public." Ibid.

25. G.A. Res. 40/61, para. 1, U.N. Doc. A/RES/40/61 (December 9, 1985).

26. Declaration on Measures to Eliminate International Terrorism, para. 12.

27. Norberg, "Terrorism and International Criminal Justice," 24; Jackson Nyamuya Maogoto, "War on the Enemy: Self-Defence and State-Sponsored Terrorism," *Melbourne Journal of International Law* 4 (2003), 406, 411.

28. S.C. Res. 731, U.N. Doc. S/RES/731 (January 21, 1992).

29. Convention on Terrorism Financing, preamble and art. 2(1).

30. Ibid., art. 2(1)(a), (1)(b).

31. S.C. Res. 1373, U.N. Doc. S/RES/1373 (September 28, 2001).

32. Saul, "Terrorism and International Criminal Law."

33. van der Vyver, "Prosecuting Terrorism in International Tribunals," 541–45.

34. *Prosecutor v. Galic*, Case No. IT-98–29-T, Trial Chamber I, Judgment and Opinion, para. 138 (December 5, 2003). See also Gasser, "Acts of Terror," 549

35. *Prosecutor v. Galic*, Case No. IT-98–29-A PP 87–90, Appeals Chamber, Judgment, paras. 88–90 (November 30, 2006).

36. Ibid., Separate and Partially Dissenting Opinion of Judge Wolfgang Schomburg, para. 21.

37. *Prosecutor v. Sesay*, Case No. SCLC 04–15-A, SCSL Appeals Chamber, Judgment, para. 1198 (October 26, 2009).
38. van der Vyver, "Prosecuting Terrorism in International Tribunals," 545–46.
39. Statute of the International Criminal Tribunal for the Prosecution of Persons Responsible for Genocide and Other Serious Violations of International Humanitarian Law Committed in the Territory of Rwanda and Rwandan Citizens Responsible for Genocide and other such Violations Committed in the Territory of Neighboring States, between January 1, 1994 and December 31, 1994, art. 4(d), S.C. Res. 955, U.N. SCOR, 49th Sess., Annex, 3453d mtg., U.N. Doc. S/RES/955 (1994) reprinted in 33 I.L.M. 1598, 1602 (1994).
40. van der Vyver, "Prosecuting Terrorism in International Tribunals," 541.
41. Nidal Nabil Jurdi, "The Subject-Matter Jurisdiction of the Special Tribunal for Lebanon," *Journal of International Criminal Justice* 5 (2007), 1125, 1126.
42. STL Interlocutory Decision on the Applicable Law, paras. 83, 85–86, 102.
43. Ibid., para. 85.
44. See, for example, Ben Saul, "Legislating from a Radical Hague: The United Nations Special Tribunal for Lebanon Invents an International Crime of Transnational Terrorism," *Leiden Journal of International Law* 24 (2011), 677, 677–79.
45. Antonio Cassese, "The Multifaceted Criminal Notion of Terrorism in International Law," *Journal of International Criminal Justice* 4(5) (2006), 933, 956–58.
46. Kai Ambos, "Judicial Creativity at the Special Tribunal for Lebanon: Is There a Crime of Terrorism under International Law?" *Leiden Journal of International Law* 24 (2011), 655, 675; Boister, "Transnational Criminal Law?" 972.
47. Cian C. Murphy, "Transnational Counter-Terrorism Law: Law, Power and Legitimacy in the 'Wars on Terror,'" *Transnational Legal Theory* 6 (2015), 31, 33, 42–43.
48. S.C. Res. 1267, U.N. Doc. S/RES/1267 (Oct. 15, 1999); S.C. Res. 1333, U.N. Doc. S/RES/ 1333 (December 19, 2000). See also Noah Bialostozky, "Material Support of Peace? On-the-Ground Consequences of U.S. and International Material Support of Terrorism Laws and the Need for Greater Legal Precision," *Yale Journal of International Law Online* 36 (2011), 59, 68.
49. S.C. Res. 1373.
50. S.C. Res. 1566; Keiran Hardy and George Williams, "What Is 'Terrorism'?: Assessing Domestic Legal Definitions," *UCLA Journal of International Law and Foreign Affairs* 16 (2011), 77, 93–94. Although Resolution 1566 was enacted pursuant to the Security Council's Chapter VII powers, it did not specifically require that Member States adopt the definition of terrorism that it provided. Hardy and Williams, "What Is 'Terrorism?'" 93.
51. S.C. Res. 2178, paras. 2, 4–5, U.N. Doc. S/RES/2178 (September 24, 2014).
52. Ibid., para. 3.
53. Myriam Feinberg, *Sovereignty in the Age of Global Terrorism: The Role of International Organisations* (Leiden: Brill-Nijhoff, 2016), 61.
54. Murphy, "Transnational counter-terrorism law," 43–44.
55. Zachary Goldman, "The Foreign Fighter Resolution: Implementing a Holistic Strategy to Defeat ISIL," *Just Security*, September 29, 2014, http://justsecurity.org/15721/foreign -fighter-resolution-implementing-holistic-strategy-defeat-isil/.
56. See, for example, Cassese, "The Multifaceted Criminal Notion of Terrorism in International Law," 935; Cohen, "Prosecuting Terrorists at the International Criminal Court," 230–31; Jordan J. Paust, "Terrorism's Proscription and Core Elements of an Objective Definition," *Santa Clara Journal of International Law* 8 (2010), 51, 54–59.

57. Gasser, "Acts of Terror," 553; Cohen, "Prosecuting Terrorists at the International Criminal Court," 230.

58. Cohen, "Prosecuting Terrorists at the International Criminal Court," 257.

59. Creegan, "A Permanent Hybrid Court for Terrorism," 267–68.

60. Ibid., 243–44.

61. Concern about Lebanon's ability to prosecute individuals in the Hariri assassination provides an example of the former, while Libya's refusal to surrender the suspects from the Lockerbie bombing case offers an example of the latter. See John P. Grant, *The Lockerbie Trial: A Documentary History* (New York: Oceana, 2004).

62. International Criminal Court, Assembly of States Parties, "Report on Working Group on Amendments," ICC-ASP/10/32, Tenth Session, Annex III, at 17–18 (December 9, 2011) (Netherlands: Proposal for the inclusion of the crime of terrorism in the Rome Statute), https://asp.icc-cpi.int/iccdocs/asp_docs/ASP10/ICC-ASP-10-32-ENG.pdf.

63. Thomas Avery, "International Justice and National Stability in Lebanon," *Human Rights Brief* 8 (2001), 71. See also John Cerone, "The Politics of International Justice—U.S. Policy and the Legitimacy of the Special Tribunal for Lebanon," *Denver Journal of International Law and Policy* 40 (2011–12), 44, 53–54.

64. Creegan, "A Permanent Hybrid Court for Terrorism," 258–59.

65. Nancy Amoury Combs, "From Prosecutorial to Reparatory: A Valuable Post-Conflict Change of Focus," *Michigan Journal of International Law* 36 (2015), 219, 229–30; H. H. Judge Peter Murphy and Lina Baddour, "International Criminal Law: Celebrating Its Achievements, Fearing for Its Future," *South Texas Law Review* 55 (2013), 307, 325.

66. Sandra L. Hodgkinson, "Are Ad Hoc Tribunals an Effective Tool for Prosecuting International Terrorism Cases?" *Emory International Law Review* 24 (2010), 515, 525.

67. Terje Einarsen, "New Frontiers of International Criminal Law: Towards a Concept of Universal Crimes," *Bergen Journal of Criminal Law and Criminal Justice* 1 (2013), 1, 19.

68. Creegan, "A Permanent Hybrid Court for Terrorism," 246

69. Einarsen, "New Frontiers of International Criminal Law," 2. See also Gerhard Werle, *Principles of International Criminal Law* (Oxford: Oxford University Press, 2003), 16–17.

70. Jürgen Habermas, "Fundamentalism and Terror: A Dialogue with Jürgen Habermas," in Giovanna Borradori ed., *Philosophy in a Time of Terror: Dialogues with Jürgen Habermas and Jacques Derrida* (Chicago: University of Chicago Press, 2004), 25, 34.

71. Saul, "Civilising the Exception," 89–90. See also European Commission, Proposal for a Council Framework Decision on Combatting Terrorism, at 6–8, September 19, 2001, COM (2001) 521 Final, 2001/0217/ (CNS), http://www.refworld.org/docid/47fdfb35d.html.

72. M. Cherif Bassiouni, "The Penal Characteristics of Conventional International Criminal Law," *Case Western Reserve Journal of International Law* 15 (1983), 27, 28–29.

73. Rome Statute of the International Criminal Court, art. 8(2), July 17, 1998, 2187 U.N.T.S. 90 (Rome Statute); Beth Van Schaack, "Finding the Tort of Terrorism in International Law," *Review of Litigation* 28 (2008), 381, 430–31.

74. Rome Statute, art. 7(2)(a); Lucy Martinez, "Prosecuting Terrorists at the International Criminal Court: Possibilities and Promises," *Rutgers Law Journal* 34 (2002), 1, 33–35.

75. Leila Nadya Sadat, "Crimes against Humanity in the Modern Age," *American Journal of International Law* 107 (2013), 334, 353–54.

76. Convention on the Prevention and Punishment of the Crime of Genocide, art. 2, December 9, 1948, 78 U.N.T.S. 277; Rome Statute, art. 6.

77. Convention on Terrorism Financing, art. 2(1)(b). See also Murphy, "Transnational counter-terrorism law," 32 (noting that many multilateral efforts to combat terrorism rely on a denial of terrorism's political nature).

78. STL Interlocutory Decision on the Applicable Law, para. 85.

79. S.C. Res. 1566.

80. Hardy and Williams, "What Is 'Terrorism?'" 84. See also Helen Duffy, *The 'War on Terror' and the Framework of International Law* (Cambridge: Cambridge University Press, 2005), 250.

81. William A. Schabas, "Perverse Effects of the *Nulla Poena* Principle: National Practice and the Ad Hoc Tribunals," *European Journal of International Law* 11 (2002), 521, 522.

82. Beth Van Schaack, "*Crimen Sine Lege*: Judicial Lawmaking at the Intersection of Law and Morals," *Georgetown Law Journal* 97 (2008), 119, 121.

83. Saul, "Civilising the Exception," 83.

84. Hardy and Williams, "What Is 'Terrorism'?" 155–59; Susan Tiefenbrun, "A Semiotic Approach to a Legal Definition of Terrorism," *ILSA Journal of International and Comparative Law* 9 (2003), 357, 363–64.

85. Jerome P. Bjelopera, *The Domestic Terrorist Threat: Background and Issues for Congress* (Washington, DC: Congressional Research Service, January 13, 2013), 3.

86. Hardy and Williams, "What Is 'Terrorism'?" 159–61.

87. Einarsen, "New Frontiers of International Criminal Law," 19.

88. Hardy and Williams, "What Is 'Terrorism'?" 159; Tiefenbrun, "A Semiotic Approach to a Legal Definition of Terrorism," 364; International Commission of Jurists, Report of the Eminent Jurists Panel on Terrorism, Counter-terrorism, and Human Rights, *Assessing Damage, Urging Action* (2009), 124, www.un.org/en/sc/ctc/specialmeetings/2011/docs/icj/icj-2009-ejp-execsumm.pdf (Report of the Eminent Jurists Panel).

89. S.C. Res. 1373.

90. S.C. Res. 1624, U.N. Doc S/RES/1624 (September 14, 2005).

91. Kim Lane Scheppele, "The International Standardization of National Security Law," *Journal of National Security Law and Policy* 4 (2010), 437, 450–53.

92. See, for example, Joined Cases C-402 and 415/05P, *Kadi and Al Barakaat International Foundation v. Council and Commission*, 2008 E.C.R I-6351 (invalidating European Community (EC) measure implementing UN Security Council asset-freezing regulations because the regulations violate fundamental rights protected by the EC legal order); Gráinne de Búrca, "The European Court of Justice and the International Legal Order after *Kadi*," *Harvard International Law Journal* 51 (2010), 1, 11–12 (discussing *Kadi* and other decisions resisting UN-led global counterterrorism measures).

93. S.C. Res. 1456, para. 6, U.N. Doc. S/Res/1456 (January 20, 2003) (calling upon states to ensure that their antiterrorism measures "comply with all their obligations under international law," including international human rights, refugee, and humanitarian law); S.C. Res. 1566, preamble (reminding states to comply with international human rights, refugee, and humanitarian law obligations); S.C. Res. 1624, para. 4 (same).

94. Norberg, "Terrorism and International Criminal Justice," 34–36; Kim Lane Scheppele, "The Constitutional Role of Transnational Courts: Principled Legal Ideas in Three-Dimensional Political Space," *Penn State International Law Review* 28 (2010), 451, 454–55.

95. Jens David Ohlin, "Joint Intentions to Commit International Crimes," *Chicago Journal of International Law* 11 (2011), 693, 694–95; Allison Marston Danner and Jenny S. Martinez, "Guilty Associations: Joint Criminal Enterprise, Command Responsibility, and the Development of International Criminal Law," *California Law Review* 93 (2005), 75, 78–79.

96. Stanislaw Pomorski, "Conspiracy and Criminal Organizations," in George Ginsburgs and V.N. Kudriavtsev eds., *The Nuremberg Trial and International Law* (Dordrecht/ Boston/London: Martinus Nijhoff, 1990), 229.

97. Ibid.

98. *Trial of the Major War Criminals Before the International Military Tribunal, Nuremberg, 14 November 1945–1 October 1946* (1947), vol. 1, 278.

99. Danner and Martinez, "Guilty Associations," 113–14.

100. Ibid., 83.

101. *Hamdan v. Rumsfeld*, 548 U.S. 557 (2006).

102. Military Commissions Act of 2006, Pub. L. No. 109–366, 120 Stat. 2600 (2006 MCA).

103. 10 U.S.C. § 950v(b)(25) (material support for terrorism); 10 U.S.C. § 950v(b)(28) (conspiracy).

104. Stephen I. Vladeck, "Military Courts and Article III," *Georgetown Law Journal* 103 (2015), 933, 937; David Glazier, "Destined for an Epic Fail: The Problematic Guantánamo Military Commissions," *Ohio State Law Journal* 75 (2014), 903, 954; Jonathan Hafetz, "Policing the Line: International Law, Article III, and the Constitutional Limits of Military Jurisdiction," *Wisconsin Law Review* 2014 (2014), 681, 683.

105. *Al-Bahlul v. United States*, 767 F.3d 1, 61 (D.C. Cir. 2014) (en banc) (Brown, J., concurring in the judgment in part and dissenting in part).

106. Margaret M. deGuzman, "How Serious Are International Crimes? The Gravity Problem in International Criminal Law," *Columbia Journal of Transnational Law* 51 (2012), 18, 19; Jonathan Hafetz, "Diminishing the Value of War Crimes Prosecutions: A View of the Guantánamo Military Commissions from the Perspective of International Criminal Law," *Cambridge Journal of International and Comparative Law* (2)4 (2013), 800, 808–09.

107. David Weissbrodt, "The Role of the Human Rights Committee in Interpreting and Developing Humanitarian Law," *University of Pennsylvania Journal of International Law* 31 (2010), 1185, 1230, and n. 176.

108. Council of Europe Convention on the Prevention of Terrorism, May 16, 2005, C.E.T.S. 196 (Convention on the Prevention of Terrorism), https://rm.coe.int/168008371c.

109. Council of Europe, Additional Protocol to the Council of Europe Convention on the Prevention of Terrorism, October 22, 2015, C.E.T.S. 217, https://rm.coe.int/168047c5ea.

110. Ibid., arts. 2–6.

111. Ibid., art. 9.

112. Convention on the Prevention of Terrorism, arts. 1(1), 5(2), 6(2), and 7(2).

113. Kai Ambos, "Our terrorists, your terrorists? The United Nations Security Council urges states to combat 'foreign terrorist fighters', but does not define 'terrorism,'" *EJIL: Talk!* (October 2, 2014), www.ejiltalk.org/our-terrorists-your-terrorists-the-united-nations -security-council-urges-states-to-combat-foreign-terrorist-fighters-but-does-not-define-ter rorism/.

114. Ibid.

115. Murphy, "Transnational counter-terrorism law," 44–45.

116. Martin Scheinin, "The Council of Europe's Draft Protocol on Foreign Terrorist Fighters Is Fundamentally Flawed," *Just Security*, March 18, 2015, http://justsecur ity.org/21207/council-europe-draft-protocol-foreign-terrorist-fighters-fundamentally -flawed/.

117. International Convention against the Taking of Hostages, December 17, 1979, T.I.A.S. No. 11081, 1316 U.N.T.S. 205 (entered into force June 3, 1983) (Hostages Convention).

118. International Convention for the Suppression of Terrorist Bombings, December 15, 1997, 2149 U.N.T.S. 284 (entered into force May 23, 2001) (Terrorist Bombings Convention).
119. Hostages Convention, art. 12.
120. Terrorist Bombings Convention, art. 19(2).
121. Scheinin, "The Council of Europe's Draft Protocol."
122. Feinberg, *Sovereignty in the Age of Global Terrorism*, 62.
123. Ibid.
124. Gasser, "Acts of Terror," 549, 557.
125. Murphy, "Transnational counter-terrorism law," 34.
126. Ibid., 36.
127. Gregory S. Gordon, "Toward an International Criminal Procedure: Due Process Aspirations and Limitations," *Columbia Journal of Transnational Law* 45 (2007), 635, 639.
128. Ibid; Laura Moranchek, "Protecting National Security Evidence While Prosecuting War Crimes: Problems and Lessons for International Justice from the ICTY," *Yale Journal of International Law* 31 (2006), 477, 478.
129. Creegan, "A Permanent Hybrid Court for Terrorism," 264.
130. Report of the Eminent Jurists Panel, 55.
131. Murphy, "Transnational counter-terrorism law," 48.
132. Creegan, "A Permanent Hybrid Court for Terrorism," 264.
133. Chris Mahony, "The Justice Pivot: U.S. International Criminal Law Influence from Outside the Rome Statute," *Georgetown Journal of International Law* 46 (2015), 1071, 1090.
134. Rome Statute, art. 12(2)(a), 12(3). In theory, the UN Security Council could refer a situation to the ICC that created the possibility for jurisdiction over US personnel. But the United States could exercise its veto power to block any such resolution.
135. Lilian V. Faulhaber, Recent Development, "American Servicemembers' Protection Act of 2002," *Harvard Journal on Legislation* 40 (2003), 537; Rome Statute, art 98.
136. 22 U.S.C. §§ 7421–7433 (2006).
137. Alex Whiting, "The U.S. Should Not Disengage from the International Criminal Court Following Palestine's Ascension," *Just Security*, January 7, 2015, www.justsecurity.org/18937/u-s-disengage-international-criminal-court-palestine-joins/.
138. Senate Select Committee on Intelligence, *Committee Study of the Central Intelligence Agency's Detention and Interrogation Program* (Executive Summary) (December 3, 2014). www.washingtonpost.com/wp-srv/special/national/cia-interrogation-report/document/.
139. Beth Van Schaack, "Don't Forget the Other Legal Issues in the 9/11 Trial," *Just Security*, December 14, 2015, www.justsecurity.org/28328/forget-legal-issues-911-trial/.
140. Mahony, "The Justice Pivot," 112–13.
141. Ryan Goodman, "The Law of Aiding and Abetting (Alleged) War Crimes: How to Assess US and UK Support for Saudi Strikes in Yemen," *Just Security*, September 1, 2016, www.justsecurity.org/32656/law-aiding-abetting-alleged-war-crimes-assess-uk-support-saudi-strikes-yemen/ (surveying US government positions).

Concluding Remarks

International criminal law has developed significantly both in scope and complexity since the International Military Tribunal conducted the first modern war crimes trial at Nuremberg after World War II. The preceding chapters have examined a number of these developments through the lens of ICL's continued effort to hold accountable perpetrators of grave crimes without compromising the fairness and integrity of the proceedings. The issues discussed can be broadly grouped into three main areas: procedural safeguards and other fair trial guarantees, such as those that enable a defendant to contest the prosecutor's evidence and present evidence in his or her defense; various modes of liability, including joint criminal enterprise, command responsibility, and co-perpetration, commonly employed to prosecute individuals who did not physically perpetrate a crime but nonetheless bear responsibility for it; and the selection of situations and cases for investigation and prosecution. In addressing these issues, international and hybrid tribunals have drawn upon various sources, including international human rights law, international humanitarian law, and fundamental principles of criminal law. They have also sought to pursue larger ends, such as restoring the rule of law in countries devastated by mass atrocities and providing redress to victims.

Each of these areas highlights the continued tension between the goals of accountability and fairness. In some respects, these tensions are endemic to any criminal proceeding that seeks to bring to justice individuals responsible for violent and destructive behavior. Yet, these tensions are amplified in ICL given the nature and magnitude of the crimes. Their resolution, moreover, is shaped not only by normative commitments, but also by a combination of practical obstacles unique to international criminal justice, such as a tribunal's limited resources, lack of enforcement power, and dependence on states for assistance with gaining access to evidence, protecting witnesses and victims, and performing other critical functions. In short, the friction between accountability and fairness may be universal in criminal law, but it assumes distinct features in international criminal trials.

The first set of issues concerns the manner in which a tribunal tries defendants accused of international crimes. On paper, the statutes for international and hybrid tribunals typically provide extensive fair trial protections for defendants modeled on and, in some cases, taken directly from international human rights instruments. The jurisprudence of these tribunals, moreover, frequently emphasizes their commitment to upholding fair trial standards and principles of legality. Other considerations, however, often pull in different directions. The wide-ranging goals of international criminal tribunals can lead courts to prioritize other interests over the fair trial rights of accused individuals. The length and complexity of some international criminal trials can undermine a defendant's right to a speedy trial and the presumption of innocence, especially when defendants are denied pretrial release. The lack of parity between the prosecution and defense has also served as a persistent source of criticism. Some of the most significant fair trial issues, however, stem from the practical obstacles that international criminal tribunals face. A defendant's access to material information may depend, for example, on the willingness of the state that supplied information to the prosecution pursuant to guarantees of confidentiality to provide that information to the court or to allow it to be shared with the defendant. While national jurisdictions similarly confront issues involving access to confidential or other sensitive information, the limited power of international criminal tribunals to compel disclosure, coupled with the sheer gravity of the offenses, magnifies the tension between preventing perpetrators from escaping punishment and scrupulously adhering to the demands of due process. International tribunals nevertheless must do all within their power to uphold fair trial standards. Further, it is especially important that they avoid compromising those standards where the obstacles are not external, such as when a state has control over particular evidence, but rather are the result of internal pressure to see that grave crimes do not go unpunished. For example, the ICC's modification of the legal characterization of the facts presented at trial illustrates the danger of a court's significantly prejudicing a trial's fairness in the name of preventing impunity. Similarly, tribunals should remain vigilant about ensuring that broader goals, such as increasing the participatory rights of victims, remain secondary to the due process rights of accused individuals.

The second constellation of issues involves the use of modes of criminal responsibility, such as joint criminal enterprise, co-perpetration, and command responsibility. These doctrines provide an important tool for prosecuting mass atrocities, where those most culpable in terms of seniority or decision-making authority are often remote from the physical commission of the crime itself. Yet, the aggressive use of these doctrines by international criminal tribunals can raise important fairness concerns, including the risk of sweeping in marginal figures based largely on guilt by association, improperly attributing responsibility to more senior officials who lack the necessary criminal intent, and failing to provide adequate notice that the alleged conduct was criminal at the time it was committed. The ICTY's past application of JCE III to crimes committed outside a common criminal plan based on their purported foreseeability represents the most expansive use of a mode of vicarious liability. But controversy persists over other doctrines that have the potential to minimize the importance of the defendant's intent, such as the ICTY's use of aiding and abetting liability in the context of assistance to foreign organizations and the ICC's use of co-perpetration and indirect perpetration. Thus, although the Nuremberg trials established the principle that criminal guilt must be personal, courts still struggle with applying this principle to situations of collective criminality where responsibility may be shared among multiple people within an organization and even across international borders.

The third group of issues relates to the selection of situations and cases for investigation and prosecution. Since Nuremberg, international criminal tribunals have grappled with the dilemma of victor's justice. They have struggled to subject officials from powerful nations to prosecution when they commit international crimes and to resist the tendency to focus on crimes committed by weaker states or non-state forces or in certain geographic regions. In many ways, selection decisions present the most intractable issues in ICL since they are directly affected by the limited authority and resources of international tribunals and are particularly vulnerable to the influence of external forces. Judges have less ability to impact choices about case selection than to ensure the sufficiency of trial procedures or proper limits on doctrines of criminal responsibility. The ICC's expected role as a permanent global court has nonetheless put it at the center of controversies over which international crimes are investigated and prosecuted – controversies that the restrictions on the ICC's jurisdiction, resources, and capacity make it more difficult for the Court to address. It is, to be sure, possible to bracket concerns about the fairness of selection decisions by emphasizing the gravity of the crimes that are prosecuted and focusing on the adequacy of the legal safeguards afforded to individual defendants in those cases. But prosecutions that consistently target weak countries or non-state actors, while effectively ignoring grave crimes committed by more powerful countries and their allies or by government forces more generally, will erode the principle of equal application of law and undermine efforts by the ICC and other tribunals to serve as credible and legitimate mechanisms for ending impunity. The ICC Prosecutor could help address these concerns not only by focusing more on international crimes committed outside of Africa, where nearly all of the Court's investigations and all of its prosecutions have been directed thus far, but also by opening a formal investigation into possible crimes committed by major powers, such as by UK forces in Iraq and US forces in Afghanistan. Despite the potential political backlash, opening such investigations would constitute an important step by expressing the norm that no individual is above the law through concrete action rather than mere words.

Focusing on accountability and fairness provides a framework for approaching procedural and substantive issues in ICL. This focus underscores how the challenges that international criminal tribunals confront are at once universal to all systems of criminal justice and unique to the prosecution of international crimes.

It also sheds light on recurring questions, such as the debate over whether terrorism should be an international crime. Providing the ICC or a new international or hybrid tribunal with jurisdiction over a crime of terrorism could help further the pursuit of accountability in several ways, especially by forcefully conveying the gravity of this offense and the threat it poses to peace and stability around the world. At the same time, prosecutions by an international or a hybrid court of a crime of terrorism would raise concerns from the perspective of all three aspects of fairness described above. First, such prosecutions would risk diminishing fair trial safeguards, for example, by limiting a defendant's access to confidential or other sensitive information. Second, the absence of a clear and precise definition of terrorism could result in overbroad applications, particularly if prosecutions relied on expansive interpretations of modes of liability to address the problem of collective criminality. Third, powerful countries would have significant incentives to pursue the selective application of an international crime of terrorism, focusing exclusively on crimes committed by weak governments or non-state actors, while seeking to insulate their own actions in combatting terrorism from prosecution. Thus, despite some benefits, treating terrorism as an international crime is unlikely to advance both accountability and fairness, two essential, but sometimes conflicting, goals of international criminal law.

Index